D0886654

Passport to Greece

Here at last is a knowledgeable, entertaining and thoroughly practical introduction to Greece for the ordinary visitor. Leslie Finer lives in Athens and has written this book to answer all those questions his friends put to him when they come to Greece for the first time. What has modern Greece to do with ancient Greece? Where and what can I eat in Athens? Is there such a thing as the Greek character? Why are all the shops closed on 28 October? Which is the most idyllic Aegean island?

Passport to Greece *combines the personal touch of a good travel book with the factual information of a guide. Motels and tavernas, ancient tragedy and modern newspapers, bathing and bouzoúki music, Greek wine and the Parthenon, motoring and Mount Athos. on all these subjects and many more Leslie Finer gives sound advice. What he has to say is enjoyable in itself; helpful to those planning a visit; and will make a holiday in the country itself really worthwhile.*

LESLIE FINER

PASSPORT TO GREECE

Illustrated by Spiros Vassiliou

LONGMANS

LONGMANS, GREEN AND CO LTD
48 Grosvenor Street, London W1
Associated companies, branches and representatives throughout the world

First published 1964

Filmset in Monophoto Times New Roman and made and printed by offset in Great Britain by William Clowes and Sons Ltd, London and Beccles

For Elsa

who guided ME to Greece –
and goaded me into writing
about it

Note

In the transliteration of Greek words and names, I have followed a simple phonetic procedure – adding only a syllable stress indication to assist the reader in the event that he may wish to pronounce the words intelligibly.

Contents

Foreword

I feel that a word of explanation, even apology, is in order. So many books have recently been written about Greece, that new-found gambit in holiday-manship, that it takes something like impertinence to believe I can add anything useful to what has already been said by the expert Hellenists and the professional exponents of fine writing.

In my reading of these books I have often responded to a fine flash of insight or penetrating analysis; often I have been moved by a purple passage of landscape painting, or a romantic-mystical appreciation in prose of Greek people and Greek monuments. Just as often, I have wondered at the sheer nerve of the back-to-nature bohemians who arrive in Greece to escape the pressures and expenses of urban existence and who, from some cosmopolitan island outpost increasingly peopled by their beatnik colleagues, venture to lay down the law about the Greeks they hardly know and the Greece they have hardly seen.

The approach to Greece in these books is specialist, or romantic, or awe-struck, or merely inadequate. The best of them are valid as art; nearly all of them, it seems to me, are too egocentric to be valid as information of the equable and apocalyptic variety which comforts the first-time visitor, soothes his restless sense of disorientation and puts into his hand a thread to the complex pattern of the country's life – a thread which ensures that, on his way through the labyrinth, he will not be missing its most important and fascinating features.

There is no lack, certainly, of books which are anything but romantic and subjective. From *The Week in Athens*, price sixpence at any kiosk, to the full-blown guide of Germanic origin or inspiration. Here is all the dry fact and objective learning that the most painstaking tourist could ask for. Like the camera and the bottle of sun-tan oil, one or more of these books will be part of his holiday paraphernalia – just as heavy to carry and just as extraneous to real enjoyment and appreciation. By definition dead-pan, unselective, hair-splitting. To possess them is like being ushered into the Louvre and being told 'now go ahead and enjoy yourself'.

These, then, are the kind of book this is not. Neither artfully literary, nor bewilderingly encyclopedic. Neither a gaudy oil painting, nor a photograph. It is, if you like, just a freehand pencil sketch; personal, incomplete but – as I hope – pleasantly illuminating. I have spent eight years in this country, reporting its light and serious side for the London Press and radio. I claim no more knowledge of the Greek people or of Greek institutions than is incidental to the competent performance of that task. I have learned the language; I have visited most parts of the country (some very briefly); I have friends among the simple islanders of Salamis and Euboia and among the far from simple politicians, artists and professional men of the city. My love for this country is genuine, but not indiscriminate; my understanding of it goes deep enough to make it easy to forgive almost everything I do not love.

When I first arrived in Greece, the questions in my mind were those which concern every first-time visitor to some extent: I wanted to know all about the country's history as reflected in its present; about its people, its language, its social habits, its art, its politics, its most absorbing sights, its most rewarding pleasures, its most characteristic quirks and, of course, its most satisfying victualling points. What I have discovered about all these facets of Greece I have tried to set down, as light-heartedly as possible, in this book. Above all, I have tried, avoiding portentous solemnity and epigrammatic obscurity, to convey the picture of a living country facing contemporary problems in a contemporary world. For, in spite of all its distinguishing charms, its exciting novelties, Greece today is not the sun-drenched museum of most novices' imagination: it is a vital, struggling and intelligent community which shares common features and problems with its neighbours in the contracting world of the twentieth century to a far greater extent than it is distinguished from them by the superficial exoticisms which fill the eye of the visitor.

To compress eight years of living into a few hours of reading is bound to lead to some distortion. My readers are asked to accept the hazards of this short-cut. They are also asked to be conscious of the personal limitations of this book: each one of them, given the chance of living eight years in Greece, would certainly derive different impressions and draw different conclusions. Never mind. The idea of writing this book (not initially my own) has gradually taken hold in my mind because of the expectation of my friends, when they first arrive in Greece, that I will be able to divulge to them, in a few moments of intensive instruction, the full fruit of my acquaintance with the country. If it should turn out that people are not willing to *pay* for this information, no great harm will have been done. I shall at least have on my bookshelf a sufficient number of free copies to keep my friends happy for a long time to come. I reflect on the time and trouble I shall save; and I am content.

Salamis, 1964

Part I
Key Patterns

I Just To Think . . . !

I remember some time ago walking along the dunes skirting the broad beach near Oropós on the north shore of Attica facing across the Gulf of Euboia. It was early in summer and the air was full of that tingling blend of ozone and pine scent which is as typical of the Greek seashore as the waft of Gauloise smoke of a Paris bar. The sea, so translucent that each variation in its depth and the texture of its bed was faithfully reflected in the range of the water's blue – from pale turquoise to Stephens' ink – was gently rippled by the *bounátsa* breeze which blows through the narrow straits at Chalkis. And, over in the forest-filled island of Euboia, the gently imposing bulk of Mount Kandíli rose through a blue-violet haze to a crest outlined with that sharp but stereoscopically gentle clarity which, we are told, results from the special properties of the light in this part of Greece.

It was, in fact, a typical summer landscape in Greece. Or seascape – call it what you will, for it is one of the delights of this country that we rarely need distinguish between the two. So typical that there would be no reason to dwell, if ever so fleetingly, on the scene were it not to set the stage for what follows.

With me was the late Dr John Papadimitríou, the urbane, learned and (I am permitted to say, since all archaeologists openly pray to the goddess of chance) remarkably fortunate Director of Greek Antiquities. We had just been visiting near-by Aulis, where the Greek fleet waited for the wind to blow towards Troy; and the Temple of Artemis at Brauron, one of Papadimitríou's last and most felicitous discoveries. As we walked, the archaeologist talked about the ancient Greece which for him lived through its vestiges. And indeed, in the timeless setting of that unpeopled seashore, it might all have happened yesterday. As if to prove the point, Papadimitríou would stop in his tracks every now and again to scuff the sand with his toe. Stooping, and almost without breaking the flow of his pleasant discourse, he would pick up a fragment of painted pottery, turn it over lazily for inspection and toss it back like an unwanted minnow, remarking 'late geometric', or (this with some aloofness) 'early Hellenistic'.

Now you or I, if we had the uncanny gift of 'divining' bits of ancient pots lying under the sand on lonely beaches in Greece, would surely wrap each fragment in cotton wool and show the treasures proudly to our friends for the rest of our lives. We might even become shard sharks, setting up a stall at Oropós to sell choice bits of ancient vases to tourists; like the shops on the fringe of the Petrified Forest reserve in Arizona where chunks of prehistoric tree-bark sell like hot cakes.

All this, since it is time to come to the point, leads up to a question which seems to me to be fundamental to the business of inquisitive travel, especially in countries with what is known as a 'glorious past': how much of our admiration of ancient relics is inspired by their intrinsic beauty, and how much springs from an ingenuous awe of anything old for its own sake? My guess would be that it is only the few specialists in the historical sciences – the geologists, archaeologists, anthropologists and, to a lesser extent, the historians themselves – who can take a reasonably detached view of human achievement in that tiny fraction of cosmic time during which humans have done anything at all. The rest of us, especially now that we are dazzled by modern achievements in the fringe-sciences of space flight and plastics manufacture, are naïve romantics, egoistically delighted and surprised to discover that a paltry few hundreds of years ago our ancestors did such 'civilized' things as to weave cloth, paint vases, carve statues and install plumbing in their houses.

It is difficult to achieve immunity from this reverence for antiquities for their own sake. Our susceptibility varies only in degree. I recall the party of transatlantic tourists who sat behind me last summer at the Herod Atticus theatre in Athens where a performance of an ancient tragedy was about to begin. Four thousand people packed the white marble tiers of the open-air Roman amphitheatre; they had only to turn their heads to see, floodlit above them on the flat plateau of the Acropolis, the fluted symmetry of the Parthenon. All was rapt expectation. And one of them said in hushed excitement to another, as she surveyed the arched niches of the Roman wall backing the stage: 'Just look at that be-ewtiful wall; it must be very, very old. Just how old would you say it is?' And our awed enquirer sank back in sighing contentment when a companion judiciously replied: 'Well, it's certainly very old, very old indeed. I'd say at least a hundred years.' But I doubt very much whether this ignorant reverence is really very different from the thrill of any non-specialist when confronted with an ancient relic. The universal wisdom of Plato and Shakespeare is often saved from relegation in our esteem to the ranks of platitude by virtue of our surprise that men who lived 'so long ago' could be at least as wise as we are. And I am dissuaded also from any tendency to taunt our Anglo-Saxon cousins when I remember the first time I saw a newly discovered Mycenean grave opened for inspection: as the tarpaulin came off, the emotions aroused by the shrivelled skeleton, and the glass and metal baubles provided to accompany the Mycenean lady to the other world, were chokingly intense. I remember how I fussed over the 'naturalness' (!) of the shrunken bones and the 'superb' workmanship of the hairpins and the bodkins. The truth being, of course, that a skeleton is a skeleton; and the ornaments were really no more than competently fashioned.

So we have established this much: we most of us have a deep-rooted reverence for the ancient. That the conception of 'ancient' is generally conditioned by a worm's-eye view of human history is neither here nor there. Just to think . . . two thousand years old! This must be the battle-cry of every eager visitor to Greece. Last year he may have spent his vacation in the Balearics or on the Riviera coast of Italy – in which case the sight of a peasant costume or two, or at most a visit to some local medieval church, was enough to fulfil his sense of obligation to the folklore and antiquity of the area. For the rest of the time he was happy enough to bask on a modern beach in front of a modern hotel on the esplanade of a modern, if quaint or picturesque, town. Nobody, after all, has ever heard of the Greatness that was Geneva or Magnificence that was Monte Carlo. But we have all heard of the Glory that was Greece. And, when we come, we mean to find out what it was all about.

There are exceptions, of course. There is not much opportunity for communion with the past when, like thousands of young Europeans these last few years, you find yourself on a package trip, set down for a fortnight in a tent or bungalow on some remote stretch of sand in, let us say, the western Peloponnese. The sand may be smoother, the sea bluer and the sun more constant than it is at Weston-super-Mare, but the contrast stops roughly there – even if you manage to squeeze in half a day among the puzzling maze of broken columns at Olympia. Or there may be individual deviations from the rule, as in the case of my friend Francis Noel-Baker, MP. Ever since his grandfather bought a delightful estate in Euboia from a Turkish gentleman in the late nineteenth century, the Noel-Baker family has tilled its acres, tapped its pines for resin and become an integral part of the countryside, giving employment to its peasants and looking after their social welfare. Francis himself takes full advantage of the long Westminster vacations to tend the needs of his other 'constituents' in Achmétaga and speaks fluent Greek of a kind which encourages Athenians to enquire politely in what village he was born. And yet, out of long tradition, the Noel-Bakers have never bothered with those features of Greece which, for the rest of us, are paramount. His grandfather, it is said, hardly ever set foot in Athens. He would travel by train from England, but long before the borders of Attica were reached, just outside Thebes, the train would make a special stop for Mr Noel to get off. A private carriage would be waiting to take him over the bumpy tracks to his estate about fifty miles away. Nowadays it is more difficult to make this kind of arrangement; the plane from London tends to make straight for Athens Airport and it is hard, as the bus turns off the coast road and heads inland to the city, to avoid a glimpse of the rearing Parthenon to the left or of the pillars of the Temple of Zeus straight ahead, forming – by some temporary optical illusion – a kind of gateway into the capital. So Francis must have *seen* the Parthenon by now; but it is rumoured that he has not yet actually set foot in it.

Most of us, however, can hardly wait to get unpacked before rushing off to add the Parthenon to our bag of compulsory travel experiences. On our way, we may feel uncomfortably confused. We are, let us assume, averagely cultivated members of some enlightened urban society. We are not, for the purposes of this argument, professional thinkers reared on a diet of Plato or teachers of the classics thoroughly at home with iambic pentameters. But we have laughed as gaily as the next man at *Beyond the Fringe*, we manage to get through half, at least, of one or two of the bulkier Sunday newspapers, we have learned not to sneer at 'pop' music, we have (or are planning to get) the latest and highest fi there is, we would prefer not to have TV (whether we have it or not), and we take an intelligent if somewhat puzzled interest in the conflicting revelations by science journalists about the latest discoveries in electronics and dietology. Some of us may have visited (rather a long time ago) the Elgin Marbles in their charming Bloomsbury setting, or the Victory of Samothrace in the Louvre. Some may even have dim memories of classical studies from which we retain the comfort of knowing what the 'hoy polloy' *really* means and, maybe, to recite the first line of Homer's *Iliad* or to recall the distinct ancient Greek words for a cow with brown markings and one with black.

What is certain is that we all of us have a firmly rooted notion of the importance of the ancient Greek civilization in the formation of the artistic, literary and political traditions of Western Europe. The Greek ideals of beauty and the democratic organization of society (which are really both reflections of a paramount respect for individual personality) are so unquestionably revered as to have become platitudes.

Vague as may be our knowledge of what these ideals were, or of the people who formulated them most aptly, or of the process by which they spread to other nations, we are as certain of their validity and their fixed place in the scheme of things as we are of the date of the next total eclipse. So, when we hear the word 'Greece', and more than ever when we are actually present on its sacred soil, it is these attributes, this universal homage, which are uppermost in our minds.

We have arrived at last. Our bags are only half unpacked in the hotel room. And we have set out on the pilgrimage to the Acropolis. We have come, of course, to spend a pleasant holiday. The prices, we have been told, are rather low; the sun shines without fail; the food, if you know your way around, is simple but good; the bathing is incomparable; the hotels modern and comfortable. But all these delights may be enjoyed in a thousand places throughout the world, many of them much cheaper to reach. This is *Greece*. And before we leave we must taste its Greekness to the full. Our very first impressions may already have raised doubts we prefer not to ponder on. Where, we may wonder uneasily, is the Greekness in the brash twentieth-century architecture we see all around us in Athens, in the rash of neon lights or the jostling workaday crowds of Omónia Square with not a Greek nose among them? The doubts are not allayed, either, at the threshold of the Acropolis where coachloads of tourists are offered bad plaster models of classical Greek statuary and iced lemonade. As we climb up towards the towering grace of those peach-coloured pillars we may well be asking ourselves: what is left, apart from the cold fragmented stone, of all that history, all that greatness? Can it all have evaporated in the two millennia of invasion, counter-invasion, civil strife and upheavals of population? Are we standing merely on the geographical site of a civilization once famous but now totally vanished except for its marble skeletons? Or, as we instinctively hope, is everything we see around us – the people, their physiognomies, the institutions, ideals and traditions of the place – linked more or less recognizably with the features of that ancient Greece of which we harbour so reverent if unprecise an image?

This is the 64,000-drachma question for which there is no ready-made answer. Greek chauvinists and foreign romantics detect the

WELLCOME
GREEK ARTS

spirit of ancient Greece all around them. The insensitive and the cynical see not a trace of it. Somewhere in-between, the scholars have their own views, carefully reasoned but conflictingly inconclusive. My own answer, based as much on everyday observation as on academic argument, will be implicit in the pages that follow. There is no reason why this should discourage the reader whose interest is in practical holiday advice. That is the primary objective of this book. But my hope is that, in conveying that practical advice, I can also draw a sketch of contemporary Greece in a perspective which illuminates the influence of the past where it exists.

This approach, it is fair to say at once, imposes slightly more strain on the reader than a plain guide-book – at least in the initial chapters. In the next of those chapters my object is to outline the mainstream of Greek history, not for its own sake but with special reference to the blunt question: what, if anything, does the Parthenon mean today for the man on the Athens omnibus? There is a similar purpose in the succeeding chapter in which I attempt to portray the basic and enduring aspects of the Greek 'character'.

The approach in both these chapters involves us necessarily with the past. They can be skipped by the reader – but only at the cost of losing much which will be of practical value for his understanding and enjoyment of the present. If he survives these initial shocks, he will proceed confidently to the remainder of Part I which deals more directly with the contemporary background of the country: in turn, its sights, sounds and general atmosphere as they strike the unfamiliar visitor; its language; its current cultural activities; its social organization; its habits and equipment in matters of eating, sleeping and travelling. Part II of the book, with chapters on Athens, the islands, the mainland and on shopping, is intended to give the reader my own personal and selective advice about the practical planning of his holiday in Greece. But it is in the main first section that I have attempted, without neglecting much information of immediate and practical purpose, to serve the growing number of visitors to Greece whose enjoyment of things seen and done is not complete unless they also understand the context of their experiences.

2 A Comforting Chronicle of Continuity

We should be wandering aimlessly in the wastes of pre-history if we tried to pin down exactly the ethnic origins of the Greek 'race'. In matters of this kind, the biblical simplicity of Adam and Eve as a practical concept seems to me more useful than earnest attempts to trace offshoots from a common stock. Certainly there has never been such a thing as a pure Greek race. If we take as our starting point the ancient Greeks of classical times, it is clear that they were a mixture of prehistoric Mediterranean peoples, whose civilization centred on Crete and the Cyclades Islands, and of northern invaders who came down in successive waves during the thousand years before Christ. Little is known of the Mediterranean civilization which mingled with the elements from the north. It was certainly in contact with Asia Minor and, later, with the flourishing civilization of Egypt, from which it adopted many features. For the Greeks of classical times, the highlights and great personalities of this civilization had the qualities of legend, they included Minos and the Minotaur, the Argonauts, Cadmus from Phoenicia who taught men the first elements of civilization, and the Cyclops. Modern archaeology has shown that the references to these legends in classical Greek literature were in fact the first written documentation of folk memories concerned with real people and historical fact. For anyone who sees the much-maligned reconstruction by Sir Arthur Evans of the complex Minoan palace at Knossos in Crete, the 'legend' of the Labyrinth and the Minotaur at once becomes vividly real.

The sophisticated architecture, the unfortified palace sites and the exquisitely delicate art of the last period of the Minoan civilization (now preserved in the breathtaking collection of the Heraklion Museum) speak eloquently of the pacific and prosperous Mediterranean society which flourished in Crete for some four hundred years and which was brought to a violent end (it is generally assumed by a great earthquake) around 1400 BC.

It had been assumed until very recently that this civilization, which dominated not only Crete but also the surrounding islands and shores of the Mediterranean by virtue of its flourishing shipping trade and colonization, was a direct development of the prehistoric Minoan civilization dating back to the third millennium BC. It came as a revolutionary shock (which some diehard scholars are still struggling feebly to resist) when, in the last few years, it was shown that the civilization of Crete in this last and finest phase was no longer directly derived from its prehistoric origins, but had been transformed by a different race of men who had established themselves across the sea on the mainland of Greece, in the Peloponnese. And this race of men was of the same stock which, in later invasions from the north, was to lay the foundations for the Greece of the Golden Age. They were, in fact, Greeks.

It is an exhilarating justification of pure scholarship that a discovery of such wide sweep and direct appeal to the imagination should have been based on the deciphering of a few stone tablets bearing the advanced hieroglyphics known as Linear B. The tablets were found at Knossos and eventually gave up their secret to the late Michael Ventris. They contain very little which adds to our knowledge of historical fact, since they are nothing more than bare lists of various commodities. But the language transliterated in these linear writings was not a pre-Hellenic language. It was clearly a language with Greek characteristics.

Tablets inscribed in the same Linear B script have also been found on the mainland of Greece, notably at Pylos in the southern Peloponnese. This was one of the centres of the Mycenean civilization which co-existed with that of the late Minoan period in Crete. This Mycenean civilization, a feudal militarist society which buried its dead chiefs in the giant 'beehive' tombs we still see at Mycenae and elsewhere, and which fortified its centres on high ground (the acropolis sites, for instance, of Mycenae, Argos, Pylos, Gla – and of Athens itself), was founded by the first wave of invaders which began to come down from the north from around 2000 BC. These invaders, of the same stock from which later waves of Greeks derived, were initially more backward than the sophisticated Cretans. But those who established themselves in the Peloponnese, the Achaeans, quickly established contact with Crete and developed a civilization very similar to that of the Cretans.

The similarities between the Minoan and Mycenean civilizations are obvious even to the casual observer in the multitude of surviving objects from both sources. Until the deciphering of Linear B, the unquestioned assumption was that the latter merely assimilated elements of the former's more advanced way of life. The presence of Linear B tablets at Pylos and Mycenae, just like those at Knossos, needed no special explanation: along with other amenities derived from Crete, the Myceneans adopted also the same language. But this assumption is shattered when, as we now know, the writing on those tablets turns out to be a kind of Greek. In other words, the language used in Crete during its last prosperous phase, was the language brought by the newcomers from the mainland – by those early representatives of the Greeks. This discovery, in the opinion of most scholars, justifies the presumption that, in its last and most glorious phase, the ancient civilization of Crete centred at Knossos was dominated by the Hellenic race from the mainland; that it was the Mycenean heroes of Homer's epics and not the Cretans who provided the impetus for the great maritime expansion which, during the fourteenth and thirteenth centuries BC, carried Creto-Mycenean trade around the Mediterranean, from Sicily in the west to Egypt and Syria in the east.

The point is not merely one of academic apportionment of merit for achievements which have long since ceased to have any kind of partisan interest. If what the majority of scholars now accept in the light of Ventris's work is true, we have a fact which goes to the heart of our attempt to trace a significant element of continuity throughout 3,500 years of Greek history: *here, at the very first appearance of a people who can be legitimately identified with the Greeks of later and better-documented ages, we have the strongest possible evidence of their unique and characteristic resilience – a capacity to assimilate without becoming assimilated, to adopt the achievements of peoples with whom they come into contact, while at the same time preserving their own identity, their own language and their own customs; and sometimes even to impose their own institutions and qualities on societies from which they have initially borrowed.* It is this quality of durability, which is both expressed in and explained by an extraordinary continuity of language, religion and psychology, that we can observe, like some dominant gene in the process of reproduction, asserting itself throughout the turbulent history of Greece.

It was certainly apparent in the shaping of what Renan called 'the Greek miracle' – the unique complex of loosely-knit city-states which emerged in the fifth century BC to set a criterion for human achievement in art, philosophy and political organization. The destruction of the Mycenean civilization in the twelfth century by new waves of iron-armed invaders from the north was followed by some four 'dark age' centuries full of turmoil and upheavals of population. The newcomers, cousins of the original Achaean invaders, were the Dorians. They were less cultivated, but spoke a variety of the same Hellenic language. The Dorian wave stretched right through the continent of Greece, established itself at Sparta, and spread as far afield as Crete, Rhodes and even Asia Minor. The turbulence of the wave during those four uncertain centuries produced new population patterns: in some regions the Dorians mingled with the earlier inhabitants, in others they drove them out as refugees to new settlements all over the East Mediterranean or even to remoter areas of the mainland, such as Arcadia in the Peloponnese. In other areas, the earlier populations were not disturbed and were even joined by refugee populations driven out from other areas – as, for instance, the Ionians who settled in Attica which, Thucydides tells, was too poor for the Dorians to bother with.

When the foam of this great wave settled, around the eighth century (the beginning of what is generally labelled the Archaic period of Greek history), the pattern of classical Greece, although it was to take another three centuries to develop fully, was already clear. Small groups organized into cities spread throughout the mainland and the near and distant coasts and islands, from southern Italy to the Black Sea. Each was different in its level of civilization, its dialect, its degree of prosperity (with the inland agricultural cities generally lagging behind the bustling maritime cities of the coasts). But all of them were Greek, speaking the same language and contributing each in its own way to the creation of the common civilization that developed.

Once more, in the transition towards the classical period of the fifth and fourth centuries, the sense of a common identity among the different city-states was a dominant characteristic, all the more remarkable when we consider the isolation of one from the other by great stretches of sea or impenetrable mountain ranges. Yet it was probably these very considerations of geography which accounted for the transformation of Hellenism from an unconscious sense of folk identity into a conscious sharing of a common civilization. The wide separation and the smallness of these city units (Athens in its heyday had no more than about 40,000 citizens and a total population of some 400,000) encouraged, in the first place, the rapid disappearance of tyrannical government and the cultivation of democratic principles. They encouraged also an intense and productive sense of rivalry – not only, or even mainly, in military strength (where a system of loose alliances and specialization proved more useful than efforts to dominate by weight of numbers), but in sculpture, drama, discussion, athletic prowess and mental culture. Each city had its own distinct divinities – distinct in their attributes even when they bore the same names. These were, like local dialects, symbols of individuality. But, just as all dialects were easily recognizable forms of a common Greek language (and a barbarian, or non-Greek, was simply somebody who did not speak Greek and instead said 'bar-bar'), so the various divinities were recognizable emanations of a common Greek religion. And the four-yearly gatherings of all the Greek states for the Olympic Games and at the Delphic ceremonies were occasions for the common worship of the Panhellenic forms of Zeus and Apollo.

We need not linger over the next couple of hundred years during which the Greeks fought off the Persians at Marathon and Salamis, advanced to new heights of achievement under Athenian leadership, and finally succumbed to long periods of inter-state wars – the result of the failure to translate the Panhellenic culture into a workable Panhellenic political system. What we are still concerned with is the survival power of Hellenism as an idea and a way of life. The very collapse of the classical Greek world proved the vitality of that way of life and its capacity to survive shocks. Whether or not the inhabitants of Macedonia in the north were ethnically Greeks (and this is a fascinating subject which has lately caused scholars on their respective sides of the iron curtain to spit nuggets of learning at each other), it is certain that, by the time Philip of Macedonia came down (around 338 BC) to take control, his kingdom on the margin of the luminous Greek world of the Aegean was beginning to absorb Greek lights. When Philip was assassinated and his son Alexander made his lightning sweep of conquest eastwards as far as the Indus, it was the spirit of Greece which his Macedonian armies carried with them. The spirit was naturally changed and enriched in contact with the civilizations of the East; it became Hellenistic – which is a way of saying Hellenic with a more universal appeal and validity. The great centres of Greek life and culture shifted eastwards, to Alexandria, Antioch, Rhodes, Pergamos. But the older centres of Hellenic civilization, although materially impoverished, continued to inspire and participate in the new but still tradition-based form of Panhellenism.

The passage of the Romans, like that of the Goths, Slavs, Franks, Normans, Sicilians, Genoese, Florentines, Venetians, Turks and Germans in the centuries to follow, made no rent in the fabric of the established order. Elements were borrowed from the store of all these visitors, and relics of their passage may still be seen, a thinly spread patchwork of cosmopolitan styles, everywhere in Greece. The Roman domination, after an initial period of hesitation, was complete enough after the destruction of Corinth (146 BC) and brought with it a considerable material decline as Greece became the cockpit for Rome's battles with the Hellenistic kingdoms and the populations of Asia Minor. Even in the relative calm which followed the defeat of Antony and Cleopatra by Octavan at Actium (31 BC) and the enjoyment by Greece, now a distinct Roman province, of the *pax romana*, Achaea (as Greece was called by the Romans) was a minor element of the mighty Roman Empire. Most of the once-prosperous city-states were reduced to little more than villages. But, in the still flourishing cities of Athens, Patras and Corinth, the Greeks continued without interruption to cultivate the Hellenic tradition – often under the admiring patronage of the Romans who, like Americans transporting culture brick by brick across the Atlantic, kept the sculptors' workshops of Athens busy making copies of classical statues to adorn courtyards of their distant homes. The Romans also took lessons from the Greeks in the arts of public speaking and philosophy. And some of their Emperors took pains to flatter and share in the Greek way of life. Nero appeared at the Olympic Games before carting shiploads of Greek treasures back to Rome; and Hadrian undertook an ambitious programme of building patronage in Athens: he finished the Temple of Olympian Zeus which the Greeks had begun to build six centuries previously.

From the first invasions of the prehistoric continent of Greece by the northern Greek-speaking tribes to the period of firmly established Roman dominion, we have rapidly crossed almost 2,500 years of history – a period absurdly long to support easy generalities. But it is broadly and impressively true that, throughout these centuries of sweeping historical tides, we may detect a dominant quality of 'Greekness'. It contained the genius needed to develop into the wonder age of its classical expression, and the resilience needed to survive after that peak was passed, not merely as a memory but as a living tradition. It was enriched and often altered by outside contribution but never overwhelmed or eroded by it.

So far so good. But now we face a problem. As long as the guiding spirit, the intellectual premise, of the Greek world was pagan, we may accept the possibility of underlying continuity. The whole context of the ancient Greek civilization was one of pagan identification of man with the deities of the physical world around him. When Paul first preached in Athens around the middle of the first century AD, he did not have much immediate success. But by the end of the fourth century, Christianity was an established creed everywhere in the Greek world. The last pagan temples were closed in AD 392, and the last Olympic Games were held, to be revived almost exactly 1,500 years later.

Can we still argue, after this apparently total suppression of the basic springs of Greek beliefs and actions, that the Christian Greek world of today has the slightest thread of continuity linking it with the remote pagan past?

The answer to this question requires a glance, if ever so fleeting, at that chilling chunk of Greek history known as 'Byzantine'. There, the word is out. But please read on. It is time that we all forgot the taboos of Anglo-Saxon education which makes us blind to ten whole centuries of live and significant history. For persons of average education in Continental countries, who 'do' the period as inevitably as we in England and America 'do' any similarly long and important period of European history, the word 'Byzantine' recalls an era of great achievement in art, architecture and even social and moral advancement. For us, the word is a bogey, a term of abuse used by all kinds of people from parliamentary orators to newspaper editorialists to suggest qualities of black cunning and devious impenetrability in their opponents. From the earliest days of the Cyprus dispute, the detractors of Archbishop Makarios, ignoring his not inconsiderable qualities of statesmanship, have referred to him as the 'Byzantine priest'. And I cannot help thinking that it was this image more than his actions which prevented his opponents from coming to terms with him as early as they should.

Maybe it was the devotion of English public school teachers to Mr Gibbon that began the trouble, for was it not Gibbon who dismissed the whole Byzantine bag of tricks as 'uniform and dull'? And it may be also that an untutored acquaintance with Byzantine art, with its traditional rather than spontaneous inspiration, tends to feed our prejudice against a world we feel to be coldly formalistic and impenetrable. Whatever the reasons may be for our tendency to shut the Byzantine period out of our minds, our effort to keep track of the continuous thread of Greek history requires that we swallow our prejudice. For it was through Byzantium that the Greek tradition, inherited from the past through the Hellenistic and Roman periods, was kept alive and enabled to influence, not only the history of Greece itself, but – through the processes of the Renaissance – the intellectual development of the whole Western world.

The name 'Byzantium', first of all, has no mystery. It is simply that of the old Greek settlement on the triangle of land surrounded by the waters of the Golden Horn, the Bosphorus and the Sea of Marmara. A delightful site which the Emperor Constantine chose in AD 324 as the headquarters for the eastern wing of the Roman Empire. When the city was officially inaugurated in 330, Constantinople was born (and, for the Greeks, has never died: to this day, the name 'Istanbul', never passes Greek lips).

Little changed when the Roman Empire was formally split into two sections in 395. In spite of Justinian's efforts in the sixth century to reunite the Empire (and in spite of the fact that a Greek today, when he wants to stress his Greek characteristics, speaks of himself as a *Romiós*) the eastern branch of the Empire remained essentially Greek, with Greek in daily use as the common language. For the Greeks, Byzantium was a continuation of Hellenism, turned Christian. Constantinople was the Greek capital and the headquarters of their religious leader, the Greek Patriarch.

The period between the sixth and fifteenth centuries is full of fresh examples of the ability of the Greeks to shrug off or absorb invading foreign elements without perceptible damage to the fabric of their own culture. The Slavs surged right through the peninsula at the end of the sixth century, reaching as far as the southernmost tip of the Peloponnese. The Greek populations often had to uproot themselves and take refuge, generally in coastal towns. But the Slavs, like others before them, were gradually assimilated and Christianized, forgetting even their own language. With the exception of a few place names, not a trace of their passage survives. Theological disputes (reflecting conflicts of political aims) and continued threats from foreign aggressors, resulting in some easterly parts of the empire being lost to the Arabs, failed to halt the steady progress of Byzantium towards its emergence as a tightly-knit and prosperous Greco-Roman world by the ninth century. This was the beginning of the great period of artistic, commercial and institutional activity in which many Greek provinces, with their own strong traditions, played a leading part. Successive invasions – by Bulgarians, Arabs, Sicilian Normans – were all resisted. For a brief period in the thirteenth century, the Venetians and Crusaders set up a Latin Empire, with French feudal lords sharing out various parts of the Greek peninsula. But this was a short interlude lasting little more than fifty years; by 1261, a Greek Emperor ruled again in Constantinople. It was after this restoration that some of the finest surviving monuments to Greek creative activity (the churches, for instance, at Árta, Castoriá and the dramatic monasteries perched improbably on the peaks of Metéora in Thessaly) were constructed. And Mistrás, last centre of flourishing Greek art and spirit before it submerged under the Turkish tide, lived on at the foot of the Taẽgetus Mountains near Sparta. The domestic architecture of Mistrás (except for some remains of the Imperial Palace in Constantinople) is the only surviving example of its period, and it was from Mistrás that the painters and neo-Platonic philosophers of Byzantium in its last phase handed on the tradition of Hellenism westwards when their Empire collapsed to the Turks.

The Byzantine world was a complex and long-lived creation evolved when the eastward expanding forces of the Roman Empire were halted and then absorbed by the dominant Greek world, as it had emerged from its Alexandrine contact with the East. The Romans contributed significant elements, particularly in the sphere of legal and institutional practices; just as the Orient had left its imprint in Byzantium's political precocity and imperial gaudiness. But, in every fundamental sphere of everyday life, and at every level of the social scale, it was Greece and the spirit of Greece which dominated the Byzantine world and was perpetuated through it.

We can now dispose, first of all, of the question we asked at the beginning of this impertinently brief probe into the complexities of Byzantium: how can we combat the assumption of a great chasm separating pagan Greece from the Greece of the Byzantine Christian Empire? The answer to that question, startlingly enough, is that Christianity, in the form it developed in Greece, not only failed to sever its faithful from their pagan past, but provided perhaps the strongest of all the links with it. The Orthodox Christian religion of Greece never came into conflict with the underlying conceptions of pagan antiquity, but was gradually blended and identified with those conceptions. Formal evidence of this process can be seen in several examples of early Byzantine art. Pagan motifs exist side by side with Christian themes, as in the depiction of the River God of Jordan in the company of John the Baptist in a sixth-century mosaic at Ravenna.

At the intellectual level, the whole of the Byzantine period was marked by a careful battle of accommodation between Orthodox Christian dogma and the teachings of outstanding philosophers who continued to represent the Platonic school.

But this process of gradual superimposition was nowhere more tentative and, therefore, ultimately complete than at the level of common folk customs and beliefs. The dogma and the saints of Christianity were identified in the popular mind with the superstitions and divinities of antiquity; and the official hierarchs of Christianity were invariably careful not to insist too rigidly on the need for differentiation. To this very day, Christianity as practised in Greece – especially in the remoter rural areas – can trace direct links with pagan beliefs and practices. The same integration of Christian dogma into the texture of everyday life can be observed also in the status of the priest in Greece. Nowhere else in the Christian world is the priest so closely identified with the life and problems of his parish. The beer-drinking curate is a well-known Anglo-Saxon type. But this kind of identification between the clergy and their flock is superficial: a public relations gambit designed to close the gap between the Church and its potential but reluctant devotees. Anyone who has spent a few hours in a Greek village will know that the role of the priest is totally different: whether sitting at the *cafeneion* in the square sipping his coffee from a small thick cup, or striding – with flowing beard and robes – down the main street, or sitting astride a donkey on the way to gather his olives or his grapes, the Orthodox priest is the natural and recognized leader of a community in which Christianity is not a set of religious rules and practices followed by the faithful and ignored by the others, but the sum total of the social, economic and spiritual tradition which permeates the community into which you are born and out of which you die.

So, if Pappa-Fotis, the village priest, is allowed to marry and have children, it is not because of any article of Orthodox faith or dogma, or even because it is considered good ecclesiastical policy to avoid the discriminatory overtones of celibacy. It is a simple consequence of the fact that Pappa-Fotis, like everyone else in his village, needs sons to help cultivate his strip of land or to go to sea and send his monthly quota of dollars from Hong Kong and Valparaiso. And whether

Pappa-Fotis is holding the Sunday morning service, or tending the sick, or helping to decide the siting of the local war memorial, or writing to a Minister in Athens on behalf of a villager who wants a licence to operate a lottery shop, or even responding to a request to exorcize evil spirits, he is, in every case, performing his proper and recognized function. This integration of a suitably adapted form of Christianity, and of its official representatives, into the web of life in Greece has not always been fully understood in the outside world. It explained the predominant and militant role of the Greek clergy in Greece's past political struggles (notably the War of Independence and the resistance against the Germans) just as it explained what was so unthinkable to so many people a few years ago: that a Primate of the Church could place himself at the head of a subversive and violent political movement of liberation in Cyprus.

The complete identification of Christianity with every aspect of life in Greece as it existed, and as it had been inherited from antiquity, was a Byzantine achievement. Another, equally significant for the preservation of continuous links with the past, was the retention and cultivation of the Greek language. At the level of formal education and literature, Greek continued throughout the Byzantine era to be the only universal language. This was true not only for scholars but for everyone. Primary education, apart from reading and writing in Greek, always included a study of ancient Greek literature. A quotation from Homer was as readily recognized by the Byzantines as we today recognize a quotation from Shakespeare (in spite of the vastly greater distance of time separating the two epochs). Higher education was largely concentrated on the traditional fields of study in ancient Greece – philosophy, mathematics and, above all, rhetoric – the characteristically Greek art of 'style' in literary and spoken expression. The legal codes, although Roman in content, were compiled in Greek. And even the basically Roman content of the codes recognized the prevalence of Greek tradition: one law, for instance, governing the application of what we now call the right to 'ancient lights', required that anyone claiming an unobstructed view from his window of monuments such as statues of ancient Greek heroes must prove his ability to appreciate the artistic and historical value of the statues in question!

It is true that in literary and ecclesiastical texts the language used by the Byzantines was not the vernacular form developed, during the early centuries of the Christian era, from the various dialects of the classical world, with predominantly Attican features. It is true also that, to some extent, their cultivation of an artificial language in imitation of specific classical authors was responsible for a confusion which has retarded and still (as we shall see) bedevils the modern Greek language and its literature. But this conscious preservation of classical tradition in the language was one of the most important factors in enabling the West (especially through the Latin countries like Italy and Spain which had already absorbed a knowledge of classical Greece) to preserve and propagate the Greek tradition during the centuries of Turkish occupation which obscured that tradition in Greece itself. Even if there is no scientific proof of the proposition, it seems to me to be reasonable to suggest that the existence of written Byzantine texts composed in a Greek language which derived directly, if artificially, from that of Thucydides or Xenophon, may well have been one important factor in the process which determined that the vernacular language in Turkish-occupied Greece (a language which, after all, was itself directly developed from classical prototypes) underwent no material changes.

The fall of Constantinople to the Turks in 1453, followed by the gradual occupation of nearly the whole of the Greek archipelago over the next eight years, might have resulted in the total eclipse of all that Greece had built up in the previous long centuries. The significant accomplishment of Byzantium was the consolidation of that achievement in a form which the West could inherit and which Greece itself, isolated from the rest of the world and exploited by Turkish masters, could preserve as a common memory from the past and a common inspiration for national resurgence in the future.

At no time throughout almost four centuries of Turkish domination, during which Greek youths were kidnapped for the Janissary Guard and Greek girls were sent to increase the variety and swell the numbers of Turkish harems, was there any sign of a weakening of national identity among the Greeks. Their language and their religion remained intact. And the few minarets which still rear their pointed towers over the Greek landscape are tolerated as quaint reminders of a dark era of

Greek history, just as the few borrowings from Turkish into the Greek language are still so lightly assimilated that, in a language-game craze which swept Athens drawing-rooms quite recently, the object was to compose funny phrases using only words of Turkish or mock-Turkish origin.

The failure of the Turks to make any kind of inroad into the fundamental pattern of Greek life can be seen often enough in the Greek countryside where, time after time, we see little churches bearing a foundation inscription dating back to the seventeenth and eighteenth centuries. And numerous acts of collective or individual resistance against the Turks, both before and during the revolution which finally drove them out, have passed into the national legend of Greece. To this day, in spite of the best efforts of statesmen to foster the policy of friendship sought more than thirty years ago by the great Venizelos, a deep-rooted feeling of mistrust between Greek and Turk is always ready (as recent events in Cyprus proved) to break out on the surface. The themes of the Greek popular shadow-theatre (itself an import from the East), which still draw crowds of children and their none-too-reluctant adult escorts to Sunday morning shows in Athenian theatres, are exclusively concerned with the exploits of one Karangyózis, a poverty-stricken, uneducated, but irrepressibly optimistic character, of infinite Greek acuity, who invariably has the best of his encounters with his powerful, brutish but inordinately stupid Turkish masters. And what Greek schoolboy does not know the by-word '*Malta yok*', which sums up the good-humoured contempt of every Greek, with a tradition of seafaring deeply rooted in his soul, for the landlubber Turks across the width of the Aegean? (The phrase '*Malta yok*' is alleged to have been used in a signal from a Turkish admiral during World War I when, after several days of fruitless wandering in the Mediterranean, he failed to find his port of destination. It means: 'Malta does not exist.')

It was the revolutionary fervour inspired by the ideas of the French Revolution which moved Greece early in the nineteenth century to set an example for the numerous movements of national liberation which followed in Europe. And it was the image of classical Greece in the minds of romantics like Byron (but also of dozens like him in other European countries) and even in the collective minds of governments abroad, which roused the support which made it possible for the popular rising of 1821 to terminate in the official establishment of the internationally recognized Greek State in 1830. But, as a former American Ambassador to Greece has drily remarked, Greece has not always been so much romantic as inspiring of romance in others. And romance will go only so far in the face of harsh realities. The history of Greece as an independent state, impoverished and backward after centuries of oblivion and exploitation, has been one of uphill struggles to gain a foothold on the plateau of prosperity and organized progress inhabited by the European countries with a briefer and less troubled past. Greek efforts, in the succeeding one hundred years, to regain Greek-speaking and Greek-thinking territories still outside the boundaries of the 1830 settlement, met with the stubborn resistance of the Great Powers whose attitude was determined not by romance, but by self-interest. The efforts, however, were slowly successful and, one by one, Greek territories returned home: the Ionian Islands, Thessaly, Árta, Crete, Southern Epirus, Macedonia, Western Thrace and, briefly (after Greek assistance to the Allies during World War I), Eastern Thrace and Smyrna. For a short moment in modern Greek history, the dream of reconstituting the Byzantine Greek Empire, including every Greek settlement on the shores of the Mediterranean and with a capital in Constantinople, seemed on the verge of becoming a reality. But the 'Great Idea', as it was called, foundered for ever in the defeat of the Greek Army which invaded Asia Minor in 1922, and the mass return of the Greek populations of Turkey.

The last fragment of Greek territory to return home was the Dodecanese group of islands, including Rhodes, which was relinquished by Italy at the end of World War II. But this was an isolated instance, the penalty for Italian iniquities and the reward for Greek virtues in wartime. For the rest, the climate of world developments during the last few decades, and Greece's preoccupation with her own internal problems, have discouraged any trend towards further Greek expansion. The fervour of the 1950s for union with Cyprus was not expansionist. It was an expression of moral solidarity with the Greek Cypriots and of a jilted lover's bitterness against Britain. The independent Republic of 1960, for all its seeds of later trouble, was greeted by Greece with relief; it enabled her, undistracted, to resume the repair of the crippling damage inflicted by war, occupation and civil conflict.

With her association in the European Economic Community, Greece has now become a part of the new international process which has replaced colonialism by co-operation as the solution for that vast majority of countries which cannot live by their own resources alone. But this does not imply the extinction of the exuberant, creative and eternally dominant spirit of the Greeks – that indomitable sperm of Greekness which, for thousands of years, has built empires and fertilized whole civilizations with its power to develop the best of which humans are capable. For a country of its diminutive size and natural resources – perhaps because of these challenging physical limitations – the vitality of Greece continues to enrich its own country and the world at large to an extent which is astonishing. There is hardly a field of man's activity in which Greeks do not continue to excel out of all proportion to their numbers: Onassis, Mitropoulos, Kazan, Callas, Niarchos, Doxiades, Kazantzakis, Seferis are only a handful of the scores of Greeks who, in our lifetime, have been world-recognized leaders in almost every branch of enterprise, art and science. And on the less rarefied level of ordinary workaday activity, there is hardly a spot on the globe, from the concrete forests of an American metropolis to the remotest corner of an Australian sheep farm, where the tough and adaptable intelligence of the Greek is not at this moment adding its quota to the sum of human achievement. The circumstance has its dangers, as I have been embarrassed to discover on several occasions when I fondly imagined that to converse in Greek with my wife was a guarantee of privacy: in the middle of an Israeli desert, in a Florentine bazaar, in a Polynesian restaurant of Los Angeles, in the precincts of an open-air theatre in Colorado, there has been a taxi-driver, a stall-holder selling straw hats, a waiter, or a man sweeping up dead leaves on hand to remind me that, however transformed and however constrained within the uniformity of twentieth-century moulds, the spirit – and the language – of Ulysses is still alive.

3 Character Part

You will, indeed, still meet Ulysses in the flesh on your travels in Greece – even if you travel no further than an Athens bar or take the electric train down to the Piraeus. Ulysses, and Phidias, and Alcibiades, and Socrates, and Plato and a host of other heroes from classical record. For baptismal purposes (the Church being broad-minded about pagan survivals only up to a point) they will all have a reserve affiliation to a recognized Christian saint, be he John (Yánnis), George (Yórgos), Harálambos, or Christ (Chrístos) himself. And it may well be that my favourite waiter Aristotle, who wields his tray with classical aplomb at Zonar's snack-bar, is otherwise known as Nikos Papadopoulos and celebrates his name day with Christian propriety each sixth of December without a thought to his remoter ancestor.

What kind of people are these latter-day Greeks? And are we justified in supposing that historical continuity, so far as we have proved it to exist, combined with fixed geographical, climatic and other material factors, implies some degree of continuity in character?

There is no reason to be shy of attempting an assessment of the Greek character. Generalizations about national character are objectionable only when they are employed to indicate a pejorative distinction from one's own. They are valid and useful enough so long as we are careful to make the elementary allowance for universal variations in individuals; so long as we concentrate on the distinctive characteristics which the Greeks share, which set them broadly apart from Germans and Hottentots.

We can rule out, straight away, any suggestion that purely racial considerations have anything much to do with character formation. Anthropologists tell us that there are still some 'ancient Greek types', physically speaking, particularly in parts of Greece like the Mani and the Aegean Islands which escaped the Slav incursions of the first millennium AD. It may well be. But it is also true that nothing distinguishes the behaviour of those populations, in basic respects, from that of the Greeks in any other part of the country. If race had a decisive influence on character, the mixture of races which now constitutes the population of Greece would make it difficult to pinpoint a single common feature of character. And that is plainly not the case. Greeks themselves, it is true, have their little regional prejudices: the inhabitants of Cephalonia are popularly written off as 'crazy', Cretans are 'fiery', the population of Corfu is 'lazy', of Macedonia 'serious-minded', of Thessaly 'bold', of Mytilene 'mean', and so on. It is a harmless kind of fun, but no more valid than allegations of Scotch stinginess.

With nations, as with individuals, it is environment which mainly determines character. Heredity enters into the reckoning mainly in the sense that characteristics acquired through environment are transmitted through the generations, even after the environment has changed. A nation's collective image of its own character is one of the most powerful forces preventing the rapid reaction of changing material circumstances. Even the sweeping changes of the twentieth century in the most advanced countries of the world have failed to alter basic character patterns more than a strong wind over the desert may shift a few million grains of sand, without changing the features of the landscape.

In Greece, urban development and the constant shift of population from the villages have obliterated some of the more overt testimonies to a continuous and uniform folk tradition, reflected in distinct character traits. Men sitting in a cinema, or a trolleybus, or sipping a cocktail tend to look and behave alike. But, happily for our purpose, this overlay is thinner in Greece than in most other countries of Europe. At the last count, 48 per cent of the population in Greece was classed as rural, and therefore still fairly close to the basic springs of character formation. Even the town dwellers of Greece are mostly first or second generation newcomers to this category, drawn in the slack tide of attraction towards urban areas which, by other standards, are still far from heavily industrialized. Athens and its surrounds now contain something like one-sixth of the total population of Greece. But, only a few decades ago, it was a smaller town than, say, Chichester; and the second biggest town in Greece, Salonika, has about 400,000 inhabitants. It has been very well said that nobody in Greece lives in towns, and nobody lives in the open countryside. Everyone lives in villages, of which Athens is the largest.

This description of Athens we shall find, when the time comes, to be remarkably apt. For now, I want only to observe that the retarded urbanization of Greece, the thinness of the cosmopolitan veneer overlying basic habits and character, makes it possible to draw character generalizations of more than average validity.

The continuity in language and religion, and the extraordinary capacity displayed by the Greeks throughout their long past to retain a collective sense of identity, suggest that, if we look hard enough, we may find basic character and folklore patterns unchanged throughout the centuries. Several scholars have worked in this fascinating field, and some have found such powerful links that they have felt justified in drawing conclusions about some unknown aspects of the Greek way of life in classical times merely by drawing analogies with the present.

Some of the outstanding analogies are worth looking at. They suggest that, however unaware he may be of the fact, my friend Aristotle shares quite a few character traits with a long dead ancestor.

One of the most striking aspects of this continuity of character is the survival today in Greece of religious practices, superstitions and customs which are plainly derived from pagan antiquity.

When, in the early part of the Christian era, the Church was making its careful attempts to suppress paganism, the cultivation of the worship of saints was one of its chief weapons. Just as Christ himself was admitted to the Pantheon (and even, it is thought, had temples built in his honour by Hadrian), so the saints were worshipped as lesser deities. And, in very many cases, the pagan gods of antiquity became associated with saints who had similar names and similar functions. St Dionysius is a good example. According to a legend which was until recently current in Euboia, and may still be a part of local folklore, St Dionysius was on his way to the island of Naxos when he saw a small plant he had never seen before. He dug it up and put it, for safety, into the bone of a bird's leg. When the plant began to grow, he had to find a larger shelter for it: the leg-bone of a lion, into which he inserted the plant together with the bird-bone from which it could no longer be detached. The plant kept growing, and the Saint had to put the whole collection into the leg-bone of an ass and, when he arrived in Naxos, he planted it. The plant (which was, of course, the vine) grew, and men made wine of it and drank. At first, after drinking, they sang like birds; then they became as strong as lions; but wound up as foolish as asses.

The transference of both the name and the qualities of the wine-god Diónysus to St Dionysius is startlingly plain in this legend. The Saint even retains his pagan predecessor's connection with the island of Naxos. And today, in Athens, you often hear quite well educated people speak of the Theatre of Dionysius, instead of the Theatre of Diónysus; and the official name of the road which skirts the theatre is St Dionysius Street.

There are many similar examples of pagan gods turned saint. Demeter, the harvest goddess, has been associated with St Demetrios, a special favourite in agricultural communities. And, in practically every Greek locality where there is a prominent hill, the site is known as the 'hill of Elijah'. The Greek for Elijah is 'Elías', an easy transcription from 'Helios', the sun god. And both the sun god and Elijah, of course, are connected with a chariot.

There are other cases where, without an identity of names between pagan gods and modern saints, there is a clear substitution of functions. Hermes, the ancient messenger of the gods, has been succeeded by the archangel Michael whose sword has replaced the wand of his pagan prototype and who has taken on the latter's duty of escorting men's souls to Hades. In the remote part of the Peloponnese where Hercules and Cerberus are supposed to have made their ascent from the lower world, emerging out of the caves of Taenarus, local legend still insists that the figure of the archangel Michael may be seen guarding the mouth of the cave.

And then we have the conversion of temples into churches where the presiding saints perform much the same functions as the former pagan denizens. Athene, the virgin goddess of Athens, fitly turns over the Parthenon to the Christian Virgin; the Church of the Annunciation on the island of Tínos, the Greek equivalent of Lourdes where thousands go each 15 August to be cured, stands on the site of the ancient sanctuary of Poseidon the Healer, and the pagan spring of water still performs healing functions.

These, and many similar examples which could be given, indicate the extent to which, for modern Greeks, the polytheism and paganism of ancient times has become accommodated within Christian forms. Up to quite recent times in Athens, for instance, you could still hear the form of blessing: 'God fit thee to find favour in the eyes of gods and men.' And, in general, the characteristics of the Christian God are very similar to those of Zeus – vague and closely related in the popular mind with the more grandiose natural phenomena, like the weather. The ancients used to say 'Zeus is wetting', and in modern Greece 'God is raining' or even 'God is taking a pee' are phrases sometimes heard in the countryside. When it thunders, God is rolling his wine-casks or shoeing his horse.

Like the ancient gods, saints often have different attributes depending on their locations: St Nicholas (successor generally to Poseidon) protects sailors and most often has his churches on the tips of capes and promontories; St John the Hunter has a monastery on Mount Hymettus; St George at Argostóli in Cephalonia is commonly known as the Drunkard because the new wine in that area is usually tapped on his day – 3 November. And like the ancient gods, Christian saints have

ΚΑΦΕΝΕΙΟΝ

to be propitiated, often in accord with a superstitious play on the name of the saint in question: St Elefthérios, for instance, when suitably approached, will give safe deliverance ('*eleftheria*'='freedom') to a woman in childbirth: St James (in Greek 'Iákovos', similar to the '*Ákoufos*', meaning 'not deaf') will come to the aid of the hard of hearing; St Andrew ('*ándras*'='man') will make weak children strong; St Triphon ('*strípho*'='twist') will not be at all pleased if you twist anything, for instance if you spin yarn, on his name day; and St Simeon ('*simeóno*'='mark') will induce birth-marks on a new-born baby if a pregnant mother touches anything black on his name day.

The ancients used to say: 'Gifts win the gods.' The modern Greeks still put this maxim into practice. Prayers are imbued with a spirit of bargaining, and some kind of return is thought essential for services rendered. The Greek islands today, particularly Mýconos, are full of tiny chapels built by supplicants who have recovered from a serious illness or by sailors who have returned home after surviving dangers at sea. The churches of Greece are full of the wafer-thin silver or gold foil trinkets with which peasants try to ensure the benign intervention of the saints. And, depending on the scope of the intervention required, these trinkets bear the imprint of eyes, limbs, sheaves of corn, chickens, ships. The giant silver candelabrum in the church at Tínos has been made by melting down thousands of these offerings. 'It is', as the popular saying goes, 'a poor kind of saint who works no miracles.'

For all the Church's strict ban on forms of idolatry, the great popularity of the ikon as an object of worship in Greece offers a similar enough substitute. Ikons, like many pagan statues which were worshipped, are also often given silver and gold overlays. These not only enhance the ikon's miracle-working properties, but are a useful protection against the erosion which would otherwise be caused by thousands of reverent lips.

Like the sick who came to be cured at the Temple of Aesculapius in Epidaurus, Greeks today will often sleep the night optimistically within the precincts of some healing divinity. A mother with a sick child will often spend the night in the village church and, on a far bigger scale, the pilgrimage to Tínos every summer brings thousands of supplicants, with their mattresses and household paraphernalia, to lie on the floor of the church. The doors of the church are locked from nine at night till early next morning. Those who cannot crowd in have to be content with a square yard or so of the exterior courtyard or one of the long flights of steps.

Nowhere is the similarity between pagan and Christian practice in Greece so startling as in the beliefs which govern communication between men and the divine power. There is even a case (existing till very recently) of a functioning Oracle situated in a Christian church and presided over by a Christian priest. This Oracle operated in the Church of St George on the island of Amórgos. It consisted of a block of marble hollowed out in the shape of an urn, without any visible inlet. Divination consisted in observing the level of water in the urn, which changed constantly: a full urn indicating good prospects for the enterprise in hand, an empty or meagrely filled urn indicating that postponement would be the wisest course. Divination was also made to depend sometimes on the various bits of vegetation and other foreign bodies found floating in the water. Travellers, including one Jesuit priest at the end of the seventeenth century, have noted what a splendid source of profit this Oracle was for the presiding priest of St George's.

One writer even claims to have reasonably reliable evidence of a case of human sacrifice to propitiate the gods performed on the island of Santoríni at the time of the Greek War of Independence less than 150 years ago. Whether or not this actually happened, it is certain that the peasant who told of the incident about sixty-five years ago had an instinctive sense of the object of human sacrifice as it was known in ancient Greece: 'We thought things over, and decided to send a man to St Nicholas to ask him to make our ships prosper in the war.'

These are isolated examples of an almost atavistic kind of continuity of folk memory and ancient pagan practices. But, in more everyday respects, there are still countless examples of similarity between pagan and contemporary notions about human communication with the divine.

The interpretation of dreams is a case in point. It was an important and widely practised art in ancient times. And in Greece today, serious discussion of the meaning of a dream is common among every section of the population. I have heard such conversation in the drawing-rooms of Athens as often as in the homes of peasants. And fat volumes of Dream Interpreters, like Bibles or Mrs Beeton, often occupy a place of honour in Greek homes and are as frequently consulted. Dreams can convey divine information about any number of things: where a holy ikon can be dug up, the method for curing a sick person, the identity of a future husband. In some villages, girls are encouraged on the eve of St Catherine's day (she being the patroness of marriage) to bake and eat salty cakes, the consequent thirst being later attacked with quantities of wine. Dreams about future husbands are not infrequently provoked by this system.

Another survival from Homeric practice is the divination of the future from the hearing of chance words or from chance meetings. An encounter with a priest is regarded as unlucky, and I have seen Greeks look really worried when they board a ship or a plane and find a priest among the passengers. A meeting with a cripple, a donkey, and a variety of other animals is a presage of bad luck. A pregnant woman, on the other hand, is a good sign. And so, strangely enough, is a madman (who is somehow regarded as being in direct contact with the divine power). Throughout Greece madmen are treated with superstitious respect and toleration.

Many of these beliefs can be traced directly to ancient tradition. And so can the superstitious belief in omens provided by birds, the most credible of all messengers between gods and men. The cries, flight, posture and roosting place of certain birds are still commonly interpreted as omens of things to come. The birds involved in this process are still the same: eagles, vultures, hawks, ravens, crows and owls. Also, in accordance with Homeric record, considerable importance is attached to whether these various bird activities are observed to occur on the right or the left of the watcher. The right is the 'lucky' and the left the 'unlucky' side. Motion from left to right is always the more auspicious. This was the direction in which, according to Homer, the gods passed the wine round. And it is in this direction (Greeks not being port drinkers) that wine is passed in Greece today, that cards are played and that, at the wedding ceremony, bride and groom are led round the altar.

Anyone who has been in Greece at Easter time and has been present at the ceremonial roasting of the Paschal lamb on a spit will have seen a survival from the ancient practice of drawing conclusions about the future from an inspection of the entrails and bones of sacrificial animals. There is always somebody among the assembled company who will sagely inspect the shoulder-blade of the sheep and pronounce on it: the degree of whiteness and freedom from blemishes seems to be the measure of favourable augury. The same kind of skill is involved in the reading of the coffee cups. It is only once a year that a sheep's shoulder-blade is readily available for the exercise of these mysterious talents. But the dregs of coffee can be read several times a day. There is always somebody among one's circle of acquaintances who is regarded as the expert in this game, which is by no means always lightly played. Turkish coffee, with its thick sediment at the bottom of the cup, lends itself ideally to the purpose. The dregs are swilled around while they are still wet, and the cup overturned on the saucer and left for a few minutes to dry off. The resulting shapes, by a process of association which recalls the ink-blot tests, provide the material on which a reading of the future can be based. Expert coffee-readers are still in high demand; our daily maid, for instance, makes a considerable extra income from this activity on her afternoons off.

In many districts of Greece, divination from sacrifice also traditionally forms part of wedding preliminaries. The various convulsions of the slaughtered animal (properly a ram, but more usually replaced by a chicken) tell the experts all kinds of fascinating things, such as whether or not the bride is a virgin, who will 'wear the trousers' in the future ménage, and the number and sex of future children. And there are many other examples of 'domestic divination' which are almost identical with those we read of in ancient literature: the ominous import of a mouse nibbling through a bag of flour, or of a dog howling in the night; the spilling of oil (bad) or of wine (good); the twitching of an eyebrow signifying an early meeting with an acquaintance – an enemy if it is the left eyebrow which twitches, a friend if it is the right eyebrow (did not the goat-herd of Theocritus exclaim: 'My right eye throbs, oh I shall see Amaryllis herself!'); a buzzing right ear, signifying kind words spoken of you by somcone, a buzzing left ear, meaning that you are being slandered; an itching right palm indicating that you will get money, an itching left palm warning that the tax inspector's demand note must be in the post; and sneezing, as a confirmation of words just spoken (as in Homer's *Odyssey*, when Telemachos sneezes aloud and Penelope says: 'Do you not see how my son sneezed in sanction of all my words?').

Perhaps the most impressive coincidence of ancient and modern customs in Greece concerns the approach to death and the ceremonial which surrounds it. In ancient Greece, as the tragedians make very plain, to be 'unwept' was as dreadful a fate as to be 'unburied' and as damaging to the repose of the dead. We read in Homer of the mourning for Hector, when 'they set singers to lead the lamentation'. The practice of hiring professional mourners to wail the set funeral dirges is still the rule in Greece, in spite of Solon's legislation in the sixth century BC to suppress the practice. About the only place in Greece where the custom is not followed is the Ionian Islands, where the Venetians stamped it out. I can understand their abhorrence: to hear one of these dirge-sessions is one of the most spine-chilling experiences imaginable.

Many of the prescribed dirges have been published. And it is remarkable how most of them still show the conception of the dead person as a messenger between those who still live and the powers of the world below. This, as we have seen, was the ancient conception of sacrifice: a deliberate despatch of a messenger to the gods to ask some favour. The same conception applied to persons who died a natural death. Euripides has Polyxeni say, as she is about to die, 'What am I to say from you to Hector or to your aged husband?' And many a modern funeral dirge conveys the same notion. For instance: 'Now I am making ready, now I am at the point to go. Whoso hath word, let him speak it, and message let him tell it; whoso hath long complaint let him write and send it.'

The same idea of the dead being messengers is found in a Greek expression used of a person who is dangerously ill: 'He is collecting letters for the dead.' And the practice of leaving a note under the pillow of a dead person's bier or whispering in his ear is still very usual in Greece. Sometimes, the purpose of the custom (which is to pass on messages to one's dead relatives) is not understood, as happened recently when the great Greek actress Marika Kotopoúli died and lay in state in Athens Cathedral. Among the long line of Athenians who came to pay their last respects was another distinguished actress (still alive and internationally famous) who had, in the past, quarrelled violently with her rival. As she passed the bier, she slipped a note under the pillow. It was found later to contain a single word (in French): '*Pardon!*'

Two other practices which Solon tried, unsuccessfully, to suppress were self-laceration by mourners and their lamenting for persons other than the one who has just died. Both these customs still survive. In particular, it is by no means rare at a Greek funeral for persons bereaved long ago to take the opportunity of joining in the lament and renewing their own mourning.

There is another basic conception about the dead which has remained unchanged in Greece throughout the centuries and which is quite distinct from the notions commonly prevailing elsewhere: the living human body is an expression of a temporary separation of the person from his soul; it is only when the body has completely disintegrated that this temporary separation is ended and the dead can find peace. Rapid and complete dissolution of the body is regarded as the essential aftermath of death, and the powerful Greek curse, 'May the earth not receive your body', still heard today, can be found over and over again in Aeschylus and Euripides. The same conception determines the unusual Greek notions about ghosts. These are not regarded as the returned spirits of the dead. The Greek ghost (*vrikólakas*) is the actual body of the dead person which has failed to disintegrate. The Church has gradually changed some of the external manifestations of these notions, but not their basic character. It was commonly believed in ancient times, for instance, that the time required for the complete disintegration of a body was forty days. This has now been changed, and the Christian practice in Greece today is for the body to be exhumed after three years, the bones carefully scrubbed and preserved in the family vault. Disintegration now being complete, the deceased is regarded as being finally at rest and no further formal acts of mourning are required. But ancient belief is still preserved in the invariable practice of holding a memorial service for the dead after forty days. At this service a sweet concoction made of grain, nuts and honey is distributed to the mourners – a survival of the sweet cakes which the ancient Greeks invariably put in a dead person's grave to provide his food for the journey to the other world. Echoes of the belief in forty-day disintegration can be detected in many other modern Greek practices: in the island of Skyros there have been cases of bodies, found to be not totally dissolved on exhumation after three years, being carried round to forty churches and then re-buried – the assumption, no doubt, being that what one burial service failed to achieve in forty days may be achieved by forty burial services in one day!

The notion that the body needs food and clothing and other essentials for sustenance until its dissolution is complete was responsible for the relics we now find in ancient graves, even toys placed in the graves of children to keep them amused, and cosmetics in the graves of women to enable them to continue their care for a good complexion. And to this day the custom of providing the dead with food both on the day of the funeral and afterwards (and even the nature of the food itself) continues unchanged. The same is true of clothing. No Greek family would dream of burying their dead except in their Sunday best or in a completely new outfit of clothes. It is true that, for reasons of economy, this outfit is often specially supplied by the undertaker, made out of new but not very durable materials. But this is a recent concession to financial stringencies, not always regarded with favour among the more traditional sections of the population. The point was amusingly brought home to me recently in a tavern half-way up Mount Parnes. We were huddled round the fire on a wintry day while the tavern-keeper grilled some lamb chops over the logs for our lunch. The only other party in the room was presided over by a burly chap, intensely cheerful, who told anecdotes incessantly. He turned out to be a mortuary attendant at one of the biggest hospitals in Athens. And not the least macabre of his Grand Guignol stories was of the patient from the village of Menídi (the ancient Acharnae, of Aristophanian fame) which, for all its proximity to the capital, preserves a strangely rustic isolation. The man from Menídi had died in hospital and had been suitably decked out for burial by his relatives. Escorted by the mortuary attendant, the body had been transported in grand state to its native village and was awaiting the last salute of the villagers before being taken to the churchyard. It was at this solemn moment that the deceased's relatives came running in great distress to find the attendant. In his anxiety to bedeck the corpse as lavishly as possible, he had completely covered its clothing with the wreaths. How, in these circumstances, was anyone to appreciate the dead man's finery? How, in particular, would anyone be able to observe that his shoes were not the usual paper-patent product supplied by the undertaker but new, real leather footwear of the best quality, purchased by the relatives? And would the attendant at once rectify this serious error of taste? Under the supervision of the anxious relatives, the attendant solemnly proceeded to extract the corpse's legs from the coffin, leaving them dangling stiffly over the sides. And in this less than dignified posture, with the real leather shoes in full view of the admiring funeral procession, the man from Menídi was slowly wheeled to his last resting place.

One final aspect of death is worth pausing to observe: the viewing of death as a kind of marriage, a union between the deceased and the divine powers. This notion is clearly and often expressed in ancient Greek literature (as in Sophocles' reference to the tomb of Antigone as a 'bridal-chamber'). And it is a common feature of modern Greek funeral dirges which are still in use, and even crops up in the continuing belief that to dream of marriage is a warning of death.

This conception of death as a kind of marriage with the gods goes to the deepest roots of the ancient Greek religion. The marriage of death was regarded as the final consummation of man's destiny by a religion which was based on the desire to draw gods and men ever closer together. This, after all, is the meaning of the anthropomorphic nature of the Greek gods, and of the apotheosis of human beauty. All of ancient Greek art, in the service of religion, emphasizes this effort to achieve communion with the gods, to discover in man divine potentialities. And what closer form of communion with the gods could be conceived than marriage itself?

These fundamental religious philosophies of ancient Greece are implicit in everything we can read or discover about its civilization. The fact that they are nowhere explicitly stated or discussed is not surprising, for it was only to the initiates of the Greek Mysteries that the doctrine was revealed. It is all too easy to accept the view sometimes put forward, that the Eleusinian Mysteries were no more than a kind of hocus-pocus by means of which the close aristocratic hierarchy of Greece played on the ignorance and superstitious fears of the masses, or that they were no more than a superior kind of harvest festival. All the great writers (including even the cynical Aristophanes) agreed as to the significance of the Mysteries as a revelationary experience through which men received a glimpse of the good things they would share with the gods in the next world. In this sense, the Mysteries were not a secret practice of esoteric rites but rather the developed and specialized celebration of rites (a kind of cabbalistic school) which grew from and acted as a preserver of doctrines which were never consciously formalized or taught, but which constituted the instinctive basis of the popular religion.

This perfunctory dip into the enthralling subject of the Greek Mysteries I have ventured only because the echoes of this greatest of all pagan rituals can still be detected in the greatest of all the Greek Christian rituals today – the ritual of Easter. Here we have the final and most impressive evidence, in sum, of the massive continuity in basic spiritual and folk feeling which is seen in countless separate expressions and customs.

It is probably a coincidence that the great Eleusinian festival occurred at the same time of the year as the celebration of Easter. But the Church was not slow to turn this coincidence to good account in the effort to tap pagan piety for its own purposes. Till quite recently, the Easter and Good Friday processions were the only exceptions in Greece to the Church's strict rule against the use of idols: effigies of Christ were commonly used in these Easter processions in many parts of Greece. And the merging of pagan and Christian tradition appears also in the fairly common belief among Greek peasants that Easter, as in the cult of Demeter at Eleusis, is the time when the fate of the crops is determined. One investigator of Greek folklore, little more than half a century ago, was struck by a general atmosphere of gloom and anxiety on Easter Saturday in a village in Euboia. When he asked why, a peasant woman told him: 'Of course we are worried; if Christ does not rise tomorrow we shall have no corn this year.'

There is an obvious relation, too, between the period of abstinence required of the initiates before the Eleusinian ritual and the period of Lenten abstinence before Easter. And it is not difficult to imagine the orgies of feasting and wine-drinking which accompanied the Eleusinian rites if you join in an Easter binge in a Greek village: after a week of boiled chick-peas and dandelion leaves, the lamb, eggs and wine of Easter are attacked with more than average enthusiasm. And the resulting gaiety is often more reminiscent of pagan excess than of Christian moderation!

Looking, too, at the deeper emotional undertones of the two ceremonies – the pagan ceremony of the Mysteries and the Christian ceremony of Easter – it is not difficult to spot several fundamental similarities: just as men mourn Christ's crucifixion, they must have shared the mourning of Demeter for her daughter who, although she was also divine, suffered the fate of mortals and was snatched away into Hades. And the rejoicing at the Resurrection of Christ is hardly different from the rejoicing at the return of Persephone from beneath the earth, proving not only that there is life beyond the grave but that there was wedded bliss there which the initiate could look forward to, just as Christians see eternal life in the Resurrection.

Time to get back to our friend Aristotle. Our inspection of his religious identity with his ancestors has not been entirely – even mainly – an academic exercise. Nor are the Aristotles you are likely to meet – unless you spend a great deal of time in the backwoods of Crete or the craggy impasses of the Mani – likely to provide many overt signs of the customs and superstitions we have been looking at. But, on the assumption that you are interested in the broad general character of the average Greek you *are* likely to meet, the extraordinary examples we have seen of the continuity and uniformity of his instinctive attitudes towards the most fundamental things in life suggest something which is of immediate relevance: that we shall find the same continuity and uniformity of national characteristics in secondary manifestations which are closer to the surface of conscious behaviour, more relevant to the immediate conditions of everyday social intercourse, and therefore of more practical interest to the uninitiated visitor whose curiosity is limited to the character quirks of the twentieth-century Aristotle. It is an obvious conclusion that the factors which have made the modern Greek such a faithful mirror of his ancestors in qualities which are at the root of man's outlook on the world around him, must also have given a recognisable shape to his everyday behaviour and attitudes.

Probably the most basic and significant of these general attitudes is the one which, in Greek, is called *métro* – a term not easy to translate, but perhaps best rendered as 'a sense of human proportion'. The gods of Olympus inhabited the cloud-capped peak of a mountain only some 9,500 feet high. For the Greeks, that dizzy altitude represented the roof of the world. And, for them, it was. For there is nothing in the natural landscape of this country which is so big, tall, hot or cold as to dwarf a human's sense of his own identity or hinder his sense of communion with his natural environment. The trees, the seas, the mountains and the valleys of Greece are man-sized, not giant-sized. In a climate which encourages contact with the outdoors, these bland and proportioned features of the Greek landscape have never debased or overawed the Greek's sense of human dignity and of the human scale of creation. A man's mind and a man's body were always the criterion of values in the philosophy of Greek religion and art; human dimensions, tangibility, balance and lucidity have always inspired the Greeks more than the elemental, the heroic, the confused and the Wagnerian.

Can this Greek characteristic of *métro* – the measurement of all values on the human scale – I wonder, be validly equated with the quality we British call 'common sense'? It is certainly a fact which needs explaining that there is a degree of natural affinity and mutual attraction between the British and the Greeks which cannot be justified in terms of historical coincidence or material interests. The British have never been very tolerant of Mediterranean 'types', whose 'charm' never quite compensates for their qualities of 'sloth' and 'hot-bloodedness'. An Englishman meeting the Greeks for the first time expects to find these dubious qualities made even less attractive by a dose of Balkan 'instability' and 'deviousness'. Yet, in almost every case, he is at once attracted and comforted by the discovery that his new Greek acquaintance is serious-minded, hard-working, direct and sensibly down-to-earth. This is not mere theory. The thousands of British troops who passed through Greece during World War II are a mass testimony to the powerful spark of recognition which flashes between the Englishman and the Greek. I have yet to meet one war-time initiate of Greece who does not speak with enthusiasm and affection for its people, and usually of a determination to renew the acquaintance.

The sentiment is even more powerful among the Greeks. Historically, there has not been much since Byron to encourage a sense of common interest. Culturally, Germany and France (and even Italy and the Middle East) have long provided the most powerful traditional links between Greece and the outside world. Thousands of Greek students still enrol regularly at universities in those countries, but still very few in England. Economically (even taking account of British preference for Greek raisins in their Christmas puddings and plum duffs), England continues to be well behind other European countries in terms of economic importance to Greece. In recent years, especially, Germany has contributed infinitely more to Greece's post-war recovery. And yet, the Greek admiration for Britain and all things British is instinctive, general and almost passionate. The list of coveted British qualities (sometimes partly imaginary, it must be conceded!) is very long: the British parliamentary system, for a start. This, along with the British Press, British justice, British fair-play and British democratic traditions in general, is the paragon of all the political virtues which no Greek politician dare question or deride. Interest in British political developments (even of such comparatively minor events as a local by-election) is widespread and painstaking. The space devoted to such things in the columns of the Greek Press would make a British foreign editor green with envy.

Then there is British punctuality. The parting shot of a Greek who makes an appointment on the phone is very often: 'English time, I mean', signifying that he expects some degree of exactitude. The average Greek notion about British punctuality is a serious embarrassment to me: to be five or ten minutes late for an appointment is to lay myself open to charges, not of simple human failing, but of apostasy and treason!

Any British product, in itself, is considered superior in quality to its rivals, and if more of them are not sold in Greece it is usually the fault of exporters' indifference to a small market. Every street-corner hawker of lengths of shoddy proclaims the British origin of his wares as the most unfailing selling gambit at his disposal. In the cinema, the Greek spectator sighs contently in the expectation of solid enjoyment when he sees Arthur Rank's muscular gong-banger go into action. And my Greek friends all assumed that my possession of a French car was the result of some unhappy but unavoidable misfortune.

British patterns tend to be followed, also, in many fields of technique and organization. For the Greeks, Scotland Yard is not merely a romantic symbol of police efficiency; the methods of the highly efficient Greek police forces are in many ways patterned on the British model. The same is true of the organization and training of the Greek armed forces: the traditions of British seafaring and aviation, in particular, seem to find an echo in the Greek temperament. Even if Columbus was not a Greek (as has been seriously argued), the traditions of a small, sea-bound country which, like Britain, has in the past become bigger than life-size because of its mastery of the sea, are reflected in that particularly balanced blend of technical skill and impetuosity which we often sense on board a Greek ship or plane.

The list of affinities could be expanded almost indefinitely. In the British the Greeks see either a reflection of themselves as they are, or an image of themselves as they would like to be. There could hardly be more persuasive evidence of a basic similarity in character and values.

But we must not push the analogy too far. I am not sure, for instance, that there is more than a superficial similarity between Greek and British notions of true courage. Of all the virtues in Greek manhood, none is more admired than that of being a *pallikári*; and, if I could translate that word accurately, I should have explained the difference I am hinting at. It implies bravery in a sense verging much more on 'bravado' than on cool, calculated courage of the kind Britons most admire. The Greek *pallikári* is daring, defiant, headstrong, rebellious. His make-up bears strong traces of an instinctive disrespect for authority and an ingenious ability to triumph over material constraints. The Greek image of a brave man, in a word, implies the ideal qualities of a guerrilla fighter. It is no accident that some of the most notable guerrilla actions in history – against the Germans in wartime Greece and, indeed, against the British in Cyprus – have been fought by Greeks. A long history of resistance against foreign occupiers, rapid and turbulent changes of government and the constant struggle against the ingrown poverty of Greece's natural resources have produced a uniquely tough alloy of spiritual defiance and physical hardihood.

This forceful individuality and resourcefulness assert themselves in many other aspects of the Greek character, in peace as well as at war. The Greek may admire and aspire to traditional British conceptions of order, restraint and polite morality. But these qualities are the veneer of an affluent society which, like Shaw's Mr Doolittle, the Greek cannot always afford. Keep a watch out of the window as you fly over Greece for the first time. Observe the heart-breaking succession of bald mountains and rocky slopes. Remember that, for every acre of olives, vines and oranges, for every picturesque village nestling in a valley, for every inviting sandy bay skirting clear turquoise water, there are a dozen more acres, villages, bays which, considering their fertility, water-supply and means of access, might as well be in the middle of the Sahara. Survival in Greece indeed demands resourcefulness; and the overtones in the scale of resourcefulness often have an unpleasant ring: sharp-wittedness, intrigue, a tough code of commercial practice, and all the other human failings of men compelled to compete for a share of far too small a pie.

The aims of this kind of competition are, however, relative. Helped by a smiling climate and, as we shall see, a much intenser sense of communal living than is possible in more urbanized countries, the Greek tends to take his pleasures simply. A 'comfortable' standard of living in Greece, by most European standards, would be regarded as next to penury; and those Greeks who fail in the contest for one of the bigger pieces of pie live on incomes which elsewhere would be thought incapable of supporting life at its simplest level. Yet nowhere in Greece does poverty bring debasement or despair; nowhere does it seem to destroy the Greek's natural sense of dignity. I have seen poverty everywhere in Greece; I have rarely seen misery. The cleanliness of even the poorest Greek cottage in a remote mountain village is somehow symbolic of its occupants' buoyant attitude to life. Even in the towns, the shoe-blacks who cheerfully take your threepence for an expert shine in all weathers keep their brass accoutrements as carefully polished as their own sharp wit and philosophical turn of phrase. I have yet to meet one who, his velvet rag flying over the glistening toe-cap, would not rather quip about the latest political rumour than moan about the manifest drawbacks of a shoe-black's life.

It is this lack of servility, this insistence on dignity and self-respect through all adversity which, among other things, is implied in that other untranslatable attribute of the Greek character which is called *philótimo*. It is not so much a recognizable set of attributes as an aura of everything desirable in a real man: forthrightness, pride, honesty, cheerfulness, respect of oneself and of one's neighbours. Nobody quite knows what it is, but a Greek who is reputed not to have it is a sorry character indeed. One aspect of it certainly shows in the patterns of Greek criminality: crimes of passion, with punishment meted out to faithless spouses or usurping lovers (or both), are certainly within the rules permitted or even encouraged by *philótimo*. The same is true of crimes to avenge family honour, however blackened (the vendetta is still a living, if somewhat attenuated part of Cretan *mores*). Thievery, on the other hand, and assaults of all kinds, are distinctly forbidden by *philótimo*; and these crimes are, indeed, remarkably rare in Greece. Recent isolated cases of breaking into lush suburban villas and pay-van hold-ups have been regarded with indignation as Hollywood-inspired exoticisms. The same has been true of what the Greeks call *teddyboyismós*: acts of hooliganism by jeans-clad youngsters received short shrift – they were not only deplorable in themselves but, even worse, a product of the juke-box rather than the *bouzoúki* (q.v. later). Drastic police action, which took the form of shearing long hair, clipping the legs of blue jeans, and parading groups of the miscreants round the town bearing placards proclaiming 'I am a teddyboy' soon put a stop to the fashion.

In this strong preference for the home-grown rather than the foreign product, even in types of criminality, I detect another aspect of the Greek character: an apparent tendency towards jingoism. I say apparent because, when we look at the phenomenon more closely, we see that it is only formal and superficial. It is natural in a country with an illustrious collective past, and a present which is often troubled and dangerous, that the ruling authorities of whatever brand of politics should seek to inspire unity and popular support by appealing to patriotic sentiment. Greek children are thoroughly schooled in the glorious landmarks of their national history. On anniversaries like that of Independence Day on 25 March and 'No' Day (the day the Greeks turned down the Italian ultimatum in 1940) on 28 October, the blue-and-white flag of Greece waves freely over the landscape, patriotic platitude is unrestrained and the stirring hymn of the poet Dionysius Solomos, which is the splendid (and reasonably brief) Greek national anthem, is heard over the land. But these are common enough formal effusions of national sentiment. I do not think they make the Greeks jingos. For jingoism implies an aggressive prejudice against foreign influences, and the Greeks are too realistic (and have too much *philótimo*) not to acknowledge their constant debt to foreign contributions to their material and cultural progress. It is fair to say, I think, that Greek knowledge of, admiration for and anxiety to benefit by foreign achievements in the technical and cultural fields is proportionate, to a remarkably honest and realistic degree, to Greek needs. The voice of the jingos is sometimes heard, even in circles which ought to know better – as when, recently, official censure was directed against the growing practice of putting up neon signs in foreign languages (Fly such-and-such; Modes; Drink so-and-so; Bar; Dancing; Cabaret, etc.), and there was a solemn committee formed to investigate and recommend corrective measures. I have not heard of this committee for a very long time, and the foreign-language signs (in keeping with the number of foreign visitors who read them) continue to increase and multiply. A distinct victory for the anti-jingos.

A strong sense of patriotism *is* a Greek characteristic, but it is a special kind of local patriotism. When a Greek is asked what is his *patrída*, his fatherland, he replies, not Greece, but Crete, or Vólos, or Corfu; and a 'compatriot' is not a fellow Greek, but a fellow Macedonian, or Spartan, or Rhodian. The geographical configuration of Greece, with its wild mountain barriers and the encompassing sea breaking the country into small and isolated regions has been largely responsible for the growth of this parochial tradition. And the tradition is still strong enough to ensure, for instance, that a man from Mytilene who applies for a job in a shop or factory owned by a Mytilenian 'compatriot' will expect (and usually get) preferential treatment over 'foreign' applicants. And the numerous Greeks who seek and make their fortunes in other countries almost invariably confine their largesse to their own birthplace rather than endow some national objective. The villages and islands of Greece are liberally sprinkled with churches, schools, hospitals and public libraries of a magnificence out of all proportion to their setting, the gifts of rich Greeks who live abroad or of old emigrants who regularly return from running a restaurant in Texas or California to live out their remaining years in the village which has never ceased to be their home.

Very often, this developed sense of local loyalty is formalized and strengthened by the unique institution of the *koumbáros*. In Orthodox practice the *koumbáros* is the best man at the wedding or the godfather at the christening. It is a solemn function which involves more than formal duties. In Greek eyes the *koumbáros* becomes a kind of honorary blood relation, not only of the married couple or the godchild, but of the whole family, and he is thereafter bound to protect and advance the family's interests. The correct choice of one's *koumbáros* is, therefore, a matter of some moment. He should, ideally, have both money and influence in reasonable measure. Members of Parliament, for instance, generally find after several years at the job that about half of their constituents are in a position to demand the considerations due not only from an elected representative, or even from a 'compatriot' (as a Greek Deputy nearly always is), but from a notional relative!

And this brings us face to face with one more dominant facet of the Greek character pattern: devotion to the gambit of the *rousfétti*. This charming word, of Arabic extraction, opens up a whole universe of subtle character expression. Originally, I believe, the word denoted the sum of money paid by a politician or a party in return for support. Now, as I apprehend it, the word describes any kind of favour given or received, on a basis of mutual interest, within the limits of the law but conferring advantages which the beneficiary could never hope to attain through the normal functioning of the administrative or social machinery. This is a formalistic, but carefully deliberate definition of a phenomenon which is an integral part of a Greek's everyday life and a faithful mirror of his character. Let us take a closer look at it. The favours bartered in this process are of vast and infinite variety: an appointment as teacher of theology in an elementary school, a transfer from lighthouse keeper in the Sporades to port officer in Hydra, a postponement of military service, a licence to operate a lottery shop – any one, in fact, of the thousand benign ambitions which seek to improve an individual's condition of life. As for the mutual interest shared by the one who receives and the one who confers the *rousfétti*, it may be based on *koumbáros*-ship, the expectation of an electoral vote, or – more often – the simple proposition that one good turn will, sooner or later, deserve another. The important thing is to have the *mésa*, that is, the 'means' or chain of acquaintances which will lead to the person who is in a position to confer the favour sought. But nowhere in this chain is any cash transaction involved. A bribe is one thing, a *rousfétti* is quite another. The former is something which, both in the giving and the taking, offends the Greek sense of *philótimo*; it is, indeed, comparatively rare in Greece. The latter, on the other hand, is a legitimate instrument of honest social exchange. And this brings us to the last element of our definition: in a poor country where a slow bureaucratic process can never keep up with the superhuman task of making a scrupulously just distribution of benefits and facilities which will not stretch to keep everyone happy, the *rousfétti* is a rough and ready, but extremely useful kind of levelling agent. It is the grease which smoothes the action of the official machine.

I prefer to regard the *rousfétti* as a significant pointer to individual Greek psychology than as a collective social phenomenon. The whole system, it seems to me, rests on a deep-rooted consciousness in every Greek that he shares a common struggle with each of his countrymen to survive and to prosper in conditions which favour neither survival nor prosperity. In every petitioner he sees himself.

The same instinctive sense of community operates, I have observed, to preserve a humane kind of elasticity in relations between the Greek citizen and officialdom. On the face of it, these relations are formidably complex and rigid. The Greek bureaucracy (perhaps because of the unspoken need to keep as many people as possible in employment) is more than somewhat devoted to rule-books and paper-chasing. Yet, in practice, the severity of the system is nicely adjusted by the fact that, in the last resort, relations between a citizen and a civil servant can always be translated into converse between one Greek and another. In my experience, there is practically nothing the rule book forbids which cannot be permitted, and nothing which should take a month to navigate the bureaucratic morass which cannot be completed in twenty-four hours – provided the matter is broached in the right spirit of appeal to the arbiter's reasonableness and *philótimo*.

The common denominator of all these aspects of the Greek character, the aspect which combines all the causes and all the effects which have operated over the centuries (the intimacy of nature, poverty, geographical isolation, sense of community, *philótimo*), is a Greek's respect for the wants of a stranger and his determination, sometimes showily, sometimes with great self-sacrifice, to supply them. This is the quality which, more than any other, makes an immediate impression on a visitor and lingers longest in his memory: the quality of Greek hospitality. If I have been a long time reaching it, it is because hospitality is the active manifestation of the deeper and more passive aspects of the Greek character which we have been looking at. We ought now to understand it better. It is not a question of polite consideration or generosity towards strangers, or even an act of obedience to a commendable moral code. For a Greek, the act of hospitality is one of self-fulfilment; it is as inevitable, as instinctive, as eternal as the act of drawing breath.

The permanence and instinctive quality of a Greek's attitude towards a stranger is indicated by the language. In Greek there is no separate word for 'stranger' and 'guest'; one is automatically also the other, and both are designated by the word *xénos*. 'Hospitality' is simply *philoxénia* (an act of friendship towards a stranger). Nor is there any provision made in the Greek language to distinguish between a 'stranger' and a 'foreigner'. The word *xénos* covers them both. And the same laws of hospitality operate, whether the *xénos* is another Greek from the next village or a black-skinned visitor from the depths of Africa. Foreigner = stranger = guest. It is as simple as that.

The antiquity of the laws governing hospitality in Greece is plain to see in literature. Without them, Odysseus would have had a much less comfortable time of it. In the ancient tragedies, a breach of the laws of hospitality often calls down punishment from the gods as dire as that reserved for crimes we should regard as much less venial.

Things have changed very little in Greece since then. In *The Frogs* of Aristophanes, Dionysus enquires about his projected journey to the nether world. 'Tell me all about the hosts who received you when you journeyed to Cerberus; tell me also of the harbours, the bakeries, the brothels, the drinking-shops, the fountains, the roads, the eating-houses, and of the hostels where there are the fewest bugs.' A stranger enquiring his way about Greece today will readily be provided with all such information. And the chances are that rather than direct a stranger to a hostel of any kind – even one with very few bugs indeed – a Greek villager will offer him a corner of his room, a heavy hand-woven rug for warmth, and a slice of home-baked bread with an olive or two.

Those unacquainted with the Greek rules of hospitality sometimes get into trouble; and a few words of instruction are in order. It is important, in the first place, to appreciate the seriousness of the whole concept. For a Greek to fail in his hospitable duties is a mark of shame which is deeply felt. Regret expressed at the refusal of hospitality is not formal, but very real. This being the case, it is most unfortunate that his gastronomic wisdom lags far behind his sense of obligation towards a stranger. To respond graciously to an offer of hospitality generally involves the visitor, at no matter what time of day, in the ingestion of something terribly sweet. It may be a lump of Turkish delight, a little glassful of banana cordial, a lump of mastic submerged in a glass of cool water (commonly known as a 'submarine'), a sticky pastry, or a spoonful of home-made jam. The latter is generally offered in a bowl from which you are expected to take a dip; it is not necessary, as one of my friends did, to apologize for being unable to finish the whole bowlful!

Offerings of this kind are regarded as a minimum token of hospitality suitable for people you don't know who call for the first time. The equipment required for the purpose (liqueur glasses, jam spoons, silver trays with dainty doyleys, etc.) is standard for newly-weds, in the town and in the country. If you find yourself in this predicament, there is one unexceptionable way out: ask for a cup of coffee instead.

More elaborate hospitality is called for when visits are of longer duration or when the visitors are of some consequence. In towns, this can be taken care of quite simply at a dinner party or in a restaurant. But village hospitality is more spontaneous. You will not only be required to consume everything the household contains of an edible nature, but you will also be loaded on departure with giant rounds of wholemeal bread, a can of local olive oil (always reputed to be the best in Greece) and one or two local cheeses (ditto). This kind of hospitality is fairly easy to take. But there are dangers. A village household, generally speaking, will not contain very much that is edible at a moment's notice. Meat once a week is the highest ambition of most

Greek villagers. The sudden descent of guests therefore presents supply problems. And these problems are usually solved by a determined bout of slaughter in the back yard. I cannot count the number of freshly killed, hastily cooked chickens I have eaten in Greece; but they have been memorable meals in the sense that they have brought home the virtues of the slightly deteriorated carcasses we more often eat.

Even among friends and neighbours, the Greek laws of hospitality are taken with considerable seriousness. I have often thought that the rarity of revolving doors in Greek public buildings is due to the fact that when two Greeks visit a bank or a hotel together it is not always easy for them to sort out the guest–host relationship between the two of them, and the resulting hesitation as to who goes first could well cause a nasty accident. The same difficulties crop up in Greek restaurants. Do not imagine, as you walk in and hear two or three rowdy altercations, that customers are complaining about the quality of the food or the service. The likeliest explanation is that parties who have dined together are arguing about who pays the bill. What we, uncensoriously, call 'Dutch treat' and what the Greeks, with considerable disdain, call the 'German system', is not countenanced in polite circles, and only with a shameful feeling of guilt in circumstances where financial stringency makes it necessary. Do not imagine, either, that an argument about who pays the bill is a formality in which the art of out-fumbling is practised. I have seen men actually come to blows over the claim to the privilege of paying. In cases where really tough resistance is anticipated, it is usual for the self-appointed host to retire somewhere out of sight about half-way through the meal. It is not possible, for obvious reasons, to enquire where he is going! And when the bill is called for at the end, it will be found to be already paid. Nothing is smugger in Greece than the smile on the face of the man who has thus out-rused his opponent. It takes a real fighter to ignore a *fait accompli* of this kind and succeed in having the money returned. But I have seen even that happen often enough! A foreigner in Greece, I should add, never gets involved in an argument of this kind. He is, under all circumstances, the guest. It is unthinkable that he should pay even when, on his insistence, he has been allowed to assume that he is acting as host.

The sincerity and power of this Greek view of hospitality is illustrated by a story I was recently told by the editor of a leading Athens morning paper who comes from a remote village in the Mani. When he visited his old uncle in his home village last summer, my friend was telling him enthusiastically of the great growth of tourism which was helping to bring prosperity to the country. 'You are out of your head, young man,' said Uncle. 'What prosperity? We've had some of your tourists here in the village this summer. Of course, we did what we could for them. But if, as you say, there are going to be more and more of them, what on earth are we to do? They'll eat us out of house and home!'

Most of the attributes of the Greek character we have discussed are generally sympathetic. I hope I have not been guilty of suppression or special pleading. It has not been my purpose to make a plea, but merely to describe and explain the Greek. And his basic qualities, I believe, are endearing and virtuous. The Greeks themselves, strangely, are not given to a self-satisfied appraisal of these virtues. They will hardly admit that they exist. They are, on the contrary, devoted to public self-criticism. The phrase 'We Greeks . . .' is a frequent introduction to a catalogue of character defects which includes practically every social vice in the book. The same kind of self-castigation is the bread and butter of the nationally famous journalists who provide the Greek Press with its most popular feature: the 'chronicle', or daily humourous homily about Greek men and matters. Take an average sample at random, and you will find that in these light-hearted but highly representative sermons by Vláchou, Psathás, Lidorikis and others, the Greeks are almost daily accused of being backward, unruly, excessively individualistic, undisciplined, talkative, demagogic, conspiratorial and in most other ways unfit representatives of an enlightened human society.

There are, indeed, traces of most of these vices in the Greek character. If I have not chosen to dwell on them it is not out of a desire to conceal flaws, but because these flaws seem to me to be superficial cracks in a substance which is sterling and solid; defects which are often the evident result of passing historical phenomena; which are subject to infinite variation among individuals; and which are mostly inherent in the admirable and dominant virtues which characterize the race of Greeks.

There could be no more persuasive evidence of this than the fact that, while he takes his virtues for granted, the Greek is perhaps the world's most persistent penitent. He knows and constantly parades his faults to himself and to his fellows. And of all the Greek virtues, the Platonic exercise of self-criticism and improvement by example is perhaps the most appealing of all.

4 That Unfamiliar Feeling

The visitor, as we have seen, is certain, through indelible custom, of a friendly reception in Greece. But, even if it were not so, he would be sure of at least a formally cordial welcome as a matter of peremptory self-interest. For, in the last five or six years, international tourism in Greece has become big business. The world's steadily increasing flock of summer migrants searching for new and untried holiday experiences has found in Greece an ideal place to roost: a country where the attractions of climate, novelty and landscape are matched by the determination of the authorities to tap an important new source of national income and to encourage faithfulness to the official assurance that 'Greece Greets You Warmly'. From a mere handful in the 1950s, the number of foreign tourists in Greece is now about a million a year and rising rapidly. The money they spend is about the biggest single source of precious foreign exchange. When we consider that, even now, tourists in Greece represent only about one in every hundred who holiday abroad in Europe, it is obvious that there is still plenty of scope for many millions to make their first acquaintance with the country. They will find everything geared to their comfort and enjoyment: new tourist roads, new hotels, new beaches, and every facility that officialdom, by direct action or persuasion, can supply. Apart from their direct material interest in this peaceful invasion, the Greeks have every reason to be pleased with it: for many radical improvements in the facilities and the external appearances of Greece, long overdue in the interests of the Greeks themselves, have now been made in the name of tourism. 'What will they think of us?' is now one of the most powerful and respected slogans heard in public discussion of public amenities.

There is always the danger that, in the attempt to adapt a country's facilities to the preconceived needs and tastes of foreign visitors, some of the genuine native patina gets rubbed off. There are, after all, very few travellers who expect or desire to find a home from home when they go abroad. The temporary sacrifice of dainty cucumber teas or chocolate malts is part of the fun, adding to the zest of adventure and discovery.

It is my experience, however, that there are fairly tight limits on this enthusiastic quest for the exotic and the unfamiliar. The limits are widest for the young, the unattached, the belligerently beatnik and bohemian. For them it is possible to spend months of unshaven nomadic bliss discovering Greece with the aid of no more than a sleeping bag and a frequently replenished bottle of *ouzo*. The majority of tourists are more mature and more conservative. They prefer to make their exciting discoveries from a comfortable ringside seat. The exotic and the unfamiliar, as observed phenomena, are the very stuff of a successful holiday abroad. But personal involvement in unaccustomed conditions of life tends to induce a sense of uneasiness, disorientation and even resentment. Involvement of this kind, particularly in a comparatively new and unspoiled tourist country like Greece, is inevitable up to a point. Which makes it worth while to identify and describe the main elements of unfamiliarity which a foreign visitor to Greece should be prepared for.

A country's internal political system may, on the face of things, be none of a tourist's business. But it is a very insensitive visitor whose mood is not influenced by the prevailing political and institutional atmosphere. It is difficult to relax and have fun in tourist blinkers in a country, for instance, where entry is subject to strict visa regulations and a prolonged scrutiny at the frontier of secret card indexes; where an omnipresent variety of armed men in uniforms seems almost to outnumber the civilians; where the threat of public disturbance, from minor street clashes to full-blooded revolution, is never entirely absent.

At many times in the last hundred years Greece would have presented drawbacks of this category. Like earthquakes which periodically disturb the cooling crust of a new planet, civil disturbance and change have punctuated the development of modern Greece: dynasties have been enthroned, exiled and reinstated; constitutions have been drafted, enacted, amended, forgotten; monarchs, republican presidents, even a dictator, have succeeded each other dizzily at the summit of power. The critical moment came after World War II when, after a near-miraculous defeat of the Italians and a brave resistance to the Germans, the Greeks were denied the respite which came to the rest of Europe in 1945. For Greece, Allied victory was the signal for a fierce civil struggle which, for four more years, continued to depreciate the human and material resources of the country. It was not till the end of 1949 that Greece, by a hair's breadth, emerged safely as a member of the Western alliance rather than a minor Soviet satellite. But it was a costly victory. A country never rich in natural resources had been cast into a situation of chaos and material ruin at a time when the rest of Europe was climbing steadily out of the wartime pit.

Allied economic assistance, given to Greece in the post-war period as a guarantee against being sucked into the Soviet orbit, helped considerably to enable Greece to recapture and then surpass her pre-war living standards. But Allied aid (never given as generously to Greece as to some other countries who used it less effectively) was equalled as a factor in the post-war recovery of Greece by the emergence of a remarkable political leader, Constantine Karamanlís. For nearly a decade after he became Prime Minister in 1955, Karamanlís worked for Greece with a flair and honest diligence which created order out of chaos and restored the country to the list of modern European states with tolerable living standards. The faults of the Karamanlís régime need not concern us here – except for the purpose of noting that they finally put an end, in 1963, to his record run of office. What matters to the visitor is that the stable and constructive years of Karamanlís effected changes deeper than can be measured in the quantitative terms of material progress: no matter what political changes occur in Greece in the years ahead, nothing is now likely to destroy the new and comforting acquisition of *predictability* and orderly development in Greek affairs. Armchair politics (or, in this case, the politics of the pavement café) have always been a popular pursuit in Greece; and some diehards can still be heard to discuss the future of the country in the old terms of plots, conspiracies, palace revolutions and military coups. It is an amusing and harmless enough accompaniment to backgammon and Turkish coffee; but it has no relation to the Greece of the present, a country which now fits snugly enough into the accepted mould of Western parliamentary democracy. Some specific procedures and institutions, as we shall see when we take a look at the Greek Press and radio, still bear the marks of a turbulent past which has not favoured the luxury of democratic standards at their purest. The close threat of communist infiltration, especially, has delayed progress in that direction. The displacement of Karamanlís in 1963 and the thaw in the cold war seem likely to speed up the process of a return to more robust democratic standards under a more insistently liberal régime. But blemishes which insufficient time and hazardous circumstance have not yet eradicated should not obscure the fact that, in the last few years, Greece has undergone a process of qualitative change in which expanding prosperity and its gradual equalization have inspired a new mood of permanency and confidence. It is only a few years since Greece's future was so uncertain and her currency so exposed to overnight depreciation that the Greeks kept their savings in the form of gold sovereigns stuffed into old socks or under the floorboards. Foreigners with money to invest would rather have risked it on a gold mine in Patagonia than on the most promising Greek enterprise. It is a vast step from that state of affairs to the present situation when the hoards of gold sovereigns in Greece have been practically liquidated, the banks bulge with deposits in drachmas (now one of the most stable currencies in the world), and private foreign capital flows continuously into Greece to finance anything from a hotel to a hardware factory.

A tourist is not directly concerned with these tokens of improving material prosperity. But he is not usually indifferent to his surroundings to the extent of remaining unmoved by extreme contrasts of wealth and poverty, by the sight of desolation, by the sense of simmering disquiet ready to erupt in strike, riot and disorder. From all these points of view, Greece today is a much pleasanter place to visit than it was a decade ago. The Greek Parliament, though it is by no means the most decorous in the world and where fisticuffs occasionally sublimate the impotent rage of mere words, on the whole conducts its business with dignity and in accord with standard democratic procedures. Greek uniforms are either charmingly colourful (like those of the skirted Evzone guards you can photograph at the Palace), or comfortingly familiar (like those of the Armed Forces which are almost indistinguishable from their British equivalents), or endearingly bizarre (like those of the Athens traffic cops with their great shining metal helmets), or attractively chic (like those of the officer cadets with their yellow tabs and little polished swords). Firearms are reserved exclusively for those who guard vital buildings. The standard police weapon is the wooden truncheon, carefully tucked out of sight. A special squad of particularly pleasant policemen, each bearing on his tunic the flag of the foreign countries whose languages he speaks, exists to cope with the problems and enquiries of foreign visitors.

Intercourse between police and public is generally on a man-to-man basis (another example, probably, of that Greek sense of communal interest). The dignity of the law lurking behind a police uniform tends to be less than overwhelming in its effect on most Greek citizens who, when challenged for some infringement by a policeman, will generally engage in verbal combat which often ends by putting the man in uniform on the defensive.

The use of handcuffs, by contrast, sometimes gives a disturbing impression of anachronistic severity. It is not too unusual to see handcuffed prisoners being escorted in the street or on a public vehicle. The practice has lately attracted some criticism and may be expected to yield to greater discretion.

Sirens, on the other hand, are not much used. They are not in the Greek capital, as they are, for instance, in New York, a constant source of physical disturbance and mental disquiet. Fire engines exist, of course, but are rarely needed. Ambulances can be seen frequently enough beating the traffic lights to the nearest first-aid post – but they generally prefer flashing lights to sirens. And police prowl cars are decorously indistinguishable in appearance and behaviour from beige-coloured taxis.

Elections, too, are quiet affairs in Greece. This is partly because the Greeks take their politics seriously, and partly because steps are taken to prevent disorders. On election day in Greece, which is always a Sunday, it is forbidden to serve or consume any alcohol in public places; and, in addition to the gendarmes at every polling station, there is a lawyer who represents the judiciary and makes sure that polling proceeds fairly and in accordance with the rules. It is between elections that the temperature sometimes goes up uncomfortably. The Constitution guarantees the right of public meeting, but the police (too often, I would say, ready to take government advice) always have the right to ban meetings on the ground that they are likely to provoke public disturbance. It is when a banned meeting is held in defiance of the ban that the police riot squads, complete with caged trucks, tear gas and fire hoses, are sometimes called into action. The centre of the capital is so constricted that, on the rare occasions when this game of cops and rioters is held, the whole of the city comes to a standstill and shopkeepers draw their shutters in resignation until the storm blows over. It is, after all, not very much more serious, and hardly at all less gay, than those occasions when traffic grinds to a halt amid the waving flags as some visiting foreign dignitary is greeted by the Mayor at Hadrian's Gate before going on to lay a wreath at the Unknown Warrior's Tomb.

In this atmosphere of recently acquired calm and stability (for my sketch of riot procedure is not to be taken as characteristic) the Greek Monarchy plays its predetermined role as the fount of constitutional safeguards and a solid anchor in a storm. It was not always so. In fact, the most serious civil discords in the history of modern Greece have centred on the issue Republic *v.* Monarchy. The first king of modern Greece, who was a Bavarian chosen by the great powers, landed at the provisional capital Nafplion in 1833. This king, Otto, abdicated in 1862 and died in exile in 1867 – not altogether forgotten since central streets of Athens (which he reinstated as capital) are still named after him and his Queen, Amalia; and German names of Bavarian families who followed Otto to Greece (including the name of Greece's most popular beer still brewed by the Fix (Fuchs) family) are still not uncommon. In 1863 Otto had been replaced by the founder of a new dynasty which, after almost exactly one hundred years, is still reigning. This time it was King George I from Denmark. But the dynasty's century has been far from uneventful or uninterrupted. George I, with the aid of a new and more liberal Constitution and the return to Greece of the Ionian Islands from Britain, stayed the course for half a century. But his reign was ended in 1913 by an assassin in Salonika, and his successor Constantine had a very brief innings indeed. The brother-in-law of Kaiser Willy, he was not very happy about Greece entering World War I on the side of the Allies and, in 1917, he was forced to abdicate in favour of his second son Alexander. Alexander was not a very willing candidate, being a young blood much more interested in motor cars than the exercise of sovereignty. His morganatic marriage to a lady not of the blood caused an uproar which was eventually calmed after negotiations with the Prime Minister in Paris, and Alexander might have lasted on the throne longer than three years had it not been for one of the pet monkeys kept at the royal country residence near Athens at Tatóï. The monkey bit the young king one day in 1920 and the blood poisoning which set in was quickly fatal.

The next few years up to 1924 (which saw the giant disaster of the Greek campaign in Asia Minor) were among the most confused and tumultuous in modern Greek history: a succession of Regencies, the recall of Constantine from exile in Switzerland, the replacement of Constantine by his son George II, Constantine's death in Palermo and finally, after a gamut of revolutions, military coups, plebiscites and every form of political upheaval known to man, the abdication of the Monarchy and the declaration, in 1924, of a Republic under Venizelos.

The next eleven years, during which George II retired to the various sites of residence frequented by Greek kings in exile, were hardly less rumbustious than those which preceded the Republic. Inevitably, George II came back, in 1935, to rule—until in 1941 the Axis compelled his withdrawal in turn to Crete, Cairo and London. For four of those six years, from 1936 to 1940, the king held the fort for the dictatorship of General Metaxas. That, among other things, made him a figure of controversy when, after the Allied victory, a plebiscite in 1946 recalled him to the throne, and the communist rebellion temporarily quelled in 1944 flared up again even more seriously. The suppression of this revolt in 1949 ensured the continuation of the Greek Monarchy which, since 1947, has been competently represented first by George II's younger brother Paul and his Queen, Frederika, and now by Paul's son, the young King Constantine.

It is difficult, considering the position of the Greek Monarchy today, to imagine the insecurity and controversy which has punctuated its history. That it is now so firmly established is the result of the general improvement we noted in the psychological stability of post-war Greece and the improved material conditions on which that stability rests. This is not to say, of course, that nobody in Greece criticizes the Royal Family. But censure has now become limited to the grumbles which are directed at most royalty: complaints about excessive pomp, excessive spending of the taxpayer's money on needless luxuries, the narrowness and remoteness of court circles, etc. Sometimes, too, in the day-to-day rough-and-tumble of politics, efforts are made – although his constitutional position is almost identical to that of most democratic monarchies – to drag the king into party disputes. But criticism and party exploitation of the monarchy in Greece now stop very far short of any kind of fundamental opposition to its place in the Greek scheme of things. Republicans, as individual idealists, still exist. But Republicanism, as an organized political force, is dead. The value of the monarchy as a guarantee of continuing calm and progress is now almost universally conceded.

Speaking in generalities, we might say that the attitude of the Greek public as a whole towards their Royal Family lies, in the scale of collective affection, somewhere between the cool utilitarian approach of the Scandinavians and the tradition-clouded, more fulsome affection of the British. In their turn, the Greek Royal Family operate somewhere about half-way along the scale between British pomp and ceremonial and the Scandinavian 'common touch'. You will not find a Greek railway station-master putting on his top hat and rubbing out the sign which reads 'Gents' when the king sets out on a journey. Nor are you likely to find him sitting unobtrusively in the next seat at an Athens cinema, or buying a newspaper at a kiosk. As members of a select and increasingly exclusive club, the Greek King and Queen keep the club rules: they almost never give interviews to the Press; they are surrounded and advised by a not particularly representative rump of Athenian 'aristocracy'; they never set foot out of doors without the whole of the police force being alerted for their protection; they marry their children decorously, and after delicate negotiation, to the most suitable candidates among overseas club members; they travel frequently to shop in Bond Street and look after their estates abroad. But, as titular heads of an adopted and frugal Greek family, they skilfully avoid offending sensibilities and arduously pursue good works: the promotion of charities; breaking red-dyed eggs and roasting lambs with the soldiers at Easter; riding on donkeys into the remotest and muddiest villages of Greece in the depths of winter; providing dowries for impecunious peasant girls. And the young king is likely to follow in his parents' footsteps.

In many ways the Greek monarch's skill in the performance of royal functions has excelled that of his colleagues in other countries: The late King Paul, for all his apparent simplicity, proved himself a splendid tactician when, in 1955, he made Karamanlís his surprise selection to form a government. And the Queen Mother Frederika, who is a woman of incisive intelligence and no mean academic attainment, can be a real charmer. Her 'small talk' on formal occasions is a masterpiece of brilliant and convincing improvisation. Their children are, if anything, even more popular. King Constantine became a national hero when, as Crown Prince, he won an Olympic gold medal in 1960; his Danish bride-to-be is extraordinarily pretty; the Princesses, Sofia who is now married and Irene, are known as unaffected, carefully brought-up young ladies, with an endearing interest in Greek archaeology.

The picture of a firmly established monarchy and a democratically elected executive which now governs Greece with stable efficiency, is beginning to be reflected in a gradually improving Greek bureaucracy. Intolerably low civil service salaries, lack of experience resulting from centuries of foreign rule, a tendency towards over-centralization and neglect of provincial interests, a cumbersome procedure resulting from failure to delegate even minor decisions to ranks below the very top – all these and many other aspects of an administration poor in the quality of its personnel and unwieldy in its system of operation now show signs of improvement.

The foreign visitor in Greece is not, fortunately, required to cultivate an intimate acquaintance with the civil service. But increasing contact with the outside world has been one of the mainsprings of its improvement. Commerical and economic interests, on the private and inter-state levels, have compelled the radical reorganization of the services concerned. Greece has at last acquired a reasonably efficient statistical service, international tariff classifications, the kilo and the litre instead of the quaint but dinosaurian Turkish *oke*, nicely designed shiny coins well made in France and Switzerland to replace grubby low-denomination banknotes, an expanding telex system, and a host of other amenities the lack of which for so long branded Greece as backward in its relations with the streamlined world outside.

These amenities are much appreciated by foreign businessmen. The individual tourist on vacation is more interested in certain other aspects of Greek officialdom. First, in time and place, is the Customs, the advance-post of any country's personality. This used to be a strangely patchy organization, a Jekyll and Hyde mixture of beguiling informality and infuriating severity. On my first visit to Greece eight years ago I crossed the Yugoslav–Greek frontier by car after midnight. At the Yugoslav barrier I had, by dint of sheer outraged resistance, won a weird battle in sign-language and tattered shreds of German with a pompous communist Customs man who evinced a desire to take the engine apart in a search for hidden treasure. It was a relief, which I still remember with emotion, to find, on the Greek side of the frontier, a radically different approach. Instead of waiting rigidly at his deserted post in full uniform at the dead of night like his Yugoslav colleague, the Greek Customs man – a benign wheezing character – turned out of bed in his pyjamas to greet me. It was clear from the start that he had no intention of prolonging the interview which had disturbed his sleep. He provided a vast printed form on which, under his gentle instruction, I wrote the word 'No' seven times above my signature. This formality completed, the laws of hospitality demanded that I drink a quick cup of coffee before being ushered kindly back to my car and on down the road to Salonika.

At less remote frontier posts, however, Greek Customs custom tended to be more peremptory – even harsh. Local shortages after the war put such a high premium on smuggled luxuries that even foreign visitors were generally greeted as *prima facie* offenders, and their luggage was meticulously searched for loot.

All this has now been changed by careful Ministry of Finance directives. The machinery of collecting duty is still absurdly complex for some purposes. I have found, for instance, that my right to import a duty-free car can be exercised only if I employ a special agent who, versed as he is in the mysterious lore and friendly as he is with the officials concerned, still needs three or four days to complete the formalities. I have often had to spend hours in a gloomy Customs office to clear a book or a magnetic tape sent by ordinary airmail but waylaid before delivery. I remember once arguing for a whole hour to persuade a zealous Customs official that one way he could *not* check the contents of an exposed roll of colour film I wanted to send to England was to open the can for inspection! But the tourist will not have to cope with this kind of problem. Provided he avoids wiring home for an extra pair of socks (in which event he will have to endure the ordeal of a visit to the aromatic regions of Sophocles Street where, among the barrels of oil and stacked salamis of the wholesale grocery warehouses, the postal Customs house is strangely hidden) he will find the Greek Customs man all benevolence and light. A quick glance at a foreign passport, a formal enquiry expecting the answer No, and the ordeal is over. These days in tourist-conscious Greece, a foreigner's bags are never opened unless there are specific grounds for suspicion; and the Customs official who fails to smile a greeting is doomed to rapid demotion.

There have been many improvements, too, in another branch of the Greek bureaucracy which the tourist inevitably meets. It is still not possible, it is true, to buy airletter forms or stamps from a machine, to send a registered package without taking it for inspection before it is sealed, or to send a parcel overseas without completing a series of formalities of which, after all these years, I remain blissfully ignorant on account of my determination never to send a parcel anywhere. It is true, also, that the scale of airmail rates (apart from being somewhat high) is so minutely calibred that the correct postage can only be ascertained on the scales at the post office – where, in any event, you have to go to post a letter since the minute blue posting boxes hung on the wall in obscure corners are so few, and so mirage-like when encountered, that they inspire no confidence whatever. Just the same, making every reservation about the convenience of a postal system which compels attendance at a post office for even the simplest transaction, it is true that, once there, the arrangements are now much smoother and more rapid than they used to be. And, when the present mammoth crumbling barn of a building which houses the main post office is finally replaced (an old and cherished dream, this one!), it may even be possible to post a letter in Athens without risking influenza. It is consoling, also, that the monotony of postal affairs in Greece is considerably livened by incessant new issues of commemorative stamps, some of which are very gay and decorative indeed.

The bank is another institution, not quite but almost official, which a tourist finds it hard to avoid. And there is nothing crumbling or barn-like about a Greek bank. Next to the grandiloquent bank-mausolea of Turkey, there is nothing to approach them for solid architectural splendour and sheer profligacy of marble majesty. No doubt there are psychological reasons for this display of air-conditioned grandeur in what are, after all, no more than money shops. Certainly there is a significant contrast between them and the rudimentary portable window-cases which line the pavement in the financial district of Athens: the shop-counters of the street traders who deal in gold sovereigns, no longer a fashionable activity.

It is fortunate that one's sojourn in a Greek bank is so comfortable, even lush. For the sojourn tends to be long, even if one's business is no more ambitious than the changing of a £5 traveller's cheque. Lavishness of the buildings seems to be matched by extravagance in staffing; and the system of work seems to be geared to the necessity for giving everybody something to do. To cash a cheque is a major operation involving scrutiny of one's identity papers by at least two clerks, the signature of an ascending hierarchy of three clerks, the verification of two adding machines, the final check by a cashier who counts the money twice – and the long, long wait in two queues while this ceremonial is proceeding. If you cannot avoid using a Greek bank, my advice is: get there as the doors open at 8.30 a.m., or slip in just as they are closing at 1 p.m. If you can avoid the banks, do – unless it is to accept an invitation to lunch from the Governor of the Bank of Greece (the biggest and marbliest of them all) who in his private suite provides the best and most attractively served food in Greece – not to mention one of the finest views of the Acropolis.

With any luck, the Customs, the Post Office and the Bank should exhaust a visitor's need for contact with Greek officialdom and semi-officialdom. For the rest, his impressions of the familiar and the unfamiliar aspects of life in Greece will be formed from the sights and sounds of ordinary people and ordinary things around him.

It is in Athens that he will form his most vivid impressions, the most intense expression of contrast with his home surroundings. But before we begin an imaginary stroll through the Greek capital, trying to get the 'feel' of the place and alert to new impressions, it might be a good idea to come briefly to grips with a subject which, wherever we are (and especially if we are on holiday) affects our mood, our appreciation, our responsiveness, our most lingering memories of a new place. I speak, of course, of the weather.

Greece does, in general, greet you warmly. Often very warmly indeed. But this is a generalization which needs analysis. The *proper* guide books can tell you all about mean temperatures, rainfall, average wind velocities and hours of sunshine. This is not what *I* mean by weather which, in Greece as elsewhere, is never average, mean or in any other way usual. Exceptional weather is the rule; wherever you go, at whatever season, you will invariably find that it has not been so hot, cold, wet, foggy or windy for at least seventy-three years. Thus, the only true guide to the weather, in my experience, must be expressed in terms of personal impressions rather than statistics.

Let me admit, at once, that I have been guilty of some exaggeration. Any time between mid-May and mid-September it is possible to count on dry weather which varies from very warm at the initial and terminal periods to very hot in the middle. And this, bearing in mind only the elementary and universal principles that it is generally hotter the further south and the more remote from the sea, holds good for the whole of the country. It would be a mistake, however, to imagine that this certainty of warm dry weather in a summer which lasts at least four months ensures comfort with no more than beachwear and a pair of sandals. However hot in daytime, the nights in Greece, blessedly, are cool. Generally, there is a lack of humidity which makes the nights in other hot climates so oppressive and sleepless. And the islands also, especially the popular Cyclades, are rarely free from a cool (not to say chill) breeze, even in midsummer. The breeze often turns into a hearty blow at the time of the *Meltémia* winds, a phenomenon so regular that the islanders have their own terminology for its degrees of strength: *cambanátos*, *kareklátos*, and – the final degree of windpower – *anthropátos*, which, translated freely, mean: 'the wind which rings the bells in the belfries', 'the wind which blows chairs over,' and 'the wind which knocks people for six'. When these winds are blowing in the more exposed portions of the Aegean, even if it is no more than a mild *cambanátos*, one's image of smooth sunlit cruising in small boats is quickly subject to revision.

For the rest of the year, the climate of Greece – although generally milder and more stable than most Europeans are accustomed to – is much more changeable. In latitudes as far south as Crete and Rhodes, winters are nearly always mild and reasonably dry. In the north heavy snowfalls and sustained temperatures below freezing point are common. In the west, from September onwards, the climate tends to be wetter than elsewhere.

Athens and the region around it tend to have the best weather conditions of all. Half-way between the familiar 'temperate' north and the near-tropical south, Athens is shielded in summer from excess heat by its closeness to water on almost every side, and from severe cold in winter by a sheltering ring of mountains – Párnes, Hyméttus, Pendéli. Cold winds and low humidity, it is true, often make winter temperatures seem lower than they are – it is sometimes hard to believe that the thermometer in Athens almost never falls below freezing point; but the great joy of an Athens winter is the certainty of frequent sunshine and the absence of that crushing succession of bleak dark days under a leaden sky. Officially, there is some rain in Athens on about one day in seven. Snow almost never falls in Athens itself; and, for hardy Anglo-Saxons, the temperature of the sea encourages heroics as late as Christmas. There is no more delightful choice than that which often presents itself during an Athenian winter: to drive half an hour up to the surrounding mountains to play in the deep snow, or to drive half an hour in the other direction to enjoy the mild sunlit seashore.

Suitably primed with an insight into public behaviour patterns, and suitably clothed to cope with the behaviour of nature, we are about ready for a reconnaissance to spot some of the less familiar features of the urban Greek landscape. The signposts to a reconnaissance of this kind – the street name-plates – must be interpreted with caution. For all the current monarchical respectability, the republican habit of honouring men and signal moments of history by constant changes of street names dies hard. The Municipal Authority of Athens is notoriously hard up (even to the point of failing to pay its electricity bills) and it is perhaps the lack of other activity occasioned by this penury which encourages this tinkering with nomenclatures. Ask any passing pedestrian, or even a policeman, where you can find the 25th of March Square; you will be met with a blank stare. Yet this, for more than thirty years, has been the official name of that central square of Athens which is universally known as Clafthmónos. The main shopping street of Athens, if I am not mistaken, is once again (after several intervening periods during which the name was temporarily out of favour) officially in the books as Churchill Street. But unless you know that its popular name is invariably Stadium Street you could easily wander around for hours looking for Winston. I really cannot say whether another main parallel of Athens at this moment honours the Academy or the memory of Franklin Delano Roosevelt; but, whatever the name-plates say, Academias is and will always remain its only accepted name.

And so on. What makes it all the more difficult is that street name-plates, previously attached to the walls of buildings at the main intersections, have nearly all disappeared in the frenzy of new building which has changed the whole aspect of Athens in the last few years. The prevailing style of the city up to ten years ago was neo-classical, with low balustraded buildings, stucco walls and red-tiled rooftops. It was a squatly attractive style, giving an impression of expansive ease and reflecting low site-values. Very few of these typical Athenian buildings still stand in the centre of town. And those that do are fast disappearing in a welter of concrete-mixers, pneumatic drills and hoardings which disappear magically overnight to reveal tall new office-blocks and hotels. One of the last of the nostalgic old buildings, daily mourned by the older generation, was the famous café of Zacharátos, on the corner of Constitution Square. The owner of the café, where Greek politics have traditionally been shaped and discussed, died not so long ago after passing his one-hundredth birthday. He would be surprised to know that the site, which he left in his will to one of his faithful waiters, is now worth somewhere around £1,000,000. On the whole, and making every allowance for nostalgic sentiment, the new Athens is a distinct improvement on the old. Building laws (which seek to protect, as far as possible, views of the Acropolis and other historic features of the city) prevent the new buildings from rearing excessively high. Seven or eight storeys is average. And the architectural style, although conservative and testifying to a uniform passion for useless balconies or mock-balconies, is on the whole gay and pleasing enough. Internally, too, these new buildings are attractive in more than a utilitarian sense: the countless new blocks of flats which line the central streets of Athens have a remarkably high lowest common denominator of comfort and cosmetic appeal. Some of them, especially the 'penthouse' apartments set back at the top of the buildings to provide a fixed minimum of light and air, have breathtaking views of the Acropolis and spacious terraces which, in the cool of a summer evening, are a very reasonable substitute for the gardens which are now so rare in any urban centre. This rapid growth of solid and attractive new residential buildings has not yet spread beyond the centre and the immediately surrounding areas of the city. Further afield, low-built stucco houses, unmade roads which turn into torrents in a rainstorm, and tumble-down collective habitations with their traditional inner courtyards adorned by lines of communal washing and pots of basil, are still the rule.

A microcosm of this galloping change in the architectural style of central Athens can be seen in another of the city's special features – one which no visitor should fail to exploit to the full. The Greek street kiosk (known as a *períptero*) is one of the most useful institutions devised by man. Sometimes I wonder how, in other cities, it is possible to survive without them. There are hundreds (maybe thousands) of kiosks in Athens, and more in every town and village of Greece. Some of them are no more than ten yards apart. In central Athens they used to reflect the neo-classical style of their surroundings: squat, square wooden structures of a uniform putty-yellow colour, bulging with a colourful assortment of anything a man may need at a moment's notice throughout the twenty-four hours. The kiosks are now housed, in the central, so-called 'touristic' areas of Athens, in smaller, more compact structures of metal. Another subject for nostalgic complaint by the ageing members of the Athens Club, between rounds of bridge. But, apart from their smarter appearance, it is said that the new-style kiosk has greater resistance to the common shocks of vehicles which mount the pavement and, almost invariably, use the kiosk as a kind of buffer. Were not the occupants of these lightly-built structures generally war-seasoned veterans (whose disablement in battle is the main qualification for the eagerly sought privilege of renting a kiosk) it is believed that the cases of nervous shock resulting from these daily collisions would be much more numerous. At many of the busiest spots in Athens the kiosks stay open all night. From them you may buy: cigarettes (from the most expensive foreign imports down to those which are sold singly from a large box), newspapers and magazines from all over the world, aspirin, indigestion tablets, pens and pencils, paper and envelopes, glue, balls of string, rubber bands, combs, chocolates and fruit drops, money purses, key-rings, streamers and masks at carnival time, stamps for official documents (nothing in Greece can be done without putting a five-drachma stamp on the appropriate application), flints for lighters, electric light bulbs, fuses, strings of beads known as *kombolói* (which suggest a religious accoutrement but are no more than the implement for an irritating kind of nervous twitch which some Greeks cultivate), toilet rolls, penknives, toothpaste, and sometimes even cheese pies and lemonade. How such a vast variety of goods is crowded into such a tiny space is a standing source of mystery.

The kiosk is a miniature complex of almost every kind of shop selling everyday articles. Both in them, and in the shops proper, it is comforting for the visitor to find articles of wide international origin. Nothing is more depressing than to find, as one still does find in some countries which hope nevertheless to entice tourists, that it is impossible to buy a newspaper in a comprehensible language or that, instead of one's favourite brand of aspirin, one has to be content with something ominously like a horse-pill. Insistence by the Greek governments of recent years on a policy of liberal trade has been more than just a matter of economic expediency, lack of foreign exchange from exports being balanced against the need for foreign participation in Greece's industrial development: it has been a reflection of the country's efforts to become an up-to-date and active member of the western world. The result can be seen on the streets and in the shop-windows: cars of almost every manufacture, from Japanese, through Russian, to Swedish, French, Italian, German, American, Czech, Australian, British; and household equipment, from radios to vacuum cleaners and cameras, from a similar variety of exporting countries. Greek grocery shops, which tend to be large and lavishly stocked, contain everything from Russian caviar to American peanut butter. Foreign imports of this kind tend, certainly, to be expensive luxuries – increasingly superfluous as Greek industry (which now makes refrigerators and washing machines and will soon be making cars and radios) gradually develops. But Greece's recent association with the Common Market (the first addition to the original Six members of the Rome Treaty) promises in the future to increase even further the variety of foreign items available and to narrow the gap between their prices and those of the equivalent local products.

Smartness is not a striking characteristic of Greek shops, which tend to have the utilitarian display arrangements of a village general store. Window-dressing, until recently an unknown art, has only just begun to set new standards – largely thanks to the efforts of a weekly magazine which now runs an annual contest for the best-dressed window in Athens. And shops tend to be small. For a city the size of Athens, it is surprising that there is still nothing approaching a general department store; and even the centre of town is scattered with one-man greengrocers, butchers, florists and furniture shops. Shops tend also to be concentrated in groups: the long line of haberdashery and dress shops along the length of Hermes Street, electrical goods, shoe-shine stands, tourist souvenirs, the gay row of flower shops outside the Parliament building, hardware down by the 'flea-market' area of Monastiráki – everything in tight compartments. It makes shopping something of a grand tour; but the extra physical effort is sometimes a small price to pay for the absence of the anonymity of the supermarket and the department store. You will not see Greek housewives wheeling their parcels home in go-carts; most Greek shops still practise service with a smile – and with errand boys.

The centre of Athens is orderly and clean. Litter is kept well under control, animals (on or off leads) are rarely seen, traffic (including the bright yellow trolleybuses) moves in regular alternation with the pedestrians who have disciplined themselves with unexpected readiness to the new system of control by red and green lights. The Athenians were quick to see the humour of these little red and green men controlling the movements of a people famed for their individuality: the little red man is universally nicknamed 'Stamátis' (a common Greek name containing a play on the word for 'stop'), and his green colleague is known as 'Gregory' (a play on the word meaning 'quick').

In daytime, trucks, horse-carts and the rudimentary covered sidecars used for conveying meat carcasses (and too often revealing obtruding members), are strictly banned from passing through the centre of the town. It is only at night, and especially in the very early hours before dawn, that the nightbird can glimpse the old unsophisticated Athens: donkey-carts loaded with fresh vegetables from the outlying market gardens; the old-iron man setting off for his distant suburban round; the piles of fresh sesame-strewn rolls crisp from morning ovens; in winter, the old man with his portable brass contraption from which he dispenses steaming hot *salépi* – a nauseous gluey concoction of Turkish origin reputed to be good for the lungs; around Easter and Christmas, long-coated shepherds with crooks and shaggy dogs driving their flocks of sheep and turkeys through the deserted heart of the city; the yoghourt man, the old woman loaded with fresh-cut mountain herbs, the knife-sharpener, the organ-grinder, the occasional horse-drawn passenger buggy – all these reminders of Athens as it was not very long ago can still be seen. But the visitor will have to stay up very late or rise very early to catch them.

From the vantage point of a pavement seat at an Athens café, you will discover that the native population of the capital is not very cosmopolitan. Greek women, if your interest lies in that direction, you will find to be dressed with a deliberate rather than spontaneous smartness. Their clothes and hair-styles seem to reflect the guidance offered in the pages of their numerous weekly magazines. Greek dress somewhat conservatively, in clothes which are extremely well tailored (there are, I believe, not a few Greek tailors in Savile Row). Even in midsummer, etiquette demands full equipment for anything other than the most informal occasions; shorts and shirt-sleeves are strictly recreational wear. The growing tourist invasion has injected an element of variety and relaxation: it is no longer only the Orthodox priest, in his tall black hat and flowing robes and beard, who provides a contrast with the restrained apparel around him; negroes in bright red robes, Swedes with blue eyes and flaxen hair, Texans with ten-gallon hats and bearded beatniks in a variety of undress now crowd the pavements. They are regarded with toleration and the mildest of interest, for the Greeks are not only innately hospitable but have never had the minority problems which engender racial prejudices. I have seen a car-load of young German tourists park (illegally) in the most central spot in Athens, begin to brew coffee, change on the pavement into warmer clothes – all under the tolerant surveillance of a policeman and without causing more than a mild flutter of curiosity.

Probably the most colourful element of the native population you will constantly meet is the small army of pavement hawkers and allied purveyors of various open-air services. One of them is the sponge-man, whose head barely pokes through the mass of porous yellow foot-balls which surround him like a golden cloud. He is one of the oldest fixtures of the Athenian scene, and his survival can only be explained in terms of our illogical preference for the real thing – even when it is less efficient than its ersatz imitation. These sponges, fished dangerously by the hardy islanders of Kálymnos from the bottom of the sea off Crete or Egypt, cost ten to fifteen times more than the plastic kind which, to my mind, are more absorbent and easier to handle. But they are still much cheaper than heavily taxed natural sponges imported into your home country. And so the Athenian sponge-man lives on – more handsomely now, thanks to you, than ever before. So does that other denizen of the Athenian pavement, the seller of pistachio nuts. His survival is an even greater mystery. His wares, the pink-shelled crisp green nut which abounds on the island of Aígina, are tasty enough in their place. But the pistachio hawker knows no such discrimination: whether you are at the beginning, middle or end of your meal, whether you are quietly dozing or engaged in heated café

ΠΑΓΩΤΑ
GLACES

controversy, he will put a sample nut on your table and wait at a discreet distance to see if you take the bait. To eat this single nut creates not only an appetite for more, but a sense of moral obligation to buy a whole packet – which is by no means cheap as nuts go. Most Athenians are practised in the art of self-denial and can easily resist the bait. The proportion of nuts sold seems to me remarkably low. The mystery of the vendors' survival in such large numbers is probably hidden in their auxiliary identity as clandestine public gamblers. To those who know the code, the approach of the pistachio man is the signal for a quiet flutter on the pavement. Most of his nuts are neatly packaged in cellophane tubes; but he always has a small mountain of them loose in the basket over his arm. For the initiates, the hawker's hand fiddling with the loose nuts in the basket is sufficient invitation to begin a game of 'odds and evens', provided there is no policeman in the immediate vicinity. To ask how (since cheating is unknown) a gamble of strictly equal chances can possibly benefit the pistachio man is to confuse mathematics with psychology: half the time, the pistachio man wins fair and square; but when he loses, at least part of his loss is compensated by the moral obligation on the winner to buy a fair quantity of nuts. Onassis, it is said, was in his Athenian youth a passionate devotee of the nut-game. Once, it is told, he encountered a pistachio man on the pavement outside Orfanídes Bar who, in reply to the budding millionaire's invitation to play the nut game, said: 'Sorry, I don't gamble.' 'That,' retorted Onassis in a flash, 'is why you are still selling pistachio nuts.'

Small boys, invariably perky and ingratiating, supply another interminable category of pavement wares: lottery tickets displayed on a long notched wooden pole, collar bones, combs, plastic hats when it rains. Then there are the chestnut-roasters who come traditionally from Epirus and who in summer, strangely out of season, turn their hand to roasting corn cobs on their street-corner pitches; self-appointed car-park attendants who, for a drachma or two, will open the door for you and wave you safely off the parking line; white-coated photographers, licensed to operate the yellow Heath Robinson contraptions on tripods which, in three minutes, will immortalize your brief acquaintance with the pigeons of Constitution Square.

These are marginal facilities, colourful but not exactly of first priority. Things like telephones, taxis, chemists' shops and medical facilities are much more closely integrated with our daily needs. And, perhaps surprisingly, they are much handier in Greece than in most countries I know. In terms of automation and adequacy of lines, the Greek telephone system is still (in spite of great recent progress) less than up-to-date. It is perhaps an unconscious sense of neighbourly obligation to share a precious commodity which accounts for the fact that public call-boxes are so few and so unnecessary. All you need do in Greece when you want to make a phone call is to walk into the nearest shop or café and use the phone. You hardly need bother to ask for permission. It is implicit in the ownership of a phone in a semi-public place like a shop that it is available to all. All you need do is leave one drachma behind when you leave. Taxis (which we must consider more closely in a later discussion of travel in general) are another example of the handiness of everyday facilities in a country where rising economic standards have not yet, as in so many other countries, transformed ordinary services (like those of maidservants, laundries, barbers and window cleaners) into untouchable luxuries. Throughout the twenty-four hours, even in the middle of a rainstorm, a willing taxi is never more than a few yards away. And if, in the middle of the night, you have urgent need of a drug – or even a cake of soap – there is no need, as in London, to undertake a major journey to a solitary all-night chemist's. Every Athenian chemist in rotation is required by law to stay open all night, and the particulars of the score of shops open on any given night are posted in lighted panels displayed outside every pharmacy.

It is not a bad idea to pack a few basic medicines for your trip to Greece – things like aspirin, Enterovioform against a possible attack of collywobbles, a tin of elastic plasters and sunburn preventives and cures. Not that these things are hard to find in Greece. Indeed, chemists' shops are heavily stocked with practically every known medicine from all over the world, in addition to very good Greek-manufactured equivalents. But they tend to be outrageously expensive.

With ordinary luck, there is no reason why any of these cures should be needed. Whether or not you come full of cautionary shots against everything from 'flu to typhoid, the Greek conditions of sanitation and laws of hygiene are strict enough to prevent all but the normal incidence of epidemic or other disease.

Inevitably, on the ordinary laws of chance, medical attention will sometimes be needed. It is readily available everywhere, except in the more remote villages. Preferably, for anything except the most minor ailments, it should be sought in Athens where the best skills and equipment are concentrated. Any hotel *concierge* (or an official of the British consulate) will be able to produce, at a moment's notice, a good doctor who has studied in England or America and will be able to converse in your own language. And, in addition to the ever-open first-aid station operated by the Greek Red Cross, there is in Athens a big network of well-equipped hospitals, one of which (in fixed rotation) is obliged each day to have several beds available for emergency cases. Private clinics, of which there are very many, should be avoided unless they are of known repute.

In general, there is no reason to fear that medical attention in Greece will be any less efficient than in your own country. In my experience, doctors in private practice are thorough and well-trained. And hospitals, combining often the best features of the American and Continental systems, are remarkably well-run, even if they sometimes lack some of the external graces. Nurses, often without the cold professionalism of their colleagues elsewhere, are none the less businesslike as well as ingratiating.

A word, only, of caution: the Greek medical profession as a whole seems to have an obsession with the liver. There seems to be no ailment, from mumps to a broken arm, which is not somehow derived from some disorder of this organ and which cannot be cured by a rigid diet of boiled carrots and an occasional grilled fish. Without attempting to teach the doctor his job, it is perhaps not unwise, in this respect, to oppose some alternative theory.

That apart, you can be ill in Greece with a perfectly easy conscience.

Among the most difficult aspects of a foreign country to attune to, and yet one which concerns the tourist most intimately, is the strangeness of the scale of prices. I doubt if there is any solution to this difficulty. Just as everyone continues, however well he knows a language learned after maturity, to count in his native language, one's native currency always carries more psychological weight than foreign money. It is arithmetically certain that £1 is worth 84 drachmas and that $1 is worth 30 drachmas. But, even after eight years, I find it impossible to attach the same respect to a 100-drachma note (worth about 25s.) as to a £1 note. In England, I would still stoop to search for a dropped sixpence; in Greece it is doubtful whether I would treat a two-drachma coin (worth almost exactly the same) with the same respect.

This 'currency block' in the mind is a danger for any tourist except the few who never count what they spend. It is very easy to toss over a 20-drachma coin for a packet of imported cigarettes or 7 drachmas for a copy of *The Observer* without stopping to calculate their equivalents in your native currency. Every tourist is, by definition, a spendthrift. To live in hotels, eat constantly in restaurants, be constantly on the move and in search of entertainment, is an expensive kind of life in any country. Considering that families in Greece live, and not too dejectedly, on as little as £6 or £7 a week, the complaint I often hear from visitors – that Greece has proved, after all, to be not nearly so cheap as it is reputed to be – is obviously misplaced. Naturally tourists will not normally be willing or able to integrate their daily needs with the standards which prevail for the Greeks themselves. Their diet, accommodation, methods of travel are bound to be on a more luxurious level. But even these facilities are considerably cheaper in Greece than their equivalents in most European countries. It is the 'currency block', the difficulty of relating drachmas to 'real' money which lures us into errors of calculation and unconscious extravagance.

Tipping is a case in point. A visitor may well be more generous than a native. But over-generosity has a snowball effect which in the end sets up two entirely different scales. No tourist need contribute thus to the future discomfiture of his successors. For general purposes (cloakroom, porter, doorman, etc.) a five-drachma tip is handy and perfectly adequate. Taxis do not expect tips, except perhaps the odd tenths of a drachma to make up the round figure (meters are calibrated in steps of two-tenths of a drachma). Restaurants may be divided, for tipping purposes, into two categories: in those which cater mainly for a Greek clientele, it is unnecessary to add anything to the 10 per cent which is automatically charged on the bill. To the boy who helps the waiter (by setting the table, bringing the beer or running out for a packet of cigarettes) a tip of one, or at most two drachmas per person is handsome enough. (Waiters in Greece are usually unsalaried; they live on their percentage, giving one-fifth of their 10 per cent – 15 per cent at Easter and Christmas time – to their boy assistants.) In the other class of restaurant, used mainly by tourists, the waiters have come to expect a tip in addition to their fixed percentage. It is, collectively, your own fault. But keep it down to an extra ten or twenty drachmas for the whole party. Out of town, tipping need be even less open-handed. And it is useful to remember that no ordinary tavern will object to supplying, for a nominal charge or no charge at all, knives and forks, a table, plates, water, bread to any traveller who arrives with his own food. Just as the notion of 'corkage' is unknown to Greek hoteliers.

On the whole, as he quickly absorbs the more strikingly unfamiliar aspects of everyday life in Greece, the visitor will soon come to appreciate its undertones of informality and its refreshing reminders that men live in communities of which the individual members share the same basic needs. It is difficult, in words, to convey the subtle flavour of a whole way of life to those who have yet to savour it. The visitor may be struck at first by the lack in Greece of some of the superficial aids to polished living: air-conditioned shops, express lifts, slot machines serving three different strengths of hot coffee, doors opening by photo-electric cells, milk in throw-away cartons, strawberries at Christmas, deep-frozen dinners and practically everything else in pressure-spray cans. Isolated examples of most of these things exist and are increasing. But they are still exotic novelties, outside the range of common habit. It would be an insensitive observer of the Greek scene who did not feel in his bones that the lack of these marginal mementoes of progress was handsomely balanced in Greece by the surviving immediacy of man's contact with his physical environment and with his fellows. For me, an eloquent symbol of this delicate but powerful difference is an ordinary Greek orange, the kind you buy at any greengrocer's shop (but only in season!): it not only tastes fresh and juicily like an orange; it actually bears a stalk and a green leaf, banner and proof at the same time of its maternity!

5 Not Quite All Greek . . .

The aspects of unfamiliarity we have been glancing at grow rapidly less unfamiliar on fairly brief acquaintance. The Greek language, on the other hand, remains obstinately foreign and impenetrable; its sounds and its hieroglyphics strike few chords of recognition.

There is no good reason why this should occasion either surprise or disappointment. It is, after all, a language which has served the Greeks well for several thousand years and was never intended as a kind of Esperanto. Nor should this refusal of the Greek language to fit into one or other of the better-known Latin or Germanic groups, painstakingly learned by Anglo-Saxons for vacation or commercial purposes, give rise to serious practical difficulties when they come to Greece. The Greeks are proud of their language, even passionate about it (as we shall see later); but they are realistic enough to appreciate its limitations as a means of communication with the outer world. The study of foreign languages in Greece is a universal and intensive preoccupation, not only in schools, from the elementary stage onwards, but in countless institutes and private classes throughout the country. No Greek is considered even tolerably well educated unless he can speak at least one language other than his own. French and German used to be the first choices for a second language, and many of the educated older generation speak one or both of these languages with charming fluency. Since the war, the emphasis has changed: English is now the firm favourite, reflecting the change in the orientation of cultural and technical outside relations. A large number of the younger Greeks you meet will be able to converse with some facility in English. The accent is fairly light and strangely indeterminate; but the prepositions are a never-ending source of trouble: you will invariably be bid 'welcome in Athens' and asked your opinion about a new suit 'made by English material'. Do not make the mistake of pointing out such errors. Greeks are not content to make themselves understood in a foreign language; they are perfectionists aiming at impeccable grammar and faultless accents; the slightest feeling of insecurity is liable to end in embarrassed refusal to utter a single foreign word. There are many Greeks who know English perfectly as a theoretical language and can read it fluently, yet never dare to speak a word.

There is no lack, either, of artificial aids to communication designed with the tourist in mind. On the roads of Greece all traffic signs are those which are current internationally; road patrols of the Greek Automobile Club are performed by vehicles labelled 'Assistance Routière'; place names, corresponding with those on your petrol company road maps, are spelt out in Latin characters. The passion for exact transliteration from the Greek is sometimes confusing: it is not too difficult to guess that 'Patrai' means 'Patras' and 'Thessaloniki' means 'Salonika'; but what, I wonder, do tourists make of the sign which, in Latin characters, blandly announces 'Stathmos'? They are apparently expected to know the Greek word for a railway station. Menus in most central restaurants and hotels, also, are available in English, French and German. A Greek waiter is disconcertingly adept at putting the right one in front of you after hardly more than a glance at your necktie. These foreign-language menus are not only of intense practical value to the hungry traveller but provide, at the same time, a wealth of exotic culinary-linguistic treasures such as stuffed wine leaves, dental fish, grilled shops, live pâté, coal slow, giant beans, fake (Greek for lentil) soup, and a variety of similar delicacies. There is no trouble, either, about calling for the bill. A sharp tap on a glass with a table knife followed by a dumb-show of writing is the way most Greeks do it.

For the rest, the growing practice of putting up neon lights and shop signs in foreign languages (the source, as we have noted, of some stiff-necked protest) takes care of the tourist's most elementary semantic needs. And, for movie fans who have endured deprivations in cinemas where Jack Hawkins improbably mouths Italian and Edward G. Robinson coos in mellifluent Spanish, it is comforting to note that all foreign films shown in Greece are sub-titled and never dubbed. It is interesting to observe, while on the subject of semantic conveniences, that Greece, too, has adopted the growing practice of distinguishing between the two varieties of private retreat by pictorial rather than linguistic differentiation of the sexes.

These aids to communication do not, of course, exist outside of the the big urban centres, or virtually outside of the capital itself. In the smaller towns and villages you will be forced back on to sign language or, at a pinch, your little phrase-book (although I have yet to find a phrase-book which is sufficiently well indexed to permit more than disjointed and usually irrelevant enquiry; or one which tells you the next move when, having asked – in precise but painfully pronounced Greek – 'Where is the nearest post office to post a letter to my aunt?', the reply comes, in voluble Greek, 'The post office is just round the corner, but it is closed for lunch'). My advice, if you need help or information in a village, is that you simply parade boldly up and down the main street talking English as loudly as possible. It will not be long before the one and only English-speaking inhabitant of the village presents himself and offers his services as host and interpreter. His knowledge of English, generally rudimentary but adequate, will have been gained as an immigrant to America several decades ago; his accent will bear strong traces of Brooklyn or Chicago. Sometimes, in the islands, the English-speaking sage will prove to be a retired sailor who served on ships sailing from British ports. These are the only people I know in the world who speak with affectionate nostalgia of places like Glasgow and Cardiff.

One way or another, an inability to distinguish alpha from omega is in no way a practical bar to the enjoyment of your stay in Greece. Yet the challenge remains. The conscientious tourist – and who is not? – is sensitive to the blocks which ignorance of the language places between him and a full communion with his surroundings. To be able to read at least the headlines of a local newspaper, to be able to pass the time of day with a villager over an *ouzo* in the central café, to be able to decipher public notices not specifically addressed to foreigners, to read posters, understand the news briefs on the radio, to share, in short, the verbal coin of the realm rather than accept the spoon-fed charity of your counterfeit mother tongue, is a compelling ambition.

The compulsion seems to me to be stronger in the case of Greek than it is for some other languages. Those who retain the merest relics of a classical education vaguely hope to find an echo of what Homer they remember in the modern Greek language. And those who nodded with Homer, or never came within a mile of a Greek unseen, find that the half-familiar appearance of the written language and the occasional sound of a half-familiar word create a disquieting and provocative sense of vague disorientation – a sense which, I fancy, is absent when we are confronted with a stranger language, say Chinese, which we are happily prepared to ignore as something totally remote and irrelevant. The rewards for those who make the attempt to approach the modern Greek language, too, are unusually satisfying. There is nothing a Greek admires more in a foreigner than his ability to babble a few words of the language, however feebly; it is regarded as a dignified compliment to his hosts and is invariably the cause of wonderment, sincere flattery and extra special attentions. I have often thought it a pity that my own Greek is no longer bad enough to qualify me for these pleasant prizes.

I am not going to suggest that I can, in the course of a page or two, reveal a secret short-cut to a knowledge of modern Greek. But I have the feeling that, by a rapid glance at the development of the language and a practical hint or two, I can clear up some troublesome misconceptions and dispel at least a part of the visitor's sense of floundering in hostile waters.

The earliest origins of language, like those of races, take us back to near-biological considerations which operate over millions rather than thousands of years. So it is perhaps interesting, but not especially significant for our present purpose, to note that Greek derives from the same Indo-European group of languages as English and many others which are now almost totally different. Only a handful of root words common to these languages can now be detected: for instance, 'father' is the Greek *patír*, and 'bear' is the Greek *féro*, the consonant changes following well-tracked etymological laws. The Greek alphabet, also, has common ancestry with the Semitic alphabet, the letters being developments of the original pictorial hieroglyphics. Greek letters are still remarkably like those in Hebrew and Arabic.

It is not until about 850 BC, with the epics of Homer, that we have a comprehensive written version of the language which we know as Greek; the language which, as we have seen, has played such a powerful and continuous role in the shaping of Greek history and institutions. But languages, however important as symbols and instruments of continuity, are living organisms subject to change. Even in its written form, the language of Homer differs substantially from that of Aeschylus; and that of Aeschylus from that of Xenophon. The differences are even more rapidly developed in the spoken or vernacular form of a language. In Greek, the gulf between the written and spoken languages began to develop noticeably in the Alexandrine period. By the early centuries of the Christian era the various dialects of the classical world had become merged into a common spoken language used throughout the Hellenic world. It was known as the *koiní* – the 'common' language. It was this language, with basically Attican characteristics, which, after further modification during the Middle Ages, developed into modern Greek. As such, modern Greek is the true and natural heir to the classical Greek language as developed in the common speech of the people.

This form of the Greek language, the form we now call 'demotic', has never had an unobstructed career. Considerations of historical necessity and national pride have always got in the way. When the Greek conscience was aroused, it was always to the language of classical Greece, as ossified in its literature, that it looked as a symbol of Hellenic unity. Educated Byzantines set the bad example. Always conscious, as we have noted, of the classical tradition, they invariably used the mummified ancient language later known as *katharévousa* (the 'pure' language). The Church, on the other hand, and others responsible for various forms of literary expression, inclined to the use of the vernacular, the language also used for poetry and folksongs from the twelfth century onwards.

Although it never officially superseded the 'pure' language, demotic Greek continued to be the living speech of the Greeks throughout the Middle Ages and during the four centuries of Turkish occupation. The liberation of Greece was a signal for the attempt to reimpose the 'pure' language. Just as very recently the creators of the new state of Israel insisted on returning to the Hebrew of the Bible as the most eloquent banner of national consciousness, so the leading lights of Greece freed from Turkish domination insisted that the dead classical language (if not of Sophocles then at least of Aristotle) was the only fit vehicle for the free and proud men of resuscitated Greece.

This was the beginning of the war between the 'Demoticists' and the 'Katharevousans' which, if it may now be said to have ended except for mild skirmishing, has made life miserable for generations of Greek schoolchildren, slowed the flowering of Greek literature and left indelible marks on the language as it exists today. In the first half of the nineteenth century, the war was a far-off rumble, barely audible. But, as the literary spirits of Greece began increasingly to resent the intolerable fetters imposed by an artificial language, the war-drums beat louder. And, as happens not rarely in Greece, politics became involved in totally irrelevant affairs. Liberals and left-wingers automatically took the side of the 'Demoticists', and conservatives rallied to the support of the 'Katharevousans'. Conversely, champions of the demotic language were instantly labelled as socialists and friends of the 'pure' language might protest in vain against charges of being tyrannical conservatives. It is hard to believe, but true, that the battle of the Greek language eventually became a battle in real earnest, with dead and wounded to remember it by: in 1901 there was rioting in the streets of Athens when a translation of the Gospel was published in demotic Greek; and, two years later, several students were killed in a clash with the soldiery when a theatrical troupe put on a performance of Aeschylus's *Oresteia* translated into the living language of Greece!

The battle has now been resolved on the basis of a compromise in which the demoticists have dictated the terms. For formal and official purposes, *katharévousa* – the so-called 'pure' language artificially based on ancient Greek – is still in daily use: an invitation from the Palace, the drafting of a legal document or parliamentary Bill, a public injunction not to spit or blaspheme against God (regularly posted in

Greek buses), traditional shop signs (a greengrocer, for instance, commonly known as *manávi*, will label himself *oporopoléion* and a *tavérna* becomes an *oinozithoestiatórion* or 'wine-beer-restaurant') – all these, and many other formal but everyday uses of the language employ *katharévousa*. In ordinary speech or writing the Greeks use *demotikí*. Nobody, for instance, would ask at the shop labelled *artopíion* (ancient Greek and *katharévousa* for bread-maker's) for a loaf of *ártos*; he would be understood but written off as a mental case. The demotic word for bread is quite different: *psomí*. The label on a matchbox reads *pyréia*; but there are not a few Greeks who would blink uncomprehendingly at this strange alternative to the ordinary word *spírta*. And so on, *ad infinitum*; not only in regard to simple nouns, but in every aspect of vocabulary, grammar and syntax there are two related but distinct forms of the Greek language existing side by side.

It would be less confusing if these two distinct forms were always used in distinctly separate compartments. Generally, the 'pure' form is used for official purposes and the *demotikí* for everyday occasions. But there are infinite shades of overlapping, both in speech and writing. Old-fashioned Athenian aristocrats, for example, and pompous fogeys in general tend to lard their everyday speech with heavy doses of *katharévousa*; their language becomes a characteristic part of their personality. Judiciously employed, however, by educated Greeks, a slight seasoning of *katharévousa* in the course of conversation often adds charming notes of humour, irony and polished style. It is an enriching ingredient, similar to a sprightly dash of a foreign language.

In the written form of the language the blending and overlapping of the two styles is even more pronounced. The character of a newspaper, for instance, is largely determined by its use of the two forms of the language. The 'heavier' papers tend to make more extensive use of *katharévousa* than the 'popular' papers. But within each newspaper there is a distinct gradation: the leading articles are generally couched in *katharévousa*-type language; the literary features are in demotic; and the news columns hesitate somewhere between the two. Or take correspondence: no normally literate Greek has any trouble writing to his uncle or his sweetheart; he uses an exact transcription of his everyday speech. But even well-educated Greeks often have to get assistance from friends with more specialized skill when they wish, for instance, to make an application to a Ministry or reply with suitable formality to an official invitation.

Not only are there infinite shades of Greek lying in the range between normal demotic and normal *katharévousa*, but two other recognizable extremes of the language which we might call 'ultra-*katharévousa*' and 'infra-demotic'. The former is used for ultra-formal occasions, like a church liturgy. It is closest of all to ancient Greek, and is of limited interest and influence within its own tight compartment. The latter, which is the language of novels, plays and poetry, is much more important. The younger generation of Greek writers, in revolt against the vestiges of 'katharévousan' trends which are still alive in the language, have been developing a kind of 'super-demotic' in which the features which distinguish demotic from the 'pure' language (such as simpler orthographic and grammatical forms, elisions, folk-expressions, etc.) are deliberately emphasized and cultivated. The language of this literary hothouse is furthest of all away from the fixed language of ancient Greece and closest of all to the folk-language which developed from it. In its turn it has begun to influence the more conservative form of the demotic language which is still in general use. When the Greek language finally settles down into a single, officially recognized and uniform instrument employed, both in speech and writing, for all occasions – an inevitable but very lengthy process – the chances are that it will be the present demotic form, absorbing the less extreme features of the modern literary language and perhaps preserving a few 'katharevousan' usages as ballast, which will emerge.

If, at the outset of this chapter, you had hopes of being helped towards an elementary comprehension of the Greek language, you are certainly downcast and desperate now. Take comfort in the fact that you are little more downcast and desperate than most Greeks; the confusion which greets them on their first day at school never really leaves them for the rest of their lives. In a way, you are luckier than they are. You have no need to go to church, or to the Palace, or decipher a solicitor's letter, or listen to a speech in Parliament, or read a poem or a novel. Your purpose is well enough served if you can read an occasional poster, a menu in Greek (less amusing but so much more informative than the foreign-language variety), a newspaper headline; and if you can exchange a simple everyday phrase with a Greek – and such do exist! – who is not a linguist and sometimes, perhaps, catch a few fascinating passages of a conversation not intended for your ears. All these desirable objects can be achieved through only one of the variety of Greek languages: the common or garden demotic.

Most visitors, especially those who have dabbled in their youth with ancient Greek, want to know the extent to which this common or garden demotic language of modern Greece resembles the language of the *Iliad* or of Plato. The answer is difficult to formulate in a few words, but it is implicit in the account of the development of the language which I have given briefly earlier. Modern demotic Greek, to be more explicit, is a direct development of the ancient language; more or less identical with it in proportion to the degree to which the various parts and usages of the language have been artificially based on the ancient language or have developed naturally through its spoken form. You will insist: does the man on the Athens omnibus understand ancient Greek? It depends. Ancient Greek is taught at all Greek schools as a distinct study (although the latest trend is to diminish the emphasis on this study, just as classical studies are no longer regarded as a *sine qua non* of a good education in European countries). The better educated the Greek, and the more intimately he retains a memory of his school tortures, the more ancient Greek he will understand. As for the Greek who never studied the classics, or remembers nothing of his schooldays or never went to school at all (and they may be the majority), his comprehension of an ancient text is, at the most, patchy. It is difficult to define his degree of comprehension arithmetically. But if I had to put it in figures, I would guess that he would understand anything from one-third to one-half of an ancient text. On my reckoning, this puts ancient Greek in relation to average modern demotic Greek about on a level with Chaucer in relation to modern English, or rather more remote. Most Greeks I have discussed the point with disagree: they maintain that Chaucer is more remote from modern English than ancient from modern Greek. But this is an insoluble kind of argument.

The thing to remember, in any event, is that the Greek of today, once out of school, never has to cope with an ancient Greek text. The whole of ancient Greek literature has been translated into the modern language. It may now appear as a glimpse of the obvious, but I will nevertheless state a fact which a large proportion of visitors to Greece seems not to understand: when they go to watch a performance of the ancient Greek drama at Epidaurus or anywhere else in Greece today, the text they are hearing is *not* the ancient Greek text, but a thorough translation of the text into modern Greek. There are, in fact, usually several well-known translations of each play by Greek men of letters who have spent their lives doing little else.

Having digested this disappointing intelligence, the former classical scholar generally wants to know whether, in spite of it all, a knowledge of ancient Greek helps in an understanding of the modern Greek language. From personal experience, I can only guess at the answer – I do not know whether a vague recollection of four years of sporadic and inconclusive tussling with Homer constitutes a knowledge of ancient Greek. But I would guess that any kind of familiarity with the ancient language is a positive help. Probably, however, not in the way you would imagine. When it is a question of reading, the former classics man will be able, certainly, to decipher most simple public signs without much trouble. He will also be able to make sense of a proportion of ordinary texts, the proportion depending on the degree to which the *katharévousa* form is used. But it will help him very little indeed in the effort to speak or to understand a conversation in ordinary demotic Greek. This is not only because of the distance between demotic and the ancient language, but especially because the pronunciation of modern Greek is totally different from that which most foreigners are taught in the course of their ancient Greek studies. The test of this difference is the fact that even the best classical scholars of Europe and America (who are accustomed to the so-called Erasmian pronunciation of ancient Greek) fail to understand even an ancient Greek text when it is spoken by a contemporary Greek who, naturally, always uses the pronunciation of his everyday speech. Occasional experiments by the BBC, using contemporary Greek actors to recite ancient Greek texts, nearly always provoke several letters of complaint from dons.

These differences in pronunciation are substantial and result in a totally different general sound, but they are fairly easy to define: all the ancient Greek diphthongs (which the scholars pronounce respectively *oy*, *ee*, *aye*, *ow*, etc.) are retained but have been simplified in modern Greek pronunciation and are given one of the exclusive six simple vowel sounds (*a* as in 'hat', *e* as in 'bet', *ee* as in 'meet', *i* as in 'fit', *o* as in 'hot' and *oo* as in 'boot'). There are no other vowel sounds in modern Greek, which makes it very simple to read out loud but severely complicates the reverse operation of spelling: any given vowel sound in modern Greek may be spelt in one of several ways, and Greeks must be about the world's worst spellers in their own language. The initial diphthongs which the classicists say *au* ('aw') as in 'automobile' and *eu* ('yew') as in 'euthanasia' are also very different to the ear in modern Greek: they become, respectively, *af* (*aftokínito*=car) and *ef* (*efthanassía*=euthanasia). The initials *b* and *d*, pronounced as hard consonants in ancient Greek according to Erasmus, have become soft in modern Greek: the *b* is pronounced like a *v* and the *d* like a soft *th* (as in 'this'). It is not difficult to understand, therefore, how perplexing it is for an ancient Greek scholar who knows the word for king as '*basilewss*' to hear the same word in modern Greek (which is spelt in exactly the same way) pronounced '*vassiléffs*'. No wonder he usually fails to recognize it, just as he fails to recognize the effect in modern Greek of ignoring all initial aspirates (although you continue to write them), making the 'hoy polloy' simply *i pollí*, and 'hubris', *ívris*.

This considerable auditory gap between ancient Greek as and if we know it and modern Greek as spoken, is widened much further still by the modern Greek stress accents. The three signs written above certain letters in ancient Greek (´ ` ˜) are still used. But, instead of indicating the pitch of vowel sounds as they used to, they are all three now employed as simple indications of which syllable in a word is stressed when it is spoken. It is probably the bitterest complaint of the classical scholar that ancient Greek verse spoken by a contemporary Greek, with his stress accents, simply does not scan. There are several answers to this, but they would take us far too deep into a specialized field I feel I have already over-cultivated – and over-simplified.

The main point is that, in approaching a comprehension of modern Greek, the ancient Greek scholar has less of an advantage than most people imagine. He may even find himself more confused than those who begin with no preconceptions whatever. If he has an advantage, I contend that it is not so much in being able to recognize the similarities between the two languages but rather in the fact that he has been trained to comprehend the abstract grammatical complexities of a highly inflected language, which modern Greek certainly is. What bothers most people in grasping even a minimum quantity of modern Greek is not so much the substantive difficulties of the language (which are less fearsome than most people imagine) but the fact that their mind is paralysed by the mere thought of anything so exotic as a third person plural past continuous passive. It is in their ability to take such devious grammatical concepts in their stride that those who know ancient Greek have a distinct edge. But this is a question of general training rather than specific knowledge; I am fairly sure that a training in Latin or any other highly inflected language is equally or almost as effective for getting to grips with the language of contemporary Greece.

What happens, then, to those who know neither ancient Greek, nor Latin, nor Sanskrit? Are they condemned to linger in total darkness? I think not. The important thing is to be alert and exercise a little ingenuity and commonsense. Panic can get you into trouble, like a former American Ambassador to Athens. Called on to make his first public address soon after his arrival, he was determined to incorporate at least one Greek word into his speech. What, he asked, was the Greek for 'thank you'. He was told that the word is *efharistó*. In doubt as to his ability to remember anything so strange, he had a brainwave: all I need, do, he told himself, is to remember the name F. Harry Stowe (he could, at this stage, be forgiven for the common error of treating a Greek *o* as though in 'blow', whereas it is invariably pronounced as though in 'orange'). The speech, full of the requisite references to the common bonds of democracy linking Plato with Jefferson, drew to its resounding close. 'And finally, ladies and gentlemen,' exulted the diplomat, 'I want to express to one and all the pride and gratitude I feel at having been invited here today. To all of you, from the bottom of my heart, I would like to say one simple but sincere word in conclusion: Harry F. Stowe.'

The publication of *The Ugly American* has revolutionized this unscientifically dangerous method of learning Greek. Officials of the American Embassy in Athens now approach the task more seriously and Greek lessons from qualified teachers are part of their daily schedule. Experience has shown that many of them do fairly well – a happy outcome which not only helps Greek-American relations but has restored harmony to many American homes in Athens where the Greek learned out of necessity to communicate with the maid has in the past given wives an unfair advantage over their husbands.

I am not suggesting that every visitor to Greece is bound to be so concerned with acquiring a smattering of the language that he is likely to take Greek lessons in advance. But I do strongly advise that everyone take the minimum trouble of familiarizing himself with the Greek alphabet. One of the most remarkable and widespread fallacies I encounter is the notion that a knowledge of the Greek alphabet which goes with a knowledge of ancient Greek is an inestimable aid to an understanding of modern Greek. Nothing could be more ingenuous – and palpably so: the Greek alphabet consists of twenty-four letters, of which ten in capitals and nine in script are exactly similar to our own. This leaves about a dozen letters which have to be 'learned' – and many of those are so similar as to be almost self-explanatory. How long can it take to learn a dozen letters? Five minutes? Ten, at the most. The barrier of the Greek alphabet, which frightens so many foreigners, turns out to be the flimsiest of veils which can be pierced in a few minutes.

Not that you will understand Greek when the veil is pierced. But you will be surprised how much of the disconcerting sense of alienation disappears. And you will be surprised how many words and phrases, previously blank and impertinently uncommunicative, begin to make friendly sense. It is no little thing, for instance, to know at a glance that the crazy-looking symbol which reads 'ΜΠΑΡ' means, simply, 'BAR'; and you will find it much easier to select your media of entertainment when you can decipher at a glance inscriptions like 'ΜΠΡΙΖΙΤ ΜΠΑΡΝΤΩ' or 'ΝΤΟΝΑΛΝΤ ΝΤΑΚ' – bearing in mind that, since *b* and *d* have become *v* and soft *th*, foreign importations have those letters represented phonetically by the combined consonants *mp* (*b*) and *nt* (*d*).

Familiarity with the Greek alphabet, combined with an appreciation of some of the basic rules of pronunciation, will do much more than reveal the comparatively few transliterations of actual foreign words and names. It is the phoney mystery of the alphabet and ignorance of a few simple principles concerning the sound of the language which obscure the startling fact that thousands of words in the Greek language itself (and most of those among the most common) are

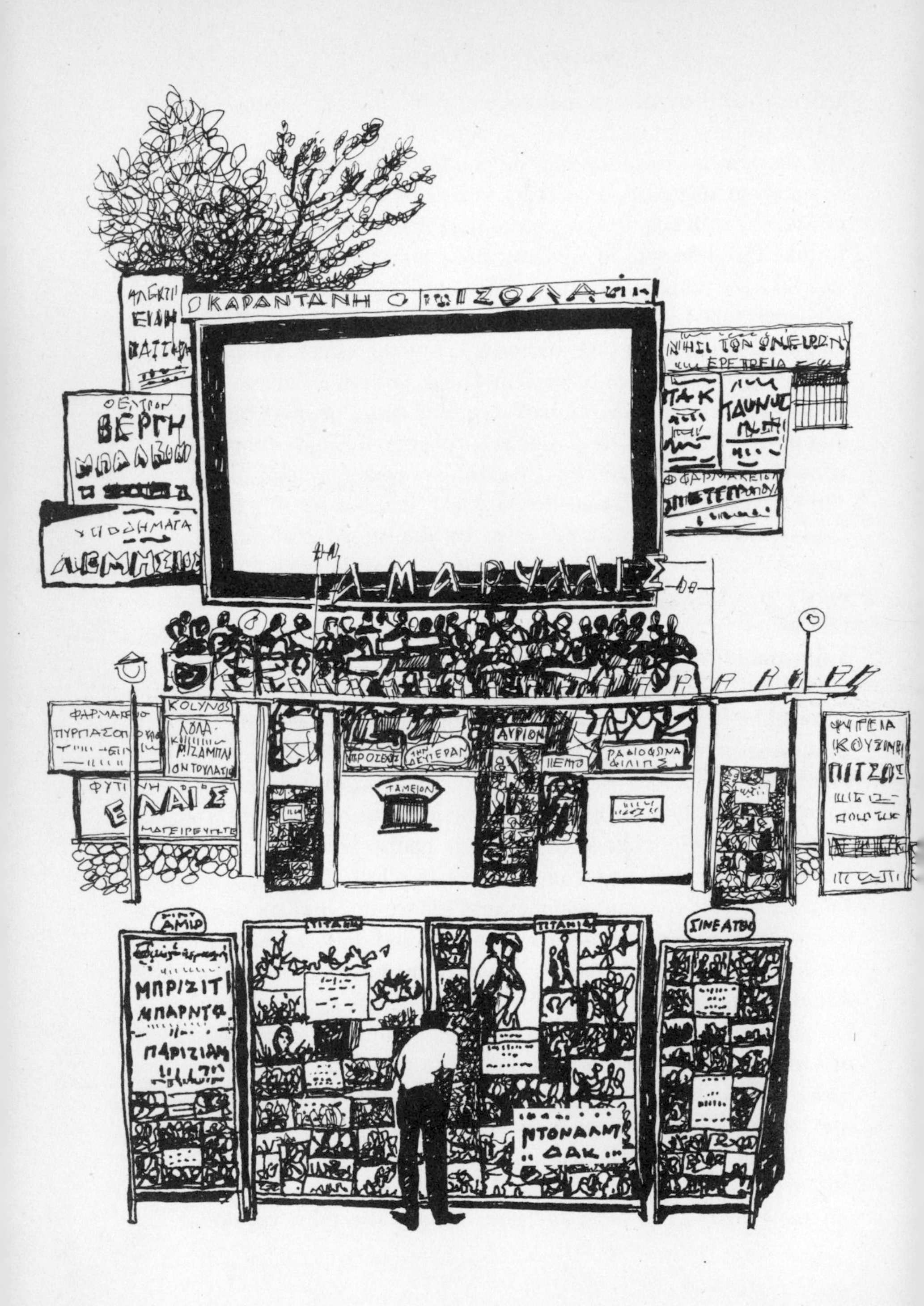
ΚΑΡΑΝΤΑΝΗ
ΖΟΛΑ
ΒΕΡΓΗ
ΥΠΟΔΗΜΑΤΑ
ΝΗΣΙ ΤΩΝ ΟΝΕΙΡΩΝ
ΕΡΕΤΡΕΙΑ
ΑΜΑΡΥΛΛΙΣ
ΦΑΡΜΑΚΕΙΟ
KOLYNOS
ΦΥΤΙΝΗ
ΕΛΑΙΣ
ΜΑΓΕΙΡΕΥΕΤΕ
ΠΡΟΣΟΧΗ
ΤΗΝ ΔΕΥΤΕΡΑΝ
ΑΥΡΙΟΝ
ΡΑΔΙΟΦΩΝΑ ΦΙΛΙΠΣ
ΤΑΜΕΙΟΝ
ΑΜΙΡ
ΜΠΡΙΖΙΤ
ΜΠΑΡΝΤΟ
ΠΑΡΙΖΙΑΝ
ΤΙΤΑΝΙΑ
ΝΤΟΝΑΛΝΤ
ΝΤΑΚ

almost identical with their equivalents in the best-known Latin languages or in English.

Italian, in particular, has been a generous donor to the Greek language in its current demotic form. The Greek word *thíra* (door), for instance, is never used except in formal *katharévousa* and in compound forms for 'doorman', 'reception desk' (*thirorós, thiroríon*), etc.: for all ordinary purposes, the word for 'door' in Greek is *pórta*, a word which no visitor from a Latin country and almost none from an Anglo-Saxon country will fail to understand. This example can be multiplied indefinitely: suitcase, bath, wardrobe, dressing-gown, kitchen, soup, fruit, blanket, boat, varnish, fan, screw, potato, brush, butter, evening, cat, drawing-room – these are just a handful of the numerous words in everyday use which have been borrowed from much more familiar languages and will be recognized at once.

The reverse process – borrowings from Greek into our own languages – results in an even greater degree of immediate recognition once you overcome the trifling obstacles of alphabet and pronunciation. Huge areas of the English language, especially in the field of the sciences (using the word in its broadest sense to cover every aspect of intellectual and technical activity) are directly borrowed from Greek. An astonishing practical proof of the extent of this identity between the two languages was given in an experiment recently performed by a Governor of the Bank of Greece (Xenophon Zolotas). Invited to address a luncheon meeting of financiers at the Guildhall in the City of London, he spoke in English from a prepared text for fifteen minutes on a contemporary economic theme without making use of a single word (except for minor conjunctions and prepositions) which was not pure Greek. If, instead of English, he had used the ordinary language spoken in Greece today, he would have said '*economikí creésis*', instead of 'economic crisis', '*teknikó próvleema*' instead of 'technical problem', '*i deenamikeé tis pseecholoyías*' instead of 'the dynamics of psychology'. Whether such words and phrases are seen in print or heard in speech, an elementary and rapidly acquired knowledge of a few Greek letters and usages in pronunciation is enough to make them instantly intelligible.

The area of language covered by this identity is so large that it is pointless to attempt to give examples. Apart from specific sciences like economics, physics, mathematics, medicine, geology, philosophy and others of which the technical vocabulary is largely Greek, the everyday language of England uses innumerable Greek words like: aristocrat, acrobat, acme, adamant, aesthetic, agnostic, agony, air, alabaster, allegory, alphabet, analogy, analysis, anatomy, anecdote, angel, anonymous, antidote, antipathy, apocalypse, apology, architect, aroma, asterisk, astigmatism, asylum, atheist, athlete, atmosphere, atom, atrophy, aura, austere, authentic, automatic, axiomatic – to name just a few words taken at random from the first pages of my *Pocket Oxford Dictionary*. All these words are still going strong in Greek today. And, with a little ingenuity, you can sometimes recognize or construe the meaning of Greek words which have not been taken directly into English: for instance, the Greek word *antípina* need not be wholly incomprehensible; since you know from English that '*anti*' means 'against' and '*pina*' possibly relates to punishment ('penal', etc.), you just *might* reach the correct conclusion that '*antípina*' means 'reprisals'. Or, as you sit at the café and see a truck go by labelled *idiotikés metaforés*, a fascinating way of passing the time would be to work out how 'idiotic metaphors' really means 'private removals' (an 'idiot' is somebody so stupid that he is a law unto himself, a man with *idio*syncrasies, or special *private* characteristics; and a 'metaphor' is simply the transfer or *removal* of the normal meaning of words to a different context).

You can, of course, have the time of your life in Greece without worrying about any of this. The simple words *né* (yes), and *stin iyiá sou* (down the hatch, or 'to your *iyía*', i.e. to your health or *hygie*nic well-being!) carry you quite a long way. And as for 'no', you need not bother even to learn a word: the most authentic way of conveying a negative known to the Greeks is contained in a single gesture which is easily copied – the head is lifted gently backwards, the eyebrows simultaneously raised upwards and a faint *tk* sound issues from behind closed teeth. This is the full treatment. But, very often, the whole sound-gesture idiogram is compressed into nothing more than a slight lift of the eyebrows which is barely visible. Until you get used to this fleeting change of expression you may often find yourself waiting for an answer to a question which has already been answered in this splendidly epigrammatic negative.

But we verge now on an intriguing side-issue: the whole repertory of Greek gesture, involving hands, eyes, arms, shoulders and heads, which is such an important complement of the language but which demands pictorial rather than literary description. We will not pursue it. Our purpose has been only to perform a superficial dissection of the modern Greek language, laying bare a little of its structure and hoping that closer acquaintance will dispel some of the fears which create an attitude of aggressive rejection identified in the phrase 'It's all Greek to me'. I am fairly certain that, with a very little application, somewhat more ingenuity and a determination not to panic, you can surprise yourselves and delight your hosts by the discovery that 'Greek' and 'incomprehensibility' are not necessarily synonyms, or, as the Greeks would say, . . . *synónyma.*

6 Bouzoúki - and Some Other Aspects of Culture

The language of art, in most of its forms, offers no barriers of the kind we have been discussing. The visitor with an interest in the arts is generally content with the packaged goods ready-served for tourist consumption. Sometimes, as with performances of the ancient drama, he is getting extremely good and representative quality; but more often he is being fobbed off with material which is neither good in itself nor typical of contemporary Greek achievement in the arts. There is no reason why, with a little preparation and a little more persistence, the foreigner in Greece should not dip into a much wider range of contemporary Greek cultural activity and satisfy, at the same time, both his curiosity and his aesthetic appreciation.

The level of achievement varies enormously from one art form to another. But there are some general considerations which, in some degree, affect them all. On the credit side, the intense individuality of the Greeks has always favoured the impulse towards personal expression which is the essence of all art. Great names, like Mitrópoulos and Callas in music, Kazantzákis in literature, Kazan in the cinema and Ghíkas in painting have risen to the surface of contemporary cultural achievement in far greater numbers than is normal for a country of Greece's size and population. There is little doubt, I think, that the artistic impulse is naturally strong in the Greeks. But between artistic impulse and successful artistic expression there is a chasm which can only be bridged in favourable material and intellectual conditions. The fact that all the famous artists I mentioned (as examples only of the long list of Greeks distinguished in the art world) reached maturity and won world recognition outside their own country is a significant clue to the proposition that Greece does not provide those favourable conditions.

However personal in origin, however sacred as a socially elevating aspect of individual expression, art is a marginal emanation of human activity, a luxury which demands hothouse cultivation. The image of the artist in his garret producing cake for people who, like himself, have no bread is romantically unreal. The lack of the material means for extensive private patronage (which sustained Greek art in classical and Byzantine times) is partially compensated in contemporary Greece by a responsible attitude of the State which, through the Ministry of Education, provides substantial subsidies to art – not only to the drama and opera through three State theatres, but to every branch of art. All the well-known reservations about this form of encouragement to art apply in Greece: the strings attached to it sometimes show too prominently. But, if we accept the principle that this is preferable to a total lack of material support, the biggest defect is that the support provided is necessarily inadequate in a country where the first call on public funds is for the development of baser necessities.

The result of these material constraints on the flowering of art in Greece is, in the first place, that many potentially talented artists never embark on the hazardous and unsatisfying career for which they are fitted. Others who take the plunge are too often compelled to attempt an impossible compromise between their art and other activities (like commerce and the law) which are more lucrative but totally incompatible. And of those who, by virtue of superlative talents, private means or unusual determination, reach final fulfilment and recognition, a large proportion find Greece too constrained a field. It is not surprising that they hasten abroad to find not only wider fame, but more encouraging material conditions than those which exist in their native country, where a first-rank actor earns up to £30 a week, a soloist's concert fee may be as little as £10, a successful book sells about 3,000 copies, and anything over £100 would be considered an impossible price for a big composition by a front-rank painter. The Greeks take great pride in their departed stars when they begin to sparkle on international horizons; they receive them like princes when, rich and famous, they return for a brief nostalgic engagement in their native land. But their absence, meanwhile, has not only deprived Greece of their art; it has created a grievous gap in the traditions and continuity of an activity which thrives on the inspiration and hero-worship a master arouses in his pupil. The studios, concert rostrums and opera houses of the world are scattered with talented Greek artists whose very presence outside of Greece acts as a magnet to attract young artists away from their country – often never to return.

I may have managed to convey the picture of a country which has been skimmed totally dry of talent. This is by no means the case. Greece has more than its fair share of gifted and prolific artists for whom native roots and a sense of national identity are necessary to their art. But these artists, more than those who leave the country, are also faced with the dilemma of internationalism: how to combine, and to what extent, the characteristically Greek elements which are part of their tradition and personality with the increasingly international content of most art forms? The problem has been confronting Greek artists throughout the 140-odd years since the liberation of their country. It was natural that after four centuries of foreign domination the artists of the new Greece should tend to express a sense of national identity by stressing traditional Greek elements which had so long been repressed: elements reminiscent of classical and Byzantine Greece, Greek folk-themes, myths, folk-art and landscapes. The tendency in the years which followed has been to liberalize and universalize – a trend which has been facilitated in the recent post-war years by the vast growth of travel and of organized cultural exchange. There is no doubt that the horizons of Greek art today are wider than they have ever been and that Greek artists share more fully than ever before in the trends of international art. Indeed, no artist considers himself or is considered by others to have 'arrived' until his work has been favourably received abroad. This is no doubt as it should be. But the old dilemma still exists: in his efforts to become internationally accepted and to share in current international trends, how far can the Greek artist risk divorce from the genuine springs of his inspiration, from the elements of his national tradition which may be the very essence of the international appeal of his art? There is no single or simple solution to this dilemma. Much depends on the individual artist and on the kind of art he practises. In general, it seems to me that Greek painters and sculptors have so far achieved the best compromise, with music and the cinema showing signs of progress in the right direction. Greek literature, on the other hand – perhaps inevitably because of the language barrier – seems reluctant to throw off its parochial chains; whereas architecture seems to have progressed to the other extreme in its aping of a lowest common denominator of international styles. It is a strange irony that it is nearly always the foreign architects invited to design buildings in Greece (like Gropius who built the new American Embassy) who contrive to produce a genuinely modern building which at the same time creates harmonious echoes of the classical style which suits the landscape so well.

Of all the art forms which represent Greece in the mind of the average visitor, there is none so familiar as the ancient Greek drama. The eternal stuff of this oldest known form of theatre never stales. And nowhere, since the ancient Greeks thronged into their amphitheatres in religious rather than secular excitement, have the ancient tragedies been so vividly brought to life as they have in contemporary Greece. There is still a minority school of thought which believes that the tragedies should be performed as museum pieces, complete with masks and buskins. But the contribution of modern Greek artists to the ancient drama has been their success, through the performances of the National Theatre, in developing a method of interpretation which preserves the super-human majesty of the original in combination with a flexibility and directness which, while it stops short of realism, is much more easily digested by a modern audience. The costumes used for these performances are unique in the world: made, to the ancient Greek recipe, with a woollen warp and a silk weft which gives the material remarkable qualities of draped grace and movement. Some of the finest actors and actresses in Greece – Paxinoú, Verghí, Sinodinoú, Minotís, Kotsópoulos – have risen to the top through their careers in the ancient drama. The same is true of producers like Rondíris and Minotís, costume designers like Anthony Fokás and a set designer like Klónis. Greek companies performing the ancient tragedies in the new style evolved in recent years have been acclaimed on their tours throughout the world. But it is impossible to appreciate the full impact of their art until you have watched a performance at one of the ancient amphitheatres in Greece – preferably at the most perfect of them all at Epidaurus. The annual Festival of Greek drama there in June and July (at week-ends) has been recently organized with a special eye to tourist interest. And thousands of tourists have thrilled to the electric atmosphere of Epidaurus as the red sun sinks over the top lip of the amphitheatre and the first ponderous notes of music announce the opening of the drama in the pine-scented dusk. The experience is made doubly memorable by the realization that they have made a genuine pilgrimage. It is rare that the theatre, which holds some 15,000 spectators, is not almost full. And it has been known to overflow!

Except for the occasional gala performance at the Athens National Theatre in honour of some visiting head of state (complete with tails, tiaras and national anthems) the presentation of the ancient dramas is strictly a summer affair. During the summer also, the open-air theatres of Athens busy themselves with popular productions of revue, light comedy and heroic costume pieces based on Greek history or folklore. They are well enough suited to the lenient demands of audiences whose main concern is to enjoy the cool of the evening; but I do not commend them to your attention.

The serious theatrical activity of Greece, apart from the ancient drama, is a winter operation, conducted from October to May each year. A measure of the intensity is the fact that the Greek capital, with a population of about 1,200,000, supports a total of twenty-one theatres.

Very few of these theatres produce the work of Greek playwrights – in spite of a differential tax which is designed to encourage such productions. Only Melás, Terzákis and, of the younger generation, Campanéllis and Peryális have shown signs of an ability to write serious theatre which escapes from the parochial tendencies of Greek literature as a whole.

For the visitor to Greece during the winter season, this is a happy circumstance. Provided he knows the play, or can find an hour or two to read it in advance, he will be able to pass an enjoyable evening at the theatre watching one of the wide selection of Broadway, West End or Paris successes of the day, performed in Greek translation but in productions of a quality which often approaches, and may even excel, that of the European and American stage. Producers abroad would scarcely believe the economics of these shows: with a maximum price for tickets ranging from seven to ten shillings (of which about 20 per cent is taken in entertainments tax), Greek theatres have to be economical and ingenious.

Greek theatre audiences are more perfunctory and harder to please than audiences generally are abroad. They do not put on black ties for first nights and are much less impressed than other audiences with the 'sense of occasion'. Their applause is hard to win when the curtain falls – all the harder, I often think, because of the custom in Greece of curtain calls between each act. If you are present in a Greek theatre where there are as many as four curtain calls at the end of the performance, you may assume you have been watching a success. And a tip about buying tickets: there are no theatre agencies in Greece. Their function is effectively performed at the box-office itself where custom has consecrated a system of tipping for the best seats. These tips (although few theatre-goers know it) are only partially retained by the box-office staff. They mostly go to swell the receipts of the theatre. And the tip you give the usherette who shows you to your seat (one or two drachmas) is her only source of income.

Most Greek actors hope to supplement their tiny earnings in the theatre by appearances in Greek films. A few of these, especially those made by Michael Kakoyiánnis, have achieved considerable success among selected audiences abroad. Some of them have not been bad films, but their success, I believe, has been a result of a vogue for the frugally exotic images of Greece they project rather than of their intrinsic quality. Compared, however, with the bulk of Greek films they have been works of genius. Greek film studios at present turn out something like eighty films every year – at a cost which rarely exceeds £12,000 per film. You will not see these films at the Cannes Festival. You will not even see most of them in Athens. The majority are broad comedies or melodramas specifically designed for Greek provincial consumption. And they are extremely profitable for the producers. The best of these films (especially those starring Greece's charming representative of the current juvenile sex-cult, Aliki Vouyoukláki) draw big audiences in the towns. But the more sophisticated audiences of the capital, especially, demand the best international films. The number and variety of such films to be seen in Athens at any given moment is abnormally large: American and British films are in the majority; but there is a substantial proportion from the studios of France, Italy, Russia, Germany, Spain, Sweden, Japan and anywhere else where films are made.

With two or three good modern studios now in operation and a gradual improvement in technical standards, the Greek film industry is certainly set on an ascending course. But one wonders, in these days of 'co-productions', with American capital, French directors, Greek actors, German cameramen and Finnish script girls, in what sense any new national film industry can ever achieve a flavour and tradition of its own.

Visiting devotees of the theatre and the cinema can look forward to a more rewarding time in Greece than they might imagine possible in advance. The outlook is less rosy for the concert fan. He is safe enough if he arrives in August or September; the two-month Athens Festival, held in the captivating theatre of Herod Atticus beneath the Parthenon, guarantees a regular supply of music performed by some of the best visiting orchestras of the world. (A word of caution: a folding back-rest or a well-stuffed pillow at least is a valuable aid to undistracted listening on the dignified but inhospitable marble tiers of this amphitheatre.) For the rest, he will have to be content with the offerings, once a week, of the Athens State Orchestra, a hard-working group of musicians who have been known to rise to unaccustomed peaks of performance on special occasions but who, for the most part, are content with uninspired renderings of well-tried programmes which pay more than average attention to the Leonora No. 3 overture. The trouble, naturally, is financial.

But irrespective of the level of performance (which is not bad so much as unexciting) attendance at Greek concerts is often a useful introduction, for those who are interested, to contemporary musical composition in Greece.

At the other end of the musical scale, you can hear the modern popular songs at any moment of the day or night by switching on the radio or eating at one of the numerous *tavernas* where intense young ladies in tight dresses compete, with the aid of powerful amplifiers, with the noise of people eating and talking.

It is in the region between the two extremes of the scale that modern Greek music has made its greatest impact on the world outside: the region of contemporary 'popular' or 'folk' music. The most representative expression of this music is that now known to all the world as the music of the '*bouzoúki*'. There is hardly a visitor to Greece these days who does not feel that he has missed a significant slice of genuine Greek life if he leaves without initiation into its mysteries. I risk the scorn and contempt of a surprising number of otherwise intelligent and cultivated Greeks when I venture the view that the music which issues from the mandolin-like instrument known as the *bouzoúki* (a word of strangely un-Greek overtones) is neither significant, nor genuine, nor even attractive. The cult, it is said, originated in the debased opium dens frequented by seamen in the Piraeus; but its temples are currently the brash, gaudy and uncomfortably crowded big taverns in the region of the Phaleron coast of Athens where you may eat bad and expensive food to the accompaniment of the *bouzoúki* band: moustachioed young bloods who strum the strident metal strings and stout unkempt songstresses who remain provocatively seated as they caterwaul the banal lyrics. The priests of the cult insist that the *bouzoúki* expresses some deep-felt sense of collective sadness which amounts to true poetry. I concede that there are occasional echoes of a wild primeval lament in the quavering harshness of the music which often inspires the well-wined single men in the company to begin their strangely introspective solo dance. And there are a few admirably competent performers, as such, on the difficult stringed instrument. But any element of genuine folk expression which *bouzoúki* may (I repeat *may*) originally have contained has been swamped in artificial propagation which has made both words and music repetitive, vulgar and cacophonous. My guess is that the *bouzoúki* would by now have died a thorough and well-deserved death, had it not been sustained by the misplaced admiration of intellectual 'slummers' and, more recently, by the considerable vogue among earnest foreign visitors. Not that anything I have said will prevent you, I fancy, from seeking out the *bouzoúki* haunts of Syngroú Avenue. But you have at least been warned.

It is often credited to the account of *bouzoúki* music that it served as the inspiration of Greece's two most gifted composers of popular music, Mikis Theodorákis and Manos Hadzidákis – both of them responsible for songs which, more than any other single expression of art, have created a world-wide link with contemporary Greece. It may be true, but if so it is fortunate that both composers have travelled a long way since. Of the two, Theodorákis is probably the most gifted as a musician: his songs and lyrics are full of pungency and poetry. But Theodorákis lacks the gifts of sheer melodiousness and invention which have made Hadzidákis as famous in Greece as Cole Porter ever was in America. It is strange that his great and growing reputation abroad should have been based on the catchy tune from *Never on Sunday*, one of his least memorable compositions. When you are in Greece, insist on hearing 'Somewhere is My Love' and 'The Postman is Dead', sung if possible by the interpreter to whom Hadzidákis owes so much – Nana Moúschouri. Then decide for yourself what this delightful music, Greek as it is to the bone, can possibly owe to the barbarian *bouzoúki*.

Next to this flowering of Greek popular music, it is probably the painting and sculpture of contemporary Greece which have won the widest recognition abroad. This is probably because the best Greek artists of the day have arrived at the most successful integration of their Hellenic identity with international trends. It was not always the case. The strongly preserved traditions of Byzantine art tended, after the liberation of Greece, to be swamped in the fashion for pseudo-classical style imported from Munich along with the dynasty of King Otto in 1830. The vogue for Impressionism reached Greece, somewhat delayed, early in the twentieth century, when the Greek landscape became the chief source of inspiration to painters. It was Constantine Parthénis, one of the earliest converts to Impressionism in Greece who now lives in almost total isolation, nearing ninety, in a house near the Acropolis, who led the way through the Parisian trends of Post-Impressionism, Fauvism, Cubism and Expressionism in turn. But his work was pioneering in the more important sense that, throughout his essays in these various foreign-inspired trends, Parthénis retained a reminiscence of the Byzantine style. Artists like Bouziánis and Gounáro branched out in a style which was purely personal; but interest in Byzantine forms, possibly encouraged by the foundation of the Byzantine and Benaki Museums in Athens, was intensified in the early Thirties especially in the work of Fotis Kóndoglou whose teaching influenced the work of one of Greece's currently most prolific and most 'Greek' painters, Spiros Vassilíou.

Tsaroúhis, Móralis, and the sculptor Kaprálos are current representatives of the school which the attachers of labels call 'Neo-Hellenic Realism'; their work shows a consciousness of the heroic but tragic events which marked Greek history in the years during and immediately following World War II. They convey the brilliant colours, harsh sunlight and geometric barrenness of the Greek landscape, all touched with a humanism which is not unrelated to the classical tradition. The same is true of Ghíkas, the most renowned of them all. The language of art appreciation is too esoteric and the variety of 'schools' too large to make it useful to mention more than a few of the other most outstanding contemporary Greek artists. The sculptures of Tómbros have a massive classic beauty of line; at the other extreme, Apérgis cultivates the spindly acuity of modern metallic sculpture. Frosso Menegáki, always pleasingly harmonious, is somewhere between the two extremes. In painting, also, the basically non-figurative work of John Spirópoulos and Alec Kondópoulos also contains sufficient hints of Greek inspiration to satisfy a visitor's quest for art which is identifiable with the country. The work of Spirópoulos, especially, is currently in considerable vogue abroad.

The establishment of a Museum of Modern Art in Athens is unfortunately one of those projects which is still at the talking stage. But an acquaintance with contemporary Greek painting can be made by visiting the most important commercial art galleries ('New Forms' and 'Zygos' are among the best). These galleries hold frequent exhibitions of works by all the most active contemporary artists, not only those who work in Greece but the many who live and work permanently abroad, especially in Paris and New York. The galleries are also the best means of introduction for serious connoisseurs of art who wish to visit the studio of a particular artist and perhaps buy a piece of his work. A good painting or piece of sculpture seems to me to be a considerably more satisfying – and not necessarily more expensive – acquisition than any number of those myriad examples of folk art (sometimes attractive enough but nearly always strangely indistinguishable from the corresponding products of other countries) with which tourists tend to stuff their suitcases.

Several factors have combined to make literature lag behind in the general trend towards the international inspiration and appeal of the Greek arts: the concern of Greek authors with their own language problems, the isolation of most Greek authors from direct contact with the literature of other countries, and the fact that, of all the arts, literature in Greece has naturally been the one most directly inspired by and concerned with the history and people of the country itself.

Poetry, inevitably, was much freer than prose from these limitations, and has consequently had a much wider international appeal. The tradition of modern Greek poetry goes back to the early nineteenth century, when Solomós and Kálvos wrote under the influence of their contemporary European romantics. The reaction against lyricism and the excessive veneration of words for their own sake rather than their meaning, came towards the end of the century under the leadership of Kostis Palamás who died, aged eighty-four, only twenty years ago. Both he and his heir Kaváfis blended their Hellenic inspiration with a universality which has made their work known in translation to large audiences abroad. Angelos Sikilianós, who died in 1951, may be described as the founder of another branch of modern Greek poetry which has influenced its development even more directly. He lit the way for a whole generation of modern Greek poets who bear strong traces of almost every trend in the contemporary poetry of the West, from T. S. Eliotism to surrealism. Poets like Papatzónis, Elýtis, Rítsos are distinguished in this group. But none has had more impact, both in Greece and abroad, than the former Greek Ambassador in London, George Seferiades, who, under the pen-name Seféris, became Greece's first Nobel Prize winner in 1963. The recognition was fitting not only for the individual merit of Seféris as a poet of the first rank, but as confirmation of the fact that poetry occupies a more important place in Greek literature and the public appreciation of it than in most countries. Relatively few people, among them Sherrard, Scott-Kilvert and Kimon Friar, are qualified to translate modern Greek poetry; their work has done much for its considerable recognition in the Anglo-Saxon countries. For the reader who would like a taste of this most accessible form of modern Greek literature, several small anthologies in English are available.

Greek poetry owes much to its popular tradition in the rich repertory of ballad and folk-song. But Greek prose has no such popular roots. In so far as a folk-tradition exists in modern Greek prose, it is in the narration of history and slices of peasant life. Fundamentally, it is this kind of prose – the 'chronicle' rather than the character plot – which is typical of the most famous Greek novelist of all, Nikos Kazantzákis, several of whose works set in Crete and Asia Minor (*Zorba*, *The Greek Passion*, *Christ Recrucified*, *Captain Michael*) have been very successfully published in English translation. The same kind of chronicle-prose is typical also of the work of many of the best-known contemporary Greek novelists – Mirivílis (several of whose best novels are now being published in English translation), Venézis, Prevelákis, Petsális. Other modern Greek novelists are perhaps closer in spirit and intention to the few isolated Greek writers of the late nineteenth and early twentieth centuries (Roïdes, Psycháris, Xenópoulos) who may be said to have laid the foundations of cosmopolitan and sociological prose in Greece. Karagátsis, in particular (who died quite young recently) was a writer in the direct line of contemporary Western writing: his novels are intent on plot, action and character; his canvas is cosmopolitan and his treatment of sex-incident, especially, is vivid and frank. It is strange that he, of all modern Greek novelists, has not, so far as I know, yet been translated. Cosmas Polítis, also, is a modern novelist whose expert treatment of adolescence and other psychological themes would find considerable favour abroad. Two fine prose writers who lie somewhere in the middle of the range between the 'chroniclers' and the 'story-tellers' are Terzákis and Theotokás. Both draw on Greek historical themes; but their primary purpose is the examination of contemporary Greek phenomena – the structure of modern Greek society, in particular, for Terzákis, and the modern Greek character for Theotokás.

Perhaps even more than in most European countries, writers in Greece (restricted to a small and generally not very prosperous local market) find it difficult to live on their earnings from books alone. A large number of them contribute to the daily Press which, in Greece, devotes much more space to novel serials, essays and criticism and much less to topical news features than the Press of the Anglo-Saxon countries. Between the 'popular' and the 'serious' papers there is, of course, a distinct difference in the boldness of headlines, the number and sexiness of pictures, the intellectual level in general of the contents. But both types of paper work on the assumption that a Greek reader (who pays 4½*d.* for a newspaper ranging from six to twelve pages) calculates the value he receives in terms of sheer reading matter. The politicians, for their part, keep the newspapers well supplied with splendidly wordy statements and counter-statements; the crime reporters are adept at stringing out even a simple case of assault and battery into two or three full columns; a leading article can comfortably run to a couple of thousand words – still leaving plenty of space for long literary contributions, either from Greek writers or from a huge variety of matter purchased or simply clipped from foreign publications and rapidly put into Greek.

The sheer volume of information imparted by Greek newspapers, even of the 'popular' category, and their wide coverage of both political and cultural developments abroad, are in impressive contrast with many corresponding publications in other countries. And there are now seven morning and eight afternoon papers published in the capital, in addition to countless local papers throughout the country. But in general, in spite of growing advertising revenues, the financial picture of the Greek Press (both daily papers and the numerous weekly magazines) is one of too many papers chasing too few readers – readers who, especially in the villages, regard a newspaper not as something to be casually read and tossed aside, but as a precious all-purpose educator to be passed from hand to hand in the café.

The financial dependency of all newspapers on some degree of subsidy from the authorities creates certain pressures which are theoretically inconsistent with a totally free Press. In practice, however, there is no kind of Press censorship in Greece; newspapers of all shades are free to print, and do print, exactly what they please within the limits of the libel and public security laws. The government of the day enjoys no kind of immunity from even the most violent and ill-informed attack. On the other hand, the government's control of or influence over several important outlets of news dissemination gives it more powerful weapons for fighting back than the more subtle means of news and comment control which are employed by governments in the Anglo-Saxon countries.

Twelve o'clock noon on the central streets of Athens is the time for the visitor to glimpse the interest and excitement which newspapers arouse, even when the news is dull. Under the watchful eye of the police, the newsboys gather at strategic corners with their huge piles of afternoon papers bulging under their arms. They are not allowed to sell a single copy a moment before noon. The hour strikes and the small army of paper-sellers, in full voice, unleashes itself in pandemonious pursuit of customers. It is difficult for anyone in their path to resist the conclusion that the world is coming rapidly to its end.

For the foreign visitor, there are four morning papers (two in English, one in German and one in French) which provide a useful and often amusingly misspelt survey of the main Greek and international news of the day. These papers are also a handy guide to tourists in search of entertainments and eating places. Some even contain translated summaries of editorial comment in the Greek Press. But, for the venturous, and especially for those who have taken my language hints to heart, the one and a half drachmas spent on a real live Greek paper is a worth-while investment: even if you understand only one word in a hundred, you will gain a faint but exhilarating feel of the nation's pulse.

The ubiquity of radios in cars, village cafés, the bedrooms of modern hotels and of transistor sets (your own and other people's) will sooner or later effect your introduction to Greek broadcasting. This is one of the media of mass communication which, with very rare and short-lived exceptions, no Greek government of whatever degree of democratic persuasion has ever had the courage to relinquish in spite of vociferous criticism. There are signs that the liberalization of the radio may happen in the not too distant future. Meanwhile, the heavily-slanted news and comment continues to defeat its own purpose by the cynicism its origins inspire in the listeners.

You, in any case, will twiddle the dial when you hear the voice of the news reader or commentator. With any luck, however, one of the three stations operating from Athens throughout the day will be found to be issuing some tolerable light music. And for me, all the faults of the Greek radio are as nothing compared to the great blessing of a fourth station: the 'Third' programme which operates from seven till midnight every evening. For five hours every night in Greece you can listen to an unbroken programme of recorded classical music performed by the best orchestras of the world. On the medium-wave dial, you will find this nightly source of calm enjoyment somewhere just short of 450. Make a note of it.

Greece will be the last country in Europe (with the exception, I believe, of Albania – which is currently more a part of Red China than of Europe) to instal a television system. It will be the tourists of two or three years hence who will see the first TV aerials atop Greek roofs, now so puzzlingly bare of rods and poles. Many people indeed suspect that Greece may turn out to be the first country where TV fails to take a powerful grip. This forecast has nothing to do with technical problems. There is no reason why the future Greek TV system should not inspire the same conviction of technical perfection which is inspired now by a visit, say, to the 'Democritus' nuclear reaction plant. If there are serious reservations about the success of TV in Greece, it is because the spread of the habit presupposes wet evenings, long distances from one's friends and a liking for the domestic hearth. Nothing, as we shall now see, could be less accurate as a description of the way the Greeks live.

7 The Pursuit of Happiness

The way the Greeks live. In many ways, to adapt a phrase from George Orwell, Greece is more average in this respect than most countries, and our generalizations will be more than usually valid.

Greece has no formal aristocracy. The Royal Family is a foreign importation which attracts affection in the competent performance of its constitutional functions. But it has no family ramifications among the Greek population, its marriages are perforce contracted with other foreign royalty, and even its closest circle of chamberlains, equerries and advisers are drawn from the normal ranks of Athenian high – but ordinarily red-blooded – society. This section of society which qualifies for the label 'high' does, it is true, contain a few members more or less remotely descended from 'genuine' aristocratic families – usually Italian, German and occasionally Russian nobility. But they are far from constituting a real aristocracy, and such faded titles as they may theoretically claim are almost never used. There is also a faint aura of aristocracy attaching to the scions of some of the traditionally wealthy – but now frequently impoverished – Greek families which, with ships and gold, sustained the glorious Revolution of 1821. The families which have historically provided the outstanding politicians and soldiers of Greece also enjoy a kind of automatic distinction.

All these categories, together no more than a handful of men and women, comprise an identifiable group which, by a long stretch of the imagination, we might describe as aristocratic. They live, not on great landed estates, but in modest four- or five-room apartments within a stone's throw of each other in Kolonáki – the Mayfair of Athens. Here they attend each other's bridge and cocktail parties and later read about these chaste occasions in the social columns of the staider newspapers. The older men, in surroundings deliberately similar to those of premises in St James's and Pall Mall, spend long hours at the dignified Athens Club, while their sons go off to Oxford and Cambridge and their daughters to finishing schools in Switzerland.

This, however, is playing at aristocracy. If there is a real aristocracy in Greece, it is an aristocracy of wealth. And, once again, the scale of it is trifling and cosily calculable compared with the dizzy stratosphere inhabited by the millionaire class of other countries. The really rich men of Greece are no longer in Greece. Those who remain, the 'kings' of enterprises which include shipping, brewing, chemicals, cotton manufacture, banking and mining, would hardly qualify for a minor dukedom in other more expansive lands. It is not easy to put this in figures: the rich men of Greece may be less affluent than their foreign colleagues in the Croesus Club, but they are at least as anxious to conceal their titles to membership from the tax-man. The ownership, however, of one (modest-sized) yacht and not more than two motor-cars (one of which is rarely a Rolls or a Cadillac) is about the measure of their claim to riches. Little enough by *Fortune* standards, or even by the standards of the growing class of Western citizens who can surpass these puny levels, without any direct participation in production, through the marginal activities of management and the stock-exchange. Real millionaires in Greece, whether in dollars or pounds, must be very few indeed.

Even at the lower levels of income attainable by ordinary persons, the scale is narrow. It is true, as we have said, that a working-class family often has to make do on as little as £6 or £7 a week, or even less. But a university professor earns no more than about £20 a week and men in the various free professions would consider their career successful when their income reached, say, £2,000 or £3,000 a year. Very few salaries in industry, even in the highest positions, exceed that figure. The salary of the Greek Prime Minister is about £125 a month; and his home is only distinguished from thousands like it by the presence of a policeman.

This constriction of the social and financial scale within fairly narrow limits today supplies psychological and material reinforcement to the group sense of 'identity' which is rooted in the even deeper soil of Greek history, language, religion and folk tradition. It would be absurd, obviously, to suggest that the everyday life of a shepherd in a lonely mountain village of the Pindus has much in common with the daily round of an Athenian industrialist. But, between those two extremes, helped by a constant shift of population from the villages to the towns and from the smaller towns to the capital, the Greek population shares an unusually uniform blend of basic ambitions, outlooks and pursuits.

Some of these basic attitudes have been superficially obscured in recent years by the rapid growth, in the more prosperous provincial towns as well as in the capital, of a bourgeois class whose habits are in many ways indistinguishable from those of their international fellows. It is their growing numbers and prosperity which has turned the ownership of a private car from a rare distinction into a commonplace, doubled the amount spent by Greek tourists abroad and sent the sales of Scotch whisky rocketing – all in the space of ten years. Possession of a car no longer involves a Greek in the moral obligation to take all his friends for a drive on Sunday morning; most of his friends have cars anyway, and those who do not soon will. There is the joke about the snobby woman who was asked where she spent her summer and languidly replied, 'Oh we had a simply heavenly time in Baden-Baden,' to which came the crushing reply, 'Really, well we've just got back from Methana-Methana!' (Méthana is a small and unprepossessing spa in the Peloponnese.) This no longer gets as big a laugh as it used to: Baden-Baden, not to mention likelier overseas playgrounds like Rome, Paris, the French Riviera and Vienna are no longer the preserves of a very few idle rich among the Greeks. And whisky (commonly known by its genteel and casual diminutive, *whiskáki*), is hardly any longer even a status symbol: in the homes of today's Greek bourgeoisie it is offered and consumed in abundance, without the former sense of defiant and uneasy participation in a daringly exotic rite. The same outward approximation of Greek middle-class habits to universal standards is evident in the constantly growing number of well-filled cinemas and theatres, the prevalence of Paris styles in clothes, the rash of *boutiques* stocked with chic imports, the generous attendance of strikingly hatted ladies at literary lectures, rummy sessions (strangely called, *koum-kan*) spring and autumn fashion shows and *thé dansants* at the big hotels.

The substitution of whisky for banana cordial and a growing predilection for cashmere sweaters, chunky costume jewellery and sheer nylons, are no more than the external evidence of two interrelated features of post-war Greece: the growing material prosperity of an expanding middle class and increased contact with the outside world. These new habits are only lightly superimposed on a much more fundamental approach to the pursuit of happiness which hardly varies from one class of Greek to another. The definition of a concept so unconsciously abstract is not easy, although it is something which makes a sharp enough impact on those who encounter it for the first time. In it, I seem to detect strong echoes of elements which, as we have seen in earlier chapters, are at the root of a continuous Hellenic tradition and character. One of these elements is the relative frugality of Greece's natural resources and the consequent earnestness, in historical as well as current economic terms, of the struggle for collective and individual survival. This, in a people as fundamentally alert and optimistic as the Greeks, seems to generate a compensating urge to seek enjoyment where they can. The notion of 'having fun' or 'enjoying one's leisure' does not, for the Greek, imply a compartmentalized activity separate from and even subordinate to the more serious business of life. Enjoyment, fun, entertainment, happiness are inextricably interwoven with life itself in its most universal aspects. The Greek does not have to be taught or encouraged to use his leisure; the positive pursuit of enjoyment is an instinctive and pervasive urge, as alive today as in the days of the Hedonists. The question

'What shall we do tonight?' is automatically posed from the moment of waking; it is not, as elsewhere, one which arises on Sundays, holidays and other special occasions. Pleasure is not something to be doled out in carefully calculated doses and planned ahead like an operation of war. To a Greek it is inconceivable that people abroad actually book seats at the theatre one or two months in advance, or make a dinner date a couple of weeks ahead. The seating plan of a Greek theatre running the biggest success of the moment will be two-thirds empty up to half an hour before the performance. One of the empty thirds will fill up in the half-hour before curtain-time; and the remaining one-third in the half-hour after curtain-time! And even then, there will still be groups of people in the foyer pleasantly debating whether to go to the theatre after all (what play is it, by the way?), or whether to slip into a cinema, or phone old Spiros and suggest dinner down by the sea. The flexibility of leisure is even recognized in official practice: an invitation, for instance, to a government reception is rarely received more than a week ahead of time; and it is not considered unpardonably rude to be asked on the day itself – everyone knows that it is not because your name has been included on the list at the last moment, but simply because *everything* is done at the last moment. And the odds are that, since you also make your decisions at the last moment, you will be free to attend. It is just a different convention, and one which most people find thoroughly refreshing when they get used to it.

The earnestness of the struggle for survival does not only create the compensating urge for enjoyment; it also determines that pleasures can be derived from the simplest activities. Growing individual prosperity may have encouraged the middle classes to borrow some of the more modest luxuries of universal currency; but they are still a long way from craving the complex and artificial aids to pleasure which have been evolved in the urban hothouses of wealthier countries. Almost every Greek, townsman and villager alike, can have all the fun he needs without spending his substance on home movie cameras, Cinerama, under-water swimming gear, colour (or even non-colour!) television, super-duper musical shows, gold swizzle sticks, vicuna overcoats, portable refrigerators, crocodile picnic baskets and fibreglass suitcases. Somehow, he seems to manage well enough on less artificial pleasures. A glass of wine, a few fried sprats and good company in the open air are enough to satisfy tastes which are still remarkably unjaded. The restraint with which even these rustic and inexpensive joys are indulged is suggested by the fact that the *per capita* wine consumption in Greece – a country which produces a large surplus of wine costing basically about 1*s*. 6*d*. a bottle – is among the lowest in the world. The *taverna*, the popular resort of every income group in Greece, differs from the pub and the bar in the sense that it is the occasion and the enjoyment of talk and song, rather than the opportunities for alcoholic intake which are the main attractions. And this might be a good point to note another feature of Anglo-Saxon behaviour which leaves the Greek gasping in astonishment: drink without food. The sight of Englishmen downing pint tankards and Americans on their fourth Martini with hardly so much as a biscuit is something no Greek easily recovers from. Drink, for the Greek, is the accompaniment to food, conversation and social intercourse.

This enjoyment of gregarious pleasures discloses another of the fundamental – one might almost say atavistic – elements which we have already observed in the Greek tradition: the active sense of community life which identifies every Greek with every other. Everyone in Greece lives in a village, of which Athens is merely the biggest in size. We have said it before. But this is the place to say it again. There is a total identity between the simplest and commonest form of leisure enjoyment in the biggest town and the smallest hamlet of Greece: just sitting and strolling in the shade of the midday sun or in the cool of the evening. Just as every inhabitant of a village, when he is not in the fields or actually eating and sleeping at home, will be gathered at one of two cafés in the village square, so, on a summer's evening, the whole million and more of the population of Athens seems to have crowded into the three or four main squares of the city, just chatting, observing, sipping lemonade and spooning ice-cream. This is pavement-squatting raised to the level of a mass ceremonial, imparting to the average Greek the same kind of spiritual sublimation as a church service to a man of religion. The ceremonial even has its recognized hieratic equipment: for example, the string of amber beads, *kombolói*, significantly reminiscent of a rosary, which occupies the idle hands of the café congregant, especially if he is a non-smoker; or the startling

array of rush-seated chairs, three or four of them, which each devotee of the café cult occupies with formalistic grace and nonchalance – one as a rocking perch to sit on, one for each languidly outspread arm, and one or two for the delicately spread-eagled legs. The habit is responsible for a phenomenon which puzzles many foreigners who visit Greece in the late autumn. A main road, as he crosses it, will seem to display a curious surface of brightly shining metal, in contrast with the ordinary tarmac of the other roads in the vicinity. How is he to guess that this section of road separates a café on the adjacent pavement from a square which, just previously, was crammed with small tables and chairs occupied day and night; and that the solid metal surface of the road is nothing but the sum total of innumerable bottle tops flipped off by waiters as they dodge the traffic between café and square and then steam-rollered into the soft summer tarmac by passing wheels?

When tired of sitting, it makes a pleasant change to stroll. In the villages or the popular quarters of towns and suburbs, this activity is a recognized exercise, '*seryáni*'; it consists simply of a mass meander, with no evident purpose, along the sea front or down the main street. It is a phenomenon so hallowed by custom that it receives official recognition in a form which puzzles the foreign motorist: driving through Greece, especially on a Saturday or Sunday night, he will frequently find himself sent on a long detour which avoids the centre of a town. If he had the curiosity to proceed on foot to discover the nature of the obstruction, he would find that it was only the complete choking of the central streets by aimless throngs of townsfolk enjoying themselves in relaxed perambulation. And even in streets not far from the central thoroughfares of Athens, the police give privileged strollers and squatters the same total protection from the invasion of fast-moving vehicles, noise and exhaust fumes.

In this simplicity of basic pleasures and the enjoyment of the gregarious life outdoors we detect another feature of modern Greek life which stretches back into the remotest Hellenic past: it is the same gentle climate, the same intimate contact with sky and sea and trees, the same confinement of Greece's natural phenomena within the scale of human proportion, which long ago determined the anthropomorphic character of Greek religion and which still makes every

Greek at heart a pagan nature-worshipper; a true descendant of the Dionysians, an initiate into the mysteries of the wood-dryads and the nymphs of the sea. Whether it is from the terrace of a luxury restaurant, a private villa by the sea, or on one of the organized country excursions which attract thousands of Greeks through the huge 'Travellers' Club', the contemplation of nature adds an important dimension to the life of the Greek town-dweller. It is identical to the dignifying sense of communion with the surrounding physical world which lends a piercing sweetness to the flute of the shepherd boy on the hillside and a calm repose to the face of the bare-footed fisherman mending his nets on a deserted beach. The sky and air of Greece are a kind of basic nourishment – not in a figurative romantic sense, but in the sense that they seem to provide an almost tangible compensation for the material deprivations which Greeks can suffer with unusual cheerfulness. The point can be proved almost statistically: many thousands of Greeks emigrate each year in search of better material conditions; it is those who go to Australia, Canada and other countries which still have wide-open spaces who tend to stay and prosper. Of those who earn undreamed-of incomes in the mines and factories of the industrialized countries of Western Europe, a very large proportion quickly reject the blessings of the gilded cage and return to the impoverished but heady air of their native villages – whether the 'village' be an Athenian suburb or a hamlet on the slopes of Mount Pelion. (We should remember, too, that some of the big new industrial projects being developed in Greece – like the great aluminium plant on the virgin beach just below Delphi and Mount Parnassus – offer opportunities of employment in surroundings which combine the best of both worlds.)

A positive attitude to enjoyments, an equable climate and the elimination of barren commuter's travel all tend towards a fuller and more varied exploitation of the day's twenty-four hours. This effect is superbly enhanced by the institution of the siesta. This is not, as foreigners wrongly assume, a testimony to indolence encouraged by high temperatures. It is difficult, certainly, to do anything much more energetic than to snooze away the hot midday hours of the summer months. But the siesta is a year-round phenomenon which plays a positive and integral role in Greek life. For many people, especially in winter, it does not involve actual sleep. But the three-hour interval when shops and offices close, when the pneumatic drills and colourful street-cries of the hawkers are silenced (by law!), and when only practical jokers (and uninstructed foreigners) set the telephone bell ringing, is a pause for recuperation as potent as the night itself. Often, it is almost as long! The Greeks retire late and rise early. A Greek restaurant is almost empty at nine in the evening, beginning to fill up at ten and reaches its peak activity between eleven and twelve. The last show at a cinema or theatre begins at ten at night in the winter, and nearer to eleven in summer. Emerging at half-past midnight or 1 a.m. those who have not yet had dinner will go off to dine; those who have will repair to a café for coffee and ice-cream; and some of those, finding that the lively conversation has not ended when the first light of dawn is faintly visible, may well decide to round up the day at one of the *patsá* joints – the Athens equivalent of the onion soup restaurants of the Paris Halles – where the main delicacy is a nourishing soup made of tripe or calves' feet on which the experts shake a generous splash of a garlic-and-vinegar sauce (*skordostoúbi*) from the bottles on the table. In any of these eventualities, it will be long after midnight – and very commonly two or three in the morning – before they are in bed. Yet they will be at work by eight or eight-thirty, and stay at work until it is time for lunch which, by the time they get home, may be eaten as late as two or three o'clock. After that, the siesta comes as a kind of night, a preparation for the new day which begins in the late afternoon and lasts for at least another eight or nine hours.

On this basis, the siesta is seen to be anything but a testimony to indolence. It is, on the contrary, the device which enables the Greeks to squeeze more out of the twenty-four hours than most people; to make two days out of every day. For many people, those who work in government offices and other large organizations, the long hours between arriving at their offices in the early morning and leaving for their late lunch leave them entirely free for the rest of the day. For the others (who tend to arrive a bit later and leave a bit earlier for lunch) there will be two or three more hours of work after the siesta. Those who can arrange their own hours, like self-employed professional men, are generally to bc found in their offices as late as nine or ten at night – unless they decide to take an evening off.

It is a much more intensive and varied schedule than we are accustomed to outside Greece. It is also much more flexible than the system of relatively brief periods of morning and afternoon work rigidly separated by commuting journeys, lunch periods and long week-ends. The system has its own terminology which can be confusing to the uninitiate: when an American official in Athens invites a Greek to see him in the 'afternoon', he means somewhere between two and four – when the Greek may not yet have had lunch. In Greece, the 'morning' means anything up to 1.30 p.m.; 'midday' means from 1.30 to around 3 p.m.; 'afternoon' means from after the siesta up to the 'little evening' (*vradáki*) beginning at about 8 p.m. and giving way, at around nine or ten at night, to the *vrádi*, or evening proper.

The non-compartmentalization of work and leisure makes the Greek week-end much less distinct as an oasis between week-days devoted to a workaday routine. For everyone, Saturday morning (and for many Saturday afternoon, too) is a normal working period. There is no long week-end, and not much of a short week-end either. Sunday is the only day of the week which has a holiday flavour: the day for sleeping an extra hour in the morning, airing the children in the park, an all-day excursion and – when elections come around – going to the polls. Sunday is also the day for football, Greece's most popular spectator sport which attracts crowds of up to 40,000 into the biggest of the many stadiums and which, in the evening, provides thousands more with a brief moment of hope as they check their entries in the official football pools which can yield prizes of more than £10,000.

Church-going is, on the whole, a more integral part of the Greek Sunday than it is in many other places. This is natural in a country where, even in the big towns, large sections of the population are recent arrivals from the countryside where the liturgical aspects of religious faith are predominant. Stand outside any church in Athens, and you will see a large proportion of those who pass by (whether on foot or in a vehicle) automatically make the sign of the cross. Even on week-days the churches receive a regular flow of visitors who buy a tallow candle at the entrance (from one to ten drachmas, depending on thickness) and offer a quick prayer after placing the lighted candle in one of the giant brass candelabra. Church attendances in Greece, however, show the same signs of falling off in proportion to rising living and educational standards as in so many other countries. The process may be hastened in Greece by the rigours of the church ceremonial: the whole congregation in a Greek church is required to stand throughout the service, and the traditional chanting of the priests and choristers is, with few exceptions, unusually monotonous and unintelligible.

Religion, however, plays an important semi-secular role in the Greek calendar (see the Table of Holidays on p. 250). Entirely non-religious holidays in the year are few: New Year's Day, 25 March (anniversary of independence), May Day and 28 October (anniversary of Greece's defiant 'No' to the Italians in 1940). These holidays are celebrated in the manner appropriate to them: New Year's Day with gifts (including the quaint custom of leaving presents at the main intersections for the benefit of the traffic police!); May Day with pastoral pursuits and the plaiting of wild-flower garlands hung on house doors; and the 'national' holidays with speeches, parades and fly-pasts. It is the Saints' Days, major and minor, which provide the most frequent calendar landmarks and provoke a succession of half-day and whole-day closures of shops and offices which only the specialists seem able to predict. To some of the older generation of Greeks these highlights of the calendar seem more familiar than the mundane days and months: 'It must have been,' they will say, 'a day or two after St Nicholas – or was it the day before St Spirídon?' These and other Saints' Days are, indeed, often memorable occasions in the sense that they are the occasion for personal celebration by the scores or hundreds of thousands who bear the name concerned. It is the custom on such days for people to set out on a round of visits to all their friends named George or John or Panayóttis, as the case may be; with them they bring the invariable gift of flowers or chocolates. On days which commemorate the more popular saints the streets seem to be swarming with delivery boys carrying the carefully wrapped orders from florists and confectionery shops; and, round about ten o'clock at night, the traffic jams formed by cars doing the rounds from the house of one Andrew or Harálambos to another are more impenetrable than at the busiest peak-hour of an ordinary non-saintly day. Once arrived, the visitors offer their traditional wish of 'Many Years' to the celebrant and his family, deliver the gift, and then sit around nibbling the cakes and chocolates which they and the other visitors have brought until it is time to move on to the next port of call. The company on these occasions is often strangely heterogeneous: sophisticated flat-dwellers sitting round the walls in cramped array side by side with kerchiefed aunts from some remote village. The conversation does not usually sparkle, and it is no wonder that the sheer boredom of these occasions seems to be gradually undermining the tradition: on each of the major Saints' Days, the newspapers print lists of people who wish publicly to declare that they are 'not celebrating' – in other words, that they will not be at home to receive visits and gifts. These lists seem to grow longer all the time.

Nothing, on the other hand, seems to detract from the universal and enthusiastic celebration of the two major religious holidays of the year. Christmas, as in most countries, has become increasingly secular in spirit, the occasion for gifts, parties, holly, mistletoe and imported fir-trees. Many of the customs which used to belong exclusively to the New Year (St Basil's Day) have now been shifted to Christmas: the traditional red-robed and white-bearded Santa Claus appears in the guise of St Basil, and the carol about that Saint, sung to the accompaniment of a tinkling triangle by groups of children collecting pennies round the houses, serves now for both Christmas and the New Year. The cutting of the *vassilópitta* ('Basil-cake') – a flat round yeast-cake divided among the family or the guests at the New Year's Eve party or among the staff of the office for good luck in the coming year – is one of the few customs attaching to the New Year which has not been shifted. Like the Christmas pudding, the *vassilópitta* always contains a charm or coin – traditionally a gold sovereign – which determines the coveted lucky slice. The *cazamías* – the satirical prediction in the newspapers of events to come during the year – is another amusing feature of the New Year season which is not specifically Greek in origin.

But there is nothing more Greek, more colourful, more intensely observed and more intimately bound up with the remotest traditions of Hellenism, both pagan and Christian, than the spring-time celebration of Easter. Apart from the advantages of the exhilarating climate and absence of big tourist crowds at this time of the year, the opportunity of observing the celebration of Easter is an excellent reason in

itself for deciding to visit Greece at that time (bearing in mind that the Orthodox Easter may sometimes be separated from Easter in other dogmas by several weeks). The complete cycle of celebrations connected with Easter lasts for about ten weeks, beginning with the three-week Carnival period which is a kind of gay 'last fling' before the lean days of Lent. The Carnival in Greece still retains many of its folklore features, most prominently the beribboned two-man 'donkeys' which, accompanied by drums and tambourines, parade the streets collecting pennies tossed down from the balconies. The remaining virtuosos of the tambourine can produce some amazing sounds from the instrument which they juggle as expertly as a drum-major twirls his long baton: by the use of knees, elbows, head and thumbs scraped over the tambourine's parchment they coax this usually feeble instrument into stirring power and range. It is specially effective when accompanied by the traditional hurdy-gurdy. But the most prominent aspects of the Carnival are now entirely social and worldly: the period is one of intensive, almost compulsory, merry-making when the taverns and night-clubs, full of streamers, masks and fairy-lights, are crowded to capacity every night and when every conceivable kind of club and association (e.g. the Friends of Byron and the Association of Cephalonians in Athens) hold their annual balls in the big hotels. The streets in broad daylight swarm with juvenile Madame Pompadours and Chinese Mandarins going to children's Carnival parties; and, at night, the mysterious 'dominoes' emerge – groups of totally masked black-robed figures who, by tradition, are permitted to enter any public place and, under the cover of anonymity, release any number of repressions by ribbing friends and acquaintances they chance to meet with utter abandon. The pace of the merry-making accelerates towards the end of the Carnival period, culminating in all-night revels in the narrow twisting lanes of the Pláka district of old Athens under the watchful but tolerant eye of policemen covered in confetti, and in the great Carnival parade, ball and chocolate-pelting war which attracts huge crowds from all over Greece to the annual Carnival celebration in Patras.

'Clean Monday', the first day of Lent, is an interval of sagely gradual transition between the revels which have passed and the self-denial which is to come. The diet for the day is a mock-frugal assortment of shellfish, spring onions, pickles, beans in oil, rice, a sweet sesame confection called *halva*, and lots of wine. The traditional bread for the day is the deliciously crisp flat loaf called *lagána* (any connection, one wonders, with the even flatter *matzo* of Jewish contritional significance?) which engenders in many the wish that 'Clean Monday' lasted the year round. All these traditionally lenten foods are consumed in great quantity in an atmosphere of *al fresco* merriment in which the flying of kites is an important feature. The Acropolis, in Athens, is the time-honoured venue for these celebrations; the sky above the Parthenon is filled with kites of many shapes and colours, many of them flown by the yoghourt sellers of the town for whom, curiously, this is a traditional annual outing.

The Lenten period which follows is observed with fasting and church attendance in proportion to individual devoutness. The Friday evening 'Salutation' services are always well attended, and the atmosphere of religious sentiment grows until, in the 'Great Week' before Easter itself, it is universal and tangible. If you are in the Greek countryside during this period, you will find it almost impossible to eat meat of any kind. Even in the cosmopolitan restaurants of the big towns a large part of the menu is restricted to lenten food, and lamb (banned by law during the pre-Easter period) is entirely absent. The most moving and spectacular feature of the 'Great Week' is the carrying of the symbolic body of the crucified Christ in procession on the evening of Good Friday. This 'Epitaph' ceremonial is deeply impressive in Athens, where, to the sound of a funeral march, the procession winds slowly through the central streets watched by silent thousands holding lighted candles. As the official procession passes by on its way back to the Cathedral, the ordinary citizens, candles in hand, join on to the tail, until – if you watch it from, say, the heights of Mount Lycabettus or the roof-garden of a big hotel – there is a giant, slowly moving snake of fairy-lights which seems to fill the city from end to end.

All this pent-up mass emotion and devotional dejection is released and transformed in an outburst of relief and joy at precisely midnight next day, when the bells begin to ring wildly and the priest intones the words 'Christ is Risen'. In Athens the Resurrection ceremony is treated as an event of national significance, with a running commentary on the radio of the service and the arrival, shortly before midnight, of the Royal Family and the Cabinet at the Cathedral. But a small church in any Greek village is the best place for a visitor to plumb the emotional depths of an occasion which, while ostensibly Christian in its outward form, seems to evoke overtones of a Hellenic tradition which is much older than Christianity. It is almost impossible to describe the complex mingling of religious fervour, human warmth, psychological relief and bursting spring-time optimism which is suggested by the pealing bells, the bursting firecrackers, the mutual embraces and the light of the Resurrection passed from candle to candle as the radiant crowds, their hearts overflowing, hurry home to break their fast on the midnight *mayirítsa* soup, made of the Paschal lamb's liver and lights, nourishingly bound with egg and lemon. After this outburst of primeval joy, the next day's leisurely roasting of lambs on spits over charcoal fires in the open air, the breaking of gaily dyed hard-boiled eggs (a kind of 'conkers' game in which points are totalled for eggs which resist fracture), and the day-long devotion to food, drink and dance, are a kind of relaxed anti-climax leading up to the secular pleasures of the cinema and football game on Easter Monday, and Tuesday's return to earth in the office.

There are other religious festivals which have their own special features of interest: Epiphany, for instance, when young lads plunge into the chilly sea to recover the cross thrown in by the priest during the ceremony of blessing the waters; and the Virgin's Day on 15 August with its mass pilgrimage of the sick and maimed to the church on the island of Tínos. But none of these contain such powerful and universal reflections of Greek life as Easter.

Your visit may well coincide also with one or more of the local village festivals which provide an insight into some special features of folklore. The Vlach Wedding at Lamía on May Day is a conscious preservation of one particular set of nuptial customs which, with certain basic common features, vary enormously in different parts of Greece. It has its interest, but a chance encounter with a wedding party in progress in any Greek village is none the worse for being less of a prearranged spectacle. The same might be said of the Tráta, the great May Day dance held at Mégara before an audience of thousands.

I have never been as absorbed by this spectacle, fascinating as it is, as I was one Sunday in a small mountain village of the Pindus when I chanced on a stately dance being performed in the village square in honour of four or five village lads who were going off for their army service. The conscripts led the dance, each joined to the other by a daintily held handkerchief, while the orchestra of violin, flute and clarinet followed behind the dancers in a close farewell embrace. There were no other spectators of this totally spontaneous ceremony except the tall, tough women of the village who, dressed in their peasant costume with its low-cut bodice of velvet and lace, sat erect and unmoving in the cold mountain air, watching the dance from their perches on the surrounding rocks.

Another local custom which attracts spectators is the annual fire-dance by a group of traditionally fanatic 'holy rollers' known as Anastenária in the Macedonian village of Langadás on 20 May. The pitch of religious fervour worked up by this strange cult enables them to dance barefoot on blazing charcoals without evident injury. I confess I have never had the curiosity to observe this event. But there is no reason to be more sceptical about the anaesthetic effects of auto-suggestion (combined with special skill and, perhaps, a gradual hardening of the skin of the feet) in the case of these Greek fire-dancers than in other well-established cases of fakirism.

More amusing, I would think, are the goings-on in the not very distant village of Monoplíssia, near Sérres in Macedonia, where on 9 January each year there is a live re-enactment of the scene envisaged by Aristophanes in his play *Ecclesiázusae*, ('The Council of Women'), where the female sex decides to take over control and clean up the mess which the men seem to have made of everything. In this annual ceremony, the women of Monoklissiá come into their own: they abandon their household chores, stroll down the village street smoking cigarettes, and take over the village café where they sit for hours drinking and discussing local politics. The men, meanwhile, are strictly confined to their homes looking after the children and attending to the cooking. Any man who appears in public becomes a 'prisoner' of the women and it is said that he is subjected to unspecified but unpleasant punishments during the secret orgy with which the women end their day of delicious domination.

Expert philologists have traced in this intriguing custom clear links with some very ancient Greek rites. This, and considerable contemporary testimony – including the evidence of Aristophanes – suggests the uninterrupted dominance of the male in Greek society ever since the disappearance of the prehistoric matriarchal system. There is no need, here and now, to explore the subject scientifically. But we can hardly conclude our sketch of how the Greeks live today without pausing to observe that, even in the enlightened era of the twentieth century, the dominance of the male is a Greek institution which dies very hard.

It is in the countryside, closest to the undiluted sources of Greek custom, that the visitor first notices strange things: women tending the goats on the hillsides, spinning wool, drawing water from the well, gathering olives – while the men sit smoking in the café; women trudging down country paths while their husbands go ahead in comfort on the back of the mule or donkey. This, in terms of rural realities, is indicative of an attitude which relegates the female to the category of a possession with only slightly more individuality than a spade or a tractor. The ulterior economic reasons for this subordination of women – the inheritance of land and wealth through the male line – are no longer fully active, following changes in the law over the course of recent years. But, in a country where under-employment is a chronic condition, it is inevitable that a woman's opportunities for advancement should be limited. The modern Greeks are not as ruthless towards their female children as the ancient Spartans, but certainly no wife considers she has done her duty until she has given birth to a male child. A son, given education and good fortune, always has at least the chance of making a career for himself and bringing honour and some extra material comforts to his parents. A girl, from the moment of birth, is something of a liability: her marriage is always 'arranged', and the arrangement invariably makes provision for a dowry which is in effect a kind of bribe or compensation to the husband for being so kind as to take the young lady off her parents' hands. In the homes of any but the poorest village family, the birth of a daughter is the signal to begin the weaving of blankets, the embroidering of sheets and the sewing of undergarments which are carefully stored away in wooden chests in anticipation of the wedding day. This store of basic worldly goods, together with a sum of money or a small parcel of land, forms the dowry without which a village girl may be doomed to spinsterhood for ever. The object of a well-known Royal charity in Greece is to provide endowments for the daughters of very poor village families which lack the means to provide even a couple of blankets and half an acre. A young couple passionately in love, he without the parents' consent and she dowry-less, may sometimes run away to live together. They are then said to have 'stolen themselves', and the consequences are not infrequently disruptive of the village calm for a long time – especially if the girl has been betrothed or even tentatively earmarked for another bride-groom.

This subordinate and dependent situation of women does not imply that they are treated with indifference or callousness by their menfolk. Greek men, it is true, tend to be the undisputed masters of their households, rarely consulting their wives on matters of importance and almost never rendering an account of their actions. A Greek would certainly find it difficult to accept British notions of equality between the sexes, and totally impossible to go along with the effective superiority of the American female. But, on the other hand, the dependent position of the female in Greece often inspires a kind of tenderness and consideration for her weakness which, in extreme cases, amounts to a cosseting which the world's liberated females might well envy. It is a rule which is still very generally observed that no son of a Greek family may marry until all his sisters have found husbands. The custom often involves hardship, but it is based on the practical consideration that brothers, exclusive possessors of the opportunity to earn, must see their defenceless sisters provided for before assuming the burden of creating their own families.

The subordinate position of Greek women is no longer a theoretical reality. Greek women voted in their first general elections in 1958 and they are no longer formally debarred from any kind of office. In practice, the women who achieve high office are still few; but there is a handful of women MPs, judges and high civil servants. There has even been one distinguished woman Minister, and the most successful publisher of newspapers in Greece is a woman, Helen Vláchou, whose talents would ensure her an outstanding place in the international field. There are expanding opportunities for women, also, in a large variety of other occupations: the arts and sciences, professional guiding, hotel administration, teaching and – at the lower levels – employment in the growing number of Greek factories.

The effects of these changes are apparent in the social behaviour of women in the towns. They drive cars, smoke in public, accompany their husbands to the cafés and in general appear to be as emancipated as their counterparts in other countries. But beneath this thin skin of sophistication, the basic pattern is not so very different from that which governs the fate of the female in the less developed areas of the country. In degrees which vary according to the economic independence which a woman may have achieved, the customs of arranged weddings, dowries and protection by the male members of the family are still fairly widely operative. The Athenian newspapers are still full of advertisements inserted by not-so-young ladies, or their families, which are frankly businesslike in their appeal for bridegrooms; and not-so-young men, in the same agony columns, consider that their willingness to accept 'only a modest dowry' and, rarely, none at all is a circumstance worthy of emphasis in their quest for a bride. If anything, the conservatism of the Greek male's attitude towards a woman, and of the woman's own conception of her role in society, seems to have outlasted the conditions which created it. For the great majority of Greek women, marriage is the supreme objective; its attainment almost always entails the abandonment of even promising careers, and not infrequently the abandonment of elementary interests outside the immediate scope of the housewife and mother. Married women tend even to abandon interest in their own feminine charms: slim, athletic and carefully dressed before they hook their man, the all-absorbing cares of child-bearing, cooking and keeping house turn them into comfortable matrons overnight. And nobody seems to mind – certainly not their children, who are over-fed, over-dressed and generally over-coddled; and not even their husbands, who tend to see in such domestic concern the epitome of wifely virtue. They may be encouraged in this attitude by the tolerant outlook of wives who, in the realization that their satisfying domestic preoccupations involve some forfeits in terms of physical and spiritual attractions, are possibly less insistent than average on total marital fidelity. Divorce, while not uncommon, is less widespread in Greece, I fancy, than the prevalence of justification for it. Very few Greeks indeed are practically incommoded by the strange relic of Byzantine ecclesiastical law which, in the total absence of civil marriage procedures, makes it impossible to marry more than three times!

8 Motels and Moussaka

And still you have not moved an inch, slept a wink or had a bite to eat! Those who have completed the familiarization course are, I dare to hope, better equipped now than they were to undertake their own reconnaissance of the country: misconceptions removed, curiosity satisfied, the main landmarks of Greek life roughly charted, they may strike out in the comforting assurance that they will not get totally lost. So much for the cake. But what about the bread? In the last analysis, a tourist is unlikely to get married or go to work in Greece; he can even get by without going to a theatre, a church or a village fête; nor is he obliged to shop, make friends, speak Greek or discuss local politics and morals. But he is, by definition, obliged to move from place to place, sleep in a succession of strange beds, and eat more or less unfamiliar food. These primordial tourist activities necessarily bring him into contact with aspects of Greek life which still remain to be discussed and which are being increasingly adapted to his special needs. It is, indeed, pertinent to wonder whether, in these respects, he is called on to share the Greek way of life, or whether it is the Greeks who are often required (by no means reluctantly) to share his. However . . . let us take a look at each of them in turn: travel, accommodation, food and drink.

TRAVEL

How to get there is always a pretty problem involving a complex time-finance-comfort equation. Taking England as a hypothetical starting-point (but bearing in mind that the same considerations apply to pretty well any country of northerly Europe), it is well to remember that, in one important sense, the marvels of modern travel have not shortened the considerable distance which separates you from Greece: broadly speaking, speed and comfort increase in direct proportion to cost. At this end of the scale, there is no doubt that the latest jet-plane services to Athens (little more than three hours from London direct) have revolutionized the journey for those who can afford the fare but not the time for cheaper and intrinsically pleasanter forms of travel. Shortly before I came to Greece, the air-journey by Viking aircraft involved an overnight stop; the Viscount came into service about ten years ago and cut flying time to about six hours – making a total of seven including the one stop on the way. By these standards, the Comet of the present is speedy to the point of bewilderment: I remember dining with some friends in Soho recently before catching the night-plane to Athens; I left them over coffee at 11 p.m. and was home in bed at 3.45 a.m., not very long after those of my friends who inhabit the more distant suburbs of London! The plane has the added advantage of affording a splendid bird's-eye view of the Greek archipelago and, at night, of the giant fairy-light expanse of Athens in skies which are almost always crystal clear. But, unless time is a vital factor in the equation, I believe that a more leisurely approach is better suited to mental preparation for a Greek holiday. There is another black mark against plane travel to Athens which nobody has yet satisfactorily explained away: the fares – whether you calculate in terms of first-class, normal tourist, or cheap night and excursion fares – are disproportionately high in relation to the distance. Why, for instance, should it cost 100 per cent more to fly to Athens than to Rome, when the distance is only about 65 per cent more? And why does it cost only

£10 more for the London–Cyprus return flight, when the return hop Athens–Cyprus costs about £30? Airline officials to whom I have put these searching questions have always mumbled incoherently about vague peculiarities of the tax and landing-dues system on this route. But I have still to hear a convincing answer.

At the other end of the cost scale (and leaving aside, always, special organized group travel which has its own tariffs and balance of merits) there is a third-class ticket on the long-distance train. Recommended, I suppose, for the young, the resilient and the desperately impecunious. But for whom else? Two or three nights of tortured vigilance in the alternating company of clucking hens, rowdy children and garrulous peasants – not to mention twenty-four hours of Yugoslav restaurant-car food – are, I would say, too high a price for most ordinary mortals to pay. And do not be fooled by the fancy names, such as Simplon-Orient Express, which still cling romantically to these smoke-grimed travesties of once-famous rail transports. How many stops, scheduled and unscheduled, turn an express into something else? And how hyphenated can a train get, as wagons are bewilderingly shunted on and off along the route, and still remain the same train? Pertinent questions, these. Of course, it is possible to remain reasonably aloof from the most intrusive of these discomforts by buying yourself a nice sleeping-berth and taking a hamper from Fortnums along with you. But (even without the hamper) we find ourselves at once in the luxury class, costing more than the fastest jet by the time you arrive.

A variation of this approach exclusively over land (after the English Channel) is for people who decide to drive all the way in their own cars. It takes about two days longer than the train (five days from London is a minimum for comfort, unless you treat the trip as a motor rally). But there the disadvantages end. For freedom of action and leisured flexibility the private car is infinitely superior to the train – and not a little cheaper if there are three or four passengers. I confess to a personal phobia about this particular approach to Greece. I adopted it – once – several years ago. As far as the frontiers of Yugoslavia, the trip went splendidly. From there until I reached Salonika (two and a half days later) the drive was crammed with nightmare incident which, to mention only some of the more memorable, included: near-assassination on a lonely road at night by a mobile bodyguard of

President Tito; near-ruin of a new car on three hundred miles of flint-strewn cart-tracks permitting average speeds of 12 m.p.h.; near-poisoning by roast swan at a new but prematurely crumbling State road station where my room for the night had flies and a blocked and smelly wash-basin; near-suffocation by crowds of children at every village who appeared to be seeing a car for the first time; near-bankruptcy by having to pay 30*s*. for a pint of engine oil in a Belgrade garage which, although asked to grease the chassis, managed to grease only the brake-drums; near-immobilization by failing in my efforts to find a drop of what passed (not without audible protest from the engine) as petrol in the third largest town of the country; and near-apoplexy in my final encounter with the pompous Customs official I mentioned earlier in this book. To be quite fair, my second-hand information is that you are no longer likely to face these hazards: the road, all but a short stretch, is now said to be good; petrol is plentiful; foreign cars less liable to attract annoying attention. I have no information about Tito's bodyguards, the garage service, the quality of food, the standard of roadside accommodation or the civility of the Yugoslav Customs. But we are entitled to assume that all these, too, have improved. So don't let my bygone experiences discourage you. Just don't ask me to come along.

The longest route to Greece is one of the pleasantest, and cheapest, of all. Instead of all land, all sea. One or two shipping lines serving the London–Australia route stop their big liners occasionally at the Piraeus (mainly for the purpose of the considerable immigrant traffic). The journey between the Port of London and the Piraeus, with stops at several Mediterranean ports, normally takes about ten days – ten days of sunny shipboard relaxation and reasonably good food. The fare, first-class return, is about 75 per cent of the return tourist-class air fare. But there is, inevitably, a snag in this idyllic perfection: the number of sailings which schedule stops in Greece are so few that you have to be lucky to find one which fits your vacation dates – and even luckier to find another which can bring you home again. But, if you have the time available, my advice is to investigate the all-sea route to Greece – at least for one half of the trip.

Of all the routes to Greece, the ones which seem to me to solve the time-finance-comfort equation most satisfactorily are those which combine land and sea travel. And this is true whether or not you decide to take your car along. These routes fall into two main groups: travel to one of several Mediterranean ports within two days of London (on your own wheels, by car train, passenger train, or even by plane), followed by two to four days on one of the ships linking these ports with the Piraeus; or similar overland travel as far as Ancona or Brindisi, with a rapid ferry crossing from there to Greece. Each of these alternatives has its advantages. The first method gives you a choice of boarding points as convenient as Marseilles, Genoa, Venice and Trieste, with a delightful short voyage to follow in well-run Greek, Italian and even Yugoslav ships on the Adriatic or the Aegean. Cars may be taken on all these vessels, but I fancy that only one line, operating from Venice, has a drive-on ferry. The Ancona or Brindisi version of the land-sea route has the advantage of being considerably cheaper and of making it very convenient to begin your Greek holiday with a few days in Corfu (first port of call) or a tour of the Peloponnese (Patras is the terminal) before plunging into Athens itself. The up-to-the minute Greek and Italian ferry ships which operate the services to and from Brindisi daily are slickly run and offer a variety of accommodation, all excellent of its kind. The rapid, smoothly oiled sea crossing, however, has to be paid for by the long drag down the leg of Italy. If only I could find more interest in the southern Adriatic coast of Italy, my choice would be the Brindisi ferry every time. As it is, I usually decide between Brindisi and one of the more accessible Mediterranean ports by the toss of a coin. One of the latest additions to the permutation is the ferry from Ancona – an appealing compromise which saves more than four hundred miles of the dreary trudge down the coast.

Greece itself, when you have arrived, does not always offer the same wide choice of transport. But each method you will be likely to adopt has its own characteristics which it is well you should know.

One method which I suggest you ignore as totally useless is the railway. It has two small and separate systems: one for the mainland and the other for the Peloponnese. They have different gauges and do not interconnect. None of the single-track system is electrified; but several of the trains are of the comfortable diesel-wagon type. That does not prevent Greek trains from being, on the whole, slower and more expensive than the best forms of road travel. There are not many places you can go to on a Greek train, and (with the possible exception of the Salonika service, which is a leg of the famous 'Simplon-Orient' we discussed earlier) those few places are better served by alternative means of travel. The Greek railways, like most others, lose a lot of money every year. And, so far as I can see, they deserve to, and will go on doing so until someone has the sense to scrap the whole system.

The internal Greek air network of Olympic Airways also, in common with most others, loses money steadily – so much money that Mr Onassis who runs the line recently threatened to throw in his hand unless the terms of his contract with the Greek Government were reviewed. They were reviewed, and Olympic flies on. Very nicely, too. We hear all sorts of plans for the replacement of the present fleet with modern planes and even of helicopter services to some of the islands at present inaccessible by air. But, for the time being, the choice of vehicle rests between Dakota, DC4 and an occasional DC6 on the longer or more popular routes. Flying in Greece is none the worse for that. Over mountains on a hot summer day the low-flying Dakota is not perhaps the smoothest of transports, but it has a charm and reliability of its own. And, with their suggestion of precisely the correct mixture of dash and skill, Greek air-crews always inspire especial confidence. I cannot remember a single careless landing in a Greek plane – which is more than I can say about many other internal airlines I have flown on. As a means of travelling quickly and pleasantly from one centre of Greece to another, the plane has much to recommend it. Fares are quite low, and there are services one or more times a day to places like Salonika, Crete, Rhodes, Mytilene, Corfu, Kaválla, Kalamáta, Yánnina and others. (Note for millionaires and other business executives: most of the above airfields are now organized to receive private planes.)

Returning to earth, we turn to consider the bus – Greece's utility transport, the cheapest and most complete in its penetration of the furthest corners of the mainland, the Peloponnese and, thanks to an improving service of large and comfortable ferry-boats, some of the islands including Euboia, Zanthe, Corfu and Thássos. Bus travel was, till recently, uncomfortable enough to make even the train preferable.

Whoever said it is better to travel than to arrive clearly had not experienced the ordeal of being dragged over pot-holed stretches of concrete with no more protective padding than that which is offered by an airless, crowded metal box without apparent springs or upholstery. Luxury 'Pullman' buses, with lounge seats, leg-room, properly circulating doses of oxygen and purring engines used to be confined to organized tourist excursions. But they are now general on most long-distance public bus routes. With the vastly improved roads of recent years, these modern buses have revolutionized not only the physical but also the aesthetic conditions of communal road travel: somewhere in the discreetly remote under-belly of these new vehicles is mercifully concealed the unappetizing array of string-secured suitcases, trussed live chickens, various baskets containing nameless rural produce and bundles of old clothes which used to clutter the roofs and rear sections of the old bone-shakers. The latter still serve a few routes, but are disappearing fast.

In most towns there is an efficient and improving urban bus system – the trolleybuses of Athens are especially comfortable, except at peak hours. Athens also has a single urban electric train, partly underground, which is useful if your destination happens to lie on the route between the Piraeus and the northern suburb of Kifíssia. But, unless pennies are important, the taxi is a much handier way of getting about in towns. They are cheap, plentiful and generally comfortable. They are not always to be recommended, however, for the timid (see below).

I used to know, but have now forgotten, the exact length of the tortuously indented coastline of the Greek archipelago. It is much longer than you would think. And it is almost impossible to imagine a visit to Greece which did not, at some point, require the use of the country's coastal shipping services. Generally speaking, there is no hardship involved in that. The Greeks have a long and distinguished seafaring tradition and, from a technical point of view, their ships are well run. But there are some physical limitations. The war destroyed the greater part of the Greek merchant fleet; and new additions since have not managed to keep pace with the enormous increase of passenger traffic on the internal sea routes. Shipboard travel is now a question of pot-luck. There are now many fast up-to-date vessels, newly built or converted for the island traffic. But there are also a number of grim hulks of which the best that can be said is that they apparently comply with the legal standards of safety and comfort. It is often consoling, on boarding one of these ancient Argos, to observe the diligence with which all sailing operations are supervised by uniformed port officials. It is even more consoling to reflect that the 'old tubs' of the island routes are being rapidly retired to the deserved pasture of the scrap-heap. With them, another hazard of Greek sea-travel has been fading fast: there are now very few islands regularly visited by tourists which lack landing facilities direct from ships tying up alongside the jetty. The once common necessity of leaping from the ship's ladder into a bucking rowboat out in the harbour was an exciting but not always popular feature of sea-travel, especially for old ladies with large hat-boxes. Perhaps the most spectacular improvement of recent years has been the introduction of the hydrofoil service between Passalimáni (one of the Piraeus harbours) and the Saronic group of islands – Póros, Hydra and Spétsas. These conveyances are more like buses than boats, with the passengers seated in fixed rows of seats above ski-like floats which skim the surface of the water. It is an expensive form of travel but, except for those who want to enjoy the sea voyage for its own sake, the huge saving of time is a decisive advantage.

The smartest means of sea-travel remains, of course, the private yacht which takes you where you like when you like. And, to judge by the forests of masts bobbing these days in Greek yacht harbours, with pennants of origin ranging from Siam to Venezuela, there are more people who can afford to scale this pinnacle of luxurious living than one might imagine. It is not necessary, of course, to set out in your own ocean-going yacht from some distant harbour for a Greek island cruise. The hiring of private yachts of all types and sizes, complete with crews and sometimes guides, is now one of the really lucrative new business activities in Greece. A converted fishing caique, adequate for two or three people, can be hired for something less than a small fortune. But anything fancier, even if we stop short of floating palaces with Chippendale furniture and gold-plated bathroom taps (which can be had for about £500 a day), demands a resilient bank account. There are now about eighty yacht-stations spread all over Greece where people with such bank accounts, and the yachts to go with them, can obtain harbourage, water, fuel and whatever other

ΑΘΗΝΑΙ
ΚΥΜΗ
ΟΡΙΖΩΝ
ΣΠΥΡΟΣ
ΛΕΣΛΗΣ

facilities are necessary, while they launch their deck-transported speedboats and put in a session of water-skiing.

Bearing in mind the possibility of reaching several of the bigger islands on four wheels (on ferries), many of the advantages of this luxury form of independent travel can be enjoyed at much less cost by visitors who use their own cars. And there are plenty of places you can reach by car which are inaccessible to the most luxurious yacht unless, like Mr Onassis, you carry a helicopter on board! It has recently become possible, without much tiresome formality, to hire self-drive cars in Greece at rates which are only slightly higher than modest – about £2 10*s*. a day up to 100 kilometres, with an additional 6*d*. for extra kilometres.

Driving yourself around Greece, however, is better done with certain cautionary principles in mind. Road and car consciousness, and the organization that goes with them, are fairly recent developments in Greece. The still comparatively light traffic on the roads is in many ways a welcome change from the congestion elsewhere. The drawback is that road habits and procedures which are second nature in countries with longer experience of driving problems cannot always be assumed to exist in Greece. It is only very recently that the precepts of international highway rules have been formally adopted in the shape of an official Greek Highway Code; they still constitute ideals to be attained rather than practices generally followed. Perhaps the most striking example of general attitudes towards traffic problems, reminiscent of the days when a man waving a red flag was obliged to walk in front of the first mechanical coaches, is the fact that until the recently issued Highway Code changed things, a driver who injured a pedestrian on the road was automatically arrested and jailed until he could prove his lack of responsibility for the accident! A child might jump out under the wheels of a passing car doing a stately 20 m.p.h., but the driver would still be temporarily locked up, no matter how many witnesses testified to his entire innocence. This terrifying practice has now been abandoned. But the conception of a car as a kind of unlawful intruder, even when it is minding its own business on the highway, lingers on. Pedestrians, encouraged by the narrowness of pavements in many towns and their total absence in many villages, tend to wander into the road and glower at drivers who invade their private domain. At dusk, as the shepherds bring their goats and sheep down from the hills, the country roads are often choked with slow-moving flocks of animals every few miles, their eyes reflecting a million pinpoints of light from oncoming headlights. It is the animals, by a kind of unspoken convention, which take precedence; let a driver make one solitary straggling sheep hop smartly out of his path and he will be rewarded by the shepherd's outraged imprecations. Even the shaggy sheep-dogs of Greece seem to resent the man behind the wheel: they frequently give chase to passing cars, with a tenacity and speed which is unbelievable – I have had a dog doing a steady 40 m.p.h. on my tail for several minutes on end, with enough breath in his lungs to keep up a constant barking!

Hazards of this kind are almost totally absent from the new national motor-roads of Greece, built to the best international standards. But the operative word is *almost*. There is always the possibility that, coming round the well-engineered bend at 70 m.p.h., you may come face to face with a pedestrian or a shepherd whose basic attitude to wheeled traffic has resisted the march of progress. The extra vigilance which this circumstance demands is not altogether a bad thing. It helps to keep drivers alert and combats road-hypnotism. It is enough to remember that, in Greece, a driver can never assume that everything is totally geared to his existence on the road.

From the viewpoint of the physical equipment at his disposal, the driver in Greece today – after the truly impressive progress in recent years – has few problems. Good-quality fuel and oil are available through a thick network of stations maintained by several of the world's leading petroleum companies. Service facilities outside of the big towns may not always be immensely up-to-date (are they anywhere in the world?); but Greek garage hands generally make up for material deficiencies by their ingenuity and speed of action. There are several road maps available, the latest of them accurate enough and given away free by the petrol companies. Road signs are the well-known international symbols. For historical reasons, most things connected with driving are linked with the English rather than the Continental system: petrol, for instance, is measured in Imperial gallons, and tyre pressures in pounds per square inch.

With few exceptions, like the new corniche tourist road between

Athens and Soúnion, the only first-class motor roads of Greece (by modern international standards) are the new national roads Athens–Salonika, Athens–Corinth, and parts of the Yánnina–Patras road. These roads, and others which will follow them in due course, are the only ones which really deserve the thick red line on the motoring maps. On them, always bearing in mind the general need for extra vigilance, it is possible to travel at speed and in comfort. You will see many other thick red lines. Treat them with reserve. They represent roads which, it is true, have been much smoothed and widened in recent years, but which are still no more than amended versions of the rutted lanes which passed for first-class roads in Greece till quite recently. They pass through, not around, a succession of villages; and many of them have uneven surfaces, crumbling verges, bumpy level crossings and frequent bends which are not only sharp but somehow treacherously difficult to predict. They are generally so narrow as to leave no more than a few feet between passing vehicles, and often no feet at all on mountain hairpins. Driving on these roads is never dull. But it is a good rule to observe the road-signs with more than average literalness. When you are warned of a bend or a rough stretch of road ahead, you can be fairly certain that the bend will be sharper and the roughness rougher than similar obstacles which are thought to merit warning signs in other countries.

The above descriptions and cautionary advice apply also to the thin red lines on the map – only more so. These are the tarmac roads connecting the centres of lesser importance. After that we reach the unblocked parallel lines, dotted lines and other indications of dirt roads, roads under construction, etc. It would be easy – and probably kind – to advise complete avoidance of these, except if you own a jeep or a tank. But the truth is that many of these channels of communication (for I will not call them roads) pass through some of the loveliest countryside in Greece: for example, Náfpaktos–Delphi, Agrínion–Karpeníssi, Mantoúdi–Aidipsós (on Euboia), Kalamáta–Sparta (in the Peloponnese). If you have a good car, with high clearance, and you feel generally resilient and adventurous, to drive on some of these routes will reveal some beauties of Greece which the less impetuous will never see.

My account of driving conditions in Greece has been misleading if it has given rise to hesitation on the part of even the most timid motorists. Generally speaking, so long as the main routes are followed, road communication is safe and rapid enough. It will be all the safer for bearing in mind that Greek driving habits have not necessarily improved at the same pace as the road system. In the towns, the native aggressiveness of men behind a steering wheel has been largely curbed by the massive supervision of special traffic police. Athens, in particular, with its brand-new system of one-way streets and 'green-wave' traffic lights, has been transformed from a battlefield of rival road-users into a city of orderly truce – a triumph of the machine over instinct. A foreign number plate is more than sufficient protection against penalties for unintentional errors – official Greek hospitality to foreign drivers even extends to the provision of special parking places for their cars. The last-ditch resistance to the new régime of peace and order in the towns is generally offered by the taxi-drivers. By a strange twist of logic, the fact that driving for them is a professional occupation is made to confer a special immunity from good driving manners rather than to impose an extra duty of public responsibility. There is no extreme of sudden stopping, traffic light jumping, maddening obstruction and unannounced change of direction which a taxi-driver will not justify, to himself, the police and his victim, on the ground that he is only trying to earn 'a morsel of bread'. Watch out, then, for taxis. You can recognize them from a distance by the red strip or red lettering across the top of their white number-plates.

On the open road, it is once more the 'professional' drivers who need watching. Recent new speed-limits on both buses and lorries, which comprise an unusually large proportion of total traffic, may gradually have their effect. But it will be a long time before all the drivers of heavy vehicles in Greece cease to operate on the principle that, in the last analysis, size and weight are conclusive advantages. Night-driving, under these conditions, can be especially trying. For all the dazzling array of rainbow-lights carried by these vehicles, they do not seem to have anything in the range between total invisibility and blinding dazzle. It used to be the convention in Greece that vehicles approaching each other at night switch out all their lights – an appalling habit even if we ignore the fact that bicycles and animal-drawn vehicles on Greek country roads are almost invariably without rear lights at night. Efforts to educate drivers into a proper use of dipped headlamps have made some progress. But not enough. If you can possibly manage it, get to your motel before dark.

ACCOMMODATION

We did say motel. There are such things now in Greece, evidence of the revolutionarily wide range of accommodation which visitors can now find. The choice till recently was effectively between one of a few international-class hotels in the capital and the lesser hostelries of which the five official gradings were clues merely to varying degrees of dilapidation and discomfort. It was fortunate that the rapid promotion of Greece in the tourist lists found the country with a hotel system so inferior to its task that it was necessary to create a completely new network of up-to-date hotels almost overnight. To be obliged to spend the night, as I once was, in the solitary E-class hotel of Kalabáka, after a tiring day among the monasteries of Metéora, is enough to spoil the fun of the sturdiest tourist. But there is now hardly a corner of the country where a visitor is likely to penetrate which does not provide one or more airy hotels on which the paint is hardly dry. Hotel accommodation in Greece, from being a drawback to be tolerated, has suddenly become one of the country's positive attractions.

The variety of new accommodation is large. In and around Athens, it includes big luxury hotels (complete with restaurants, swimming pools, cabarets and shops), service apartments and groups of rather expensive service bungalows down by the sea. But the important innovation for the majority of visitors is the large number of efficiently run new second-class hotels; there is no longer any temptation in Athens, for the sake of comfort and pleasant surroundings, to stay at one of the top few hotels and ruin your holiday budget.

In the countryside and the islands recent improvement has been even more impressive. There is no need to dwell unduly on the motels. There are only one or two of them; and they lack the distinctive features which, for me, make motel the ideal form of hotel: the almost complete relief from dealings with desk-clerks, bell-boys, lift-boys, waiters and chamber-maids. The delight of an American motel is in the sense it creates of total freedom and privacy; once you have paid the man in the office in advance and collected your key, there is no need to speak to another soul before piling your bags in the boot next morning and driving away. The Greek motels, like many other imitations of an American prototype, are misnamed: they are really no more than hotels with individual parking places for cars. But, whether they are called motels or hotels, the new hostelries of the Greek outdoors are probably the most notable of all aids to the practical enjoyment of a visit to the country. Some of the hotels in this new string encircling the whole country are directly owned by the tourist authorities of Greece. These include the series of hotels named 'Xenía' and the small tourist pavilions which have been built at the most popular archaeological sites and, in addition to food and refreshment, provide a few rooms for archaeologists and others who decide to stay on the spot. Other country and island hotels are privately owned. But they are all designed and operated under official supervision. Carefully sited to afford and not obstruct views of the landscape, and with prettily laid-out gardens, nearly all these hotels have a uniform architectural style which admirably suits their surroundings: they are light, clean-cut structures, with individual balconies opening on to the sea and sun; the furnishing is simple, utilitarian but graceful; the decor makes full use of Greek folk artistry, with a strong emphasis on local stone and glistening marble expanses warmed by thick, bright-coloured peasant rugs. In these hotels, even those situated far from the cosmopolitan hub of the country, there is no longer any need to order breakfast in sign language. The staff will have been put through a complete course in hotel keeping, often with the assistance of Swiss hotel firms which have invested in Greece.

In the category of less formal accommodation, there are several good organized holiday camps with bungalows (usually rented through inclusive arrangements which include visits to the other main tourist spots in the vicinity), half a dozen or more organized caravan sites, and a great deal of open country for the considerable number of young tourists who like to pitch their own tents where the fancy takes them. The latter are very often hard put to it to make hospitable villagers understand that they prefer their tent to the proffered bed! There is a special charm, too, in staying at one of the local houses which, especially in the busier tourist islands, offer a bed for the night under the supervision of the local tourist authorities. The beds will not be over-soft, and the other facilities are correspondingly spartan – 'running water', for instance, is generally that which flows cold and thin from a tap-regulated tin container nailed to the wall above an enamelled or plastic hand-basin. But, in their whitewashed spotlessness and simplicity, these houses are more in tune with the mood of the Greek islands in summer than the lusher hotels. They are also, of course, much cheaper.

For visitors who plan fairly long stays with the family, there is an increasing number of villas available for rent. Some of them have attractive furniture in the distinctive island style which makes effective use of woven straw and gracefully carved, dark-stained wood. And many come complete with maids who will cook, clean and do the washing. (The rising standard of living in Greece has not yet reached the point of putting domestic help completely out of reach; even in Athens, an excellent cook-housekeeper can still be employed for as little as £4–5 a week.)

I can think of no special advice for successful hotelmanship in Greece. The newer and more expensive hotels are organized along lines which in no way differ from world-wide practice. Service, in general, is willing and efficient. Tipping may be confined, and then only at the end of your stay, to those who have given you specially useful attention. During the busier seasons, most hotels which have restaurants charge for one meal a day, whether you have it or not. In the smaller and older hotels, traces of specifically Greek customs still survive. There is a tendency, for instance, to charge for the room rather than the person. Since very few of these hotels have single rooms, it is a good idea to negotiate in advance for a suitable reduction if you are alone. On the other hand, many of these hotels would not charge extra if you asked them to put an additional bed in the room to accommodate a party of three! In these hotels, also, it is a good idea to bring your own soap. You will not generally find it already provided. And a few precautions are in order if you are among those who simply must have breakfast in your room. Foreign breakfast habits have gradually become known even to the managers of backwoods hotels; but you may easily still strike trouble in some places where the conception of breakfast has not progressed beyond the basic Greek approach – namely a small cup of Turkish coffee. Thus, assuming you order a normal breakfast of coffee, toast, butter, honey and a boiled egg, you may well find the following on your tray: a small cup of Turkish coffee, a saucer containing a thin spread of white Greek butter over which a sea of honey has been poured, a sawdusty rusk, and an almost raw egg rolling about on a plate. You then call the man and tell him you meant coffee with milk, and he will smile understandingly and reappear with a full glass of hot sugary milk with fat globules floating on the surface. Into this he will expect you to tip the Turkish coffee. Don't do it! The result is nauseating. Don't try, either, to explain that you want a four-minute egg in an egg-cup, fresh toasted bread and the butter and honey in separate containers. He will simply be confused and saddened, without being able to comprehend or comply. The rapid incursion of the instant-coffee habit in Greece provides a fairly acceptable solution to the breakfast coffee problem. But the maxim 'If you can't lick 'em, join 'em' seems to me, in such circumstances, to contain much wisdom. Provided you have eaten dinner the night before at a suitably late Greek hour, a Greek breakfast of Turkish coffee is not totally inadequate, and saves a lot of trouble. The business of serious eating can be tackled later in the day.

FOOD AND DRINK

These are, of course, a serious business at all times. For the tourist they can easily become an obsession. Liberation from the chains of domestic routine and snatched lunches between office hours at once turns a man who is normally content with a diet of poached eggs, chips and shepherd's pie into a budding Brillat-Savarin, in leisured and single-minded search of new and memorable gustatory experiences.

I will try to be his guide in Greece, difficult as it is, in a matter which cannot be divorced from personal tastes, to set up any kind of objective standard. For the record, I am a fairly earnest eater and drinker in the qualitative rather than quantitative sense. I believe there is no food in the world like good French food (unless it is good Chinese food); I find Italian food on the whole insipid; I am specially fond of meat dishes, preferably with complicated sauces and lots of spices; I am only moderately fond of fish in general; I like most cooked vegetables but cannot swallow a mouthful of raw salad; all cheeses are welcome, from the most fragrant to the smelliest; I like fruit cold and varied, and desserts hot and sweet. Using this brief dietary confession as a 'control' the hungry reader may make the necessary mental modifications to my remarks about food in Greece.

I do not propose to join in the sterile argument about whether there is any such thing as Greek cooking or whether it is a blend of Turkish, Balkan and European cuisine. The phrase 'Greek food', for our purposes, means no more than the food you eat in Greece, irrespective of its parentage. I will only say at once that Greek food is much more distinctive than the vaguely Hellenized versions of international dishes which are generally served at 'Greek' restaurants abroad. To plunge in with a few carefully considered generalizations, I would say that, for the truly dedicated gourmet, Greece offers little in the way of exquisite satisfaction; there are some fine dishes which appeal at once to most tastes, and some doubtful ones which, to say the least, demand perseverance; there are some good complicated Greek concoctions, but few are as good as the best of the simple dishes. To sum up, I have eaten lots of good food in Greece, varied, interesting and highly palatable; but all the memorable meals I can recall – and there have been many – have been memorable much less for the food than for the circumstances of the eating: the turning spit in a poppy-grown garden; fresh-caught river perch grilled on a wood fire and eaten with pickled dill flowers and hunks of country bread in a Peloponnesian forest; bacon and eggs under the fig-trees of an Euboian shore, with a school of dolphins inquisitively close by; crisp whitebait at a table on a jetty looking out over the moonlit landscape of Salamis on a summer night; coarse bean soup, heavy with olive oil, in a remote mountain village after a day's long excursion. These are the gustatory joys I most remember; and they all depend less on the simple food than on the landscape, the climate and the outdoor exhilaration which were its perfect accompaniment.

Where you eat in Greece is, then, at least as important as what you eat. Whether you are eating in the garden of a simple tavern, under the awning of an unpretentious sea-shore restaurant or on the terrace of a luxury hotel, it is the pleasure of eating outdoors which is important.

This may be why indoor restaurants, with the exception of a few large luxury establishments, tend to be bare and forbidding places. When the Greeks eat indoors, it is a perfunctory and utilitarian operation. They cannot easily be tempted by soft lights, deep pile carpets and expensive decoration. The cosy intimate type of small speciality restaurant which makes 'eating out' an objective in itself in most countries of the world is totally lacking in Greece. If they did exist, as one or two gallant attempts have proved, they would be half-empty in winter and completely empty in summer, no matter how much air-conditioning was installed. A Greek gladly lingers over his food in the open air. But when the weather forces him indoors he likes to eat up and leave. The typical Greek restaurant, therefore, is not a place of beauty. With its bare marble or 'mosaic' chip floor, large square tables covered with plain white cloths and set with clean but clumsy tableware, soaring whitewashed ceilings, plain wooden chairs and sentinel coat-racks, it resembles a railway waiting-room more than a place for convivial enjoyment.

The *taverna* has more charm. It differs from the restaurant proper in containing some elements of local colour. At the lowest level these are no more than a few large barrels of wine exposed to view and maybe some hollow gourds, corn-cobs and strings of garlic hung from the ceiling. For the rest, the furnishing and equipment are even more frugal than in the ordinary restaurants: rickety rush-seated chairs, coloured metal mugs for serving the wine and tinny forks which bend under slight pressure. There are *tavernas* which, while they retain the same basic character, incorporate some more luxurious variations of these themes: gaily coloured tablecloths, walls covered with cane-work decorations, samples of folk-art, plaster grottoes and musical background varying from a single mendicant guitarist to a full orchestra complete with floor-show. It is in these so-called 'social' *tavernas* that the Greeks in winter meet and drink, sing and converse in an atmosphere much less devoted to the hushed appreciation of good food than to perpetuating a semblance of *al fresco* pleasures.

The general-purpose *taverna* has three recognizable affiliated types: the seaside *taverna* devoted almost exclusively to seafood; the *psistariá* type which has a special line in various specialities grilled over charcoal; and the *hassapotavérna* or 'butcher's tavern', which is a glorified butcher's shop serving choice cuts of charcoal-grilled meat with nothing but the barest minimum of accompanying food (bread, wine, salads and fruit). All three sub-types, together with the general-purpose *taverna*, have one important feature in common: the kitchen is part of the public domain, with all the food, cooked or waiting to be cooked, on display in casseroles or refrigerated glass cases. This is not merely, or even primarily a concession to public interest in hygiene – although it happens also to be a guarantee of cleanliness; the kitchens are open to the public because it is the invariable practice for the *taverna*'s customers to order their food after a personal inspection of the pots and refrigerators rather than from a menu. They will be served the precise lamb-chop or fish or portion of cooked food that they themselves choose. The custom is not only amusingly novel but, for foreigners, solves the problem of deciphering an unfamiliar menu.

The normal restaurant and the various types of *taverna* between them cover the majority of eating ambiences. Apart from the few Athenian luxury restaurants, hotel and night-club dining-rooms serving a filtered version of Greek-international food, there are a few other minor types to note: the '*patisserie-confiserie*' (*zacharoplasteíon*) a favourite and often luxuriously appointed kind of venue for coffee, snacks, ice-creams and Greece's first-rate pastries (specially recommended for late evening pavement squatting in summer); the *galaktopoleíon*, generally very modest cafés specializing in various kinds of milk foods, like egg-custards, cold rice puddings, hot *bougátsa* (a kind of custard pie with flaky pastry), cheesy things and eggs fried in butter – these are useful places to look out for in the provinces if you are in search of a light meal and a change from second-rate *taverna* food; *souvláki* stands – rough and ready kiosks or wheeled hand-carts serving chunks of hot grilled lamb on tiny cane skewers or wrapped in a kind of semi-crisp flannelly bread, with or without raw onion and tomato – useful as a stand-by on journeys; 'ouzeries', a kind of popular bar serving *ouzo* (the standard apéritif) in little carafes, or draught beer, with a large variety of (mainly fishy) *hors d'œuvre*; vegetarian restaurants, with menus based largely on various oil-cooked vegetables – not recommended for the uninitiate. There are no self-service restaurants, automats or similar rapid action establishments, except for one in Salonika. And there are no 'foreign speciality' restaurants since the failure of an unlikely so-called 'Chinese' place a few years ago.

It is useful to bear in mind one or two basic attitudes to food which differ in Greece from those which are conventional elsewhere. The 'composite' dish (e.g. roast beef, Yorkshire pudding and two vegetables) is not native to Greek eating habits. Deep down, the Greek is devoted to the custom of eating a large variety of separate delicacies rather than one central dish topped and tailed by minor 'courses'. There is a tendency, certainly, to concentrate on piquant things at the beginning and sweet things or fruit at the end, with the meaty things in the middle. But the ordered succession of a three- or four- or five-course meal becomes something much less predeterminate. It is quite usual, for instance, to see Greeks continuing to eat a fishy *hors d'œuvre* concurrently with a meat dish; and cheese can well last from the beginning to the very end of a meal. The individual 'unit' of food which comprises this somewhat disordered succession of delicacies which we would call a meal, but for which the Greeks significantly have no separate word (calling it merely 'food'), is known as the *mezés* (plural *mezédes*). This is a fairly untranslatable term, but it involves the connotation of something small, appetizing and existing in large variety. So prized is the *mezés* as a type of food that a Greek will praise a dish by saying: 'Why, this is a *mezés*!' There is no higher praise than that – unless it be a nomination for the category of *becromezés*, the kind of *mezés*, in other words, most enjoyed by the *bekrís* or wine-tippler because of its special wine-absorbent properties.

The significance of this general food concept for the visitor is not direct, for he is unlikely to change his native eating philosophy overnight. But it has certain side-effects which the visitor may well find useful. In any except the more expensive internationalized restaurants and *tavernas* of Greece, it is possible for the visitor to satisfy his curiosity about Greek dishes by ordering one of each in which the company is collectively interested. This collection of dishes may then, with perfect propriety and absolutely no embarrassment, be shared among the group, each digging into whatever dish he fancies ranged in the centre of the table. This is not merely a practice permissible for foreigners; it is what the Greeks themselves do. And even in more formal restaurants, it is rare to see a company of Greek diners who do not constantly offer each other sample forkfuls of the food which each has ordered. Up to a point, it is even possible for the lone eater to achieve the same added variety: in many Greek restaurants, and in all except the most chic *tavernas*, a half-portion of any dish may be ordered without the semblance of a blush. The institution of half-dishes (called *olígo* – 'a little') exists not to facilitate economy so much as to encourage variety.

A few other general-purpose remarks before we begin our highly personalized description of specific foods and drinks in Greece:

It is well to make up your mind as early as possible about your attitude to olive oil. This is the primary and universal fat of the country, taking the place both of butter and of meat and vegetable fats. The distinctive flavour of olive oil varies according to the degree of refinement; but it tends generally to be much more intense than that of the very highly refined product preferred in most countries abroad. This flavour is, of course, much more obtrusive when the oil is used raw than when it is an ingredient in cooked dishes. If you like the flavour of olive oil (and many foreigners do) there is nothing to worry about. If you don't, a few precautions are necessary: for salad dressing, for instance, make sure (if you can) that the oil is of the refined type; if you order grilled fish, make a point of telling the waiter that you want it without oil – for, otherwise, it is almost certain to be served already smothered in a sauce of beaten oil and lemon juice; if you want fried eggs, they will generally be cooked in oil unless you insist that they be fried in *fresh* butter (and the word 'fresh' is important here, because 'butter' otherwise may well be taken to mean the special and to my mind unpleasant kind of clarified butter sometimes used for cooking in Greece).

For those who like chips with everything, Greece can be a disappointment. Lots of fried potatoes are consumed, but nobody (with one or two lone exceptions which I will signal in the appropriate place) yet seems to have learned the simple secret of having a constant supply of crisp hot fried potatoes available. In restaurants, fried potatoes tend to be soggy and limp; in *tavernas* they are generally soggy, limp *and* cold. They are fried early in the day and kept as a kind of basic stodge to garnish plates of freshly grilled food. If you want fried potatoes, insist that they be freshly cooked for you – but only if you have plenty of time to spare. (One of the basic drawbacks of *taverna* food, incidentally, is the general indifference of the Greeks to proper temperatures in their food; they often ice their beer and fruit to the point of extinguishing all flavour, and are quite content with lukewarm soup and other ready-cooked food. This is often one excellent reason for preferring food cooked to order.)

Salads (venturing on to ground I know only at second hand) also require special foresight. An average Greek salad consists of the various ingredients (lettuce, cucumber, tomato, cabbage and often white cheese and capers) chopped or sliced and arranged symmetrically on a flat plate to receive the baptism of oil and vinegar poured direct from their bottles or of lemon juice squeezed from the cut fruit placed on the side of the plate. This procedure, I understand, is less than satisfactory to salad eaters accustomed to carefully blended dressings. The solution, apparently, is to ask for your salad to be brought in a deep plate (a soup plate, generally, since salad bowls are not standard equipment) and then to mix your own dressing with oil and mustard or whatever it is.

Spices tend to be more varied and obtrusive than you may be used to. Oregon, for instance, is almost invariably sprinkled on grilled meat before it is served. Some people love it. I always ask the man to skip it. Spearmint is often used in certain minced-meat dishes. I find it about as inappropriate as the cinnamon which also finds its way into meat sauces and which, much more successfully, is sprinkled liberally over many kinds of dessert. Bay leaves and celery leaves, whole pepper, garlic (generally used in moderation except in one special dish which is pure garlic and mashed potato!) are among the other more acceptable aids to piquancy. If you have a special aversion to any of them, it is not a bad idea to ask for a list of the pot's contents.

One final tip for lazy fruit-eaters: the waiter will always bring your fresh fruit ready-peeled and segmented if you ask him. This has the added advantage that the responsibility for making sure the fruit is good is thrown fairly and squarely on the restaurant, which cannot openly serve a dud.

We are now about ready to open the menu and choose a meal. If you are still eating bread with your food, make up your mind at once that you will eat less of it than usual in Greece. It varies, of course. But it is mostly heavy and enjoyable only when it is still warm from the oven – not a very usual circumstance in a restaurant. Some of the bread rolls are an improvement and, better still, you can always ask for black bread. This is a cheaper kind of bread mostly regarded by Greeks as a badge of indigence; but it is much tastier than the average white bread. The coarse kind of wholemeal bread found in the country and in some town *tavernas* is also a pleasant variation and can sometimes be extremely good. The best bread of all comes in the form of twisted 'hoops' covered in sesame seed (*kouloúria*) which are sold on the streets of Athens early in the morning. They must be eaten very fresh, and the slightly re-freshened versions which are sold outside cinemas and theatres at night are a parody of the real thing. In a very few *tavernas* close to the northern Athenian suburb of Ekáli they have a quaint speciality known by the inexplicable name of *peinirlí* – certainly not a Greek word. This is, basically, a kind of bread. It seems to be semi-leavened and baked in backyard ovens; while still piping hot the boat-shaped flat loaf is 'stuffed' with fresh butter and cheese, or with minced meat, and served at once. Try the plain butter-and-cheese type for preference, and get the waiter to show you the trick of cutting it most expertly so as to inject the stuffing right inside the loaf.

Iced water is automatically served with bread. There is no reason not to drink it. The water all over Greece, although it may sometimes taste different from the particular blend of H_2O and chemicals you are accustomed to, is pure and palatable. Some visitors, quite unnecessarily, stick to mineral waters to be on the safe side of the colly-wobbles. For them, there is a large choice of sparkling and flat bottled water from a variety of spas throughout Greece. They are all very pleasant and guaranteed to cure you of anything from arthritis to gall-stones. Also highly recommended are the various Greek soft drinks: the orangeade, especially (bottled with or without fizz), is the best and most genuinely fruity of any I know. It makes it much easier to live with the burden of a total ban on the import of Coca-Cola and other internationally hallowed beverages of the kind. In season, there is also excellent apricot, apple and strawberry juice; and at least two unusual soft drinks worth a try: *soumáda*, a kind of almond cordial, and *vissináda*, made of bitter cherry.

That should take care of the teetotallers. For the rest of the thirsting summer crowds beer is undoubtedly about the most popular drink in Greece. It is not specially cheap, but it is very good indeed – of the lager type, but with considerably more flavour and body than many Continental lagers. There used to be only one brand: 'Fix', a corruption of the name Fuchs, a family of Bavarian brewers who followed the dynasty of King Otto into Greece in the last century. Lately, a new brand – 'Alpha' – has come onto the market. It is not appreciably different. The Fix 'Binding' beer, a new variety based on a current German lager, is specially good. Dark lagers have been tried, but without success. Many bars and some restaurants also serve a good draught beer – Fix again.

Greece has a considerable wine surplus. Strange that more of it is not drunk, for it is sometimes very good. The *vin ordinaire* of the country, especially in the region of Attica, is – as every schoolboy now knows – *retsína*. This, quite simply, is normal dry wine, usually white but sometimes *rosé* (in which case it is called *kokinélli*) drawn from barrels into which a quantity of pine-resin has been introduced. The result is a strange-tasting wine which tends to revolt or captivate the novice. I find both extremes of reaction over-hasty. I doubt if anyone who tastes *retsína* for the first time can immediately (and honestly) fall in love with its unusual and somewhat acrid flavour. On the other hand, with a little perseverance, you come to be very fond of the sharp, clean qualities of a wine which seems to suit simple food, especially fish, eaten in a hot climate. My advice is to reserve your first attempt for an occasion when you are at a little seaside *taverna* and have ordered some grilled freshly caught fish. If you don't like *retsína* then, the chances are that you never will. Always prefer *retsína* from a barrel rather than a bottle, and avoid drinking it with food which is in the slightest degree complicated or delicately flavoured. The *retsína* habit, which is peculiar to Greece, certainly goes back to classical times. Sir Mortimer Wheeler said in a lecture I heard that several ancient Greek wine-vases he had found as far afield as India, where Greek wine was apparently imported, contained distinct traces of resin residues. The usual theory that resin was used as a preservative is not, I believe, chemically tenable. The chances are that the habit of dropping a lump of resin into the barrel developed because, in the very early days of storing wine in barrels, pine-wood barrels were used and imparted a distinct pine-flavour to the wine. When other wood was preferred by the coopers, the wine-makers introduced resin itself as a substitute for the flavour which the Greeks had grown accustomed to.

There is no need to be despondent if *retsína* resists your best effort to come to terms. Greece is full of wine which has no connection whatever with pine-trees. And many of them compare very well with the wines of better-known producing countries. In general, Greek white wines are much better than the red. This is true, at least, of the standardized wines which are freely on sale and served in restaurants. For one of the problems about Greek wine is that a large number of splendid local wines are not marketed in an organized fashion and can generally be tasted only if you happen to be passing through the area where they are produced – or at the annual Wine Festival near Athens when about two hundred different kinds of wine from all over Greece are served to visitors by girls dressed in the costume of the relevant district.

Of the standard dry white wines, among the best are Pallíni, St Helena and Mínos. Cáva Kambá is also excellent if you are feeling expansive, but it is not really worth its much higher price. These are all fairly light, fragrant dry wines which seem to lie somewhere between hocks and burgundies in the ranges of flavour and body. None of them, good as they are, touch the unique quality of a good Verdéa wine from the island of Zanthe. This is a strange pink-amber coloured wine which manages to combine dryness with fullness in a remarkable degree. Sad to say, only a little of it reaches Athens – and only in bottles, not nearly as good as the barrelled stuff of Zanthe itself. With the exception of some curiously fruity yet unsweet products I have struck in various remote villages, I know of no red Greek wine I can recommend with much enthusiasm. It tends to be either too thin or too rough. The red wine generally regarded as the best is the Boutári from Macedonia. It is certainly not bad stuff, but, just as you are beginning to think it has the qualities of a fairly good Burgundy, the slight acidity and roughness spoils it as it goes down. I am not sure that one of the best all-purpose red wines is not the mundane and quite cheap Deméstica; it is a little 'muddy' to look at and undistinguished to taste, but otherwise palatable enough. Another wine to look out for is the Pallíni 'semi-sweet' – a splendid Rhine-type wine which is unfortunately produced in quite small quantity.

The sweet wines of Greece have been famous for much longer than those now more in fashion. The 'malmsey and malvoisie' which Simon the Cellarer kept and which reputedly drowned the Duke of Clarence were none other than the sweet wines of Monemvásia, a medieval town in the extreme south of the Peloponnese. The town is now barely more than a relic and produces no wine that I know of. But other well-known Greek sweet wines continue to have a steady world market: especially the amber-coloured sweet Samos and the dark purple Mavrodáphni of Achaia in the western Peloponnese. Both are worth trying with your nuts and raisins.

Before the meal, *ouzo* is the standard Greek apéritif – although there are several excellent vermouths (none extremely dry) if you prefer. *Oúzo* (not 'ouzoo' as it is strangely pronounced by many foreigners) is a spirit distilled from the residue of the wine-presses, like many similar spirits in wine-producing countries. Its apéritif properties are conferred by its aniseed flavouring, and it is pretty heady stuff – like the French *pastis* drinks. Specially recommended before lunch in summer – with lots of ice, which turns it beautifully cloudy, and always with a little something to eat. Most people water it down fairly hard. I think that ice gradually melting in the glass is much less destructive of its intriguing flavour.

There are one or two passable Greek liqueurs for after the meal: one made from Chinese cumquat oranges which comes from Corfu; another from Rhodes which has some strange crystalline forms and a thick twig of some tree or other inside the bottle; and, often, home-made cherry brandy if it comes your way. Generally, however, the liqueurs are not much to write home about. There is a much larger production of brandy, much prized in some parts of the world. The average three- or five-star brandy, for all that it seems to attract the inexplicable admiration of French visitors, is a hopelessly weak and strangely perfumed product. Drier brandies have been produced lately and many of them are passably good. (Votris and Camba are two brands you might try.) There are some first-class Greek brandies of great age. But these are about as expensive as imported Cognac. One useful tip for cocktail drinkers: a brandy-sour, made with local brandy, is excellent and much cheaper than other cocktails which have to be made with imported gin and whisky.

If you have recovered from the hangover, we can go on to consider breakfast. We have already discussed some of the problems involved. There is only one other tip worth pausing on: make a point of trying the honey of the area you are visiting. The honey of Hymettus is famous all over the world. But the different wild flowers of practically every part of Greece produce a superb variety of honey flavours. Be wary if you are offered *marmeláda*. This will generally turn out to be a pulpy kind of apricot jam – not very interesting. If you like bitter orange marmalade, insist on *marmeláda neránzi*.

There is almost no end to the variety of dishes, of distinctly Greek associations, which belong to the main meals of the day. The following annotated menu is no more than an indication of some of those most frequently served.

Hors d'Œuvre (*Orektiká*)

Enough variety for a complete meal. Apart from the usual kinds of fishy things (smoked herring fillets, anchovies stuffed with capers, etc.) there are these less usual ones: *taramosaláta* (an excellent paste of red fish-roe mixed with oil, onion, etc.); *lakérda* (tender slices of smoked fish – tunny, I think – in oil); *tsíri* (strips of dried mackerel marinated in salt, oil and some kind of herb). This begins to read like an American menu, but I can see no way out. *Brick* (globules of red caviar, from some fish other than the sturgeon – rather salty, but preferable to much inferior 'real' caviar one meets); *avgotáracho* (a very expensive product of Míssolonghi – a kind of compressed fish-roe pâté preserved in sausage-shaped wax covering – interesting, but not worth its luxury rating to my mind. It is strangely transliterated on English-language menus as 'butarge' or some such thing.) The ordinary anchovy, unfilleted, is perhaps the only *hors d'œuvre* of this kind you are certain to find even in the most out-of-the-way and humble tavern. Generally too lean and finicky to bother with; but watch out for the lush corpulent anchovies from the island of Mytilene, called *calloní*.

Greek *charcuterie* is not distinguished in general. Some taverns will grill you an interesting type of home-made sausage (*loukánika*), generally over-spiced and suggesting too much bread among the meat. Salami (same word) is often good, if somewhat coarse, when it comes from the island of Lefkáda. Best of all is the home-made pork brawn (*pichtí*), with egg and chopped gherkins in it.

Pickles are too blatantly salty and vinegary. An exception, sometimes, are the tiny pickled aubergines, stuffed with pimentoes and celery. These *melidzanákia* are worth a try. And, for those who like ready-made stuff in bottles, there are now very passable versions of foreign-inspired piccalilli and tomato ketchup. And there is no end to the variety of olives (*eliés*) from every part of the country: fat green ones, tiny green ones with an attractive bitterness of their own, black wrinkled ones, smooth black oval ones from Kalamáta, and bottled ones stuffed with either pimentoes or almonds.

Special mention for one extremely unusual type of *hors d'œuvre*, sadly limited to some 'ouzerie' bars and a few special taverns: *zadzíki*, a memorable concoction of thinly sliced fresh cucumber, garlic and yoghourt. Keep asking for it; you might be lucky.

The internationally known Greek dish *dolmádes* is frequently served as a hot *hors d'œuvre* – rice and minced meat wrapped in vine leaves. I find the *dolmádes* made with cabbage leaves are better – the vine leaf frequently resists the boiling process. But either version, served with an egg and lemon sauce, is much preferable to the cold so-called *yalandzí-dolmádes* ('mock *dolmádes*') which have a meatless stuffing of oil-soaked rice inside the tough vine-leaf. Some people like them, though. Almost all the large variety of Greek dishes made with minced meat are often served as hot *hors d'œuvre*, although they are all capable of being treated as main dishes also. *Moussakás* is, of course, the daddy of them all: a very tasty dish of sliced potatoes (or aubergines, or courgettes, or artichokes, or a combination of any of those vegetables) alternating with spiced layers of minced meat, topped with a béchamel sauce and baked in the oven. I always think it would be rather more digestible without the béchamel. But don't miss it on that account. The list of minced-meat dishes is long and generally worth investigation: *papoutsákia*, a variation of *moussakás*; *kolokithákia yemistá*, courgettes stuffed with rice and meat and served with egg and lemon sauce; stuffed tomatoes and pimentoes; *soudzoukákia*, spicy meatballs in tomato sauce; fried meatballs, *keftédes*; and grilled hamburger-type minced-meat patties known generally as *biftekákia*. Another hot *hors d'œuvre* you should say yes to is the tiny triangular hot pie made of flaky pastry and stuffed generally, with cheese, spinach, or minced chicken (*tirópites*, *spanakópites kottópites*).

You will need, as you see, to eat several meals before you have run the gamut of *hors d'œuvre*. Do not try too many at one sitting, or you will have no room for the rest. As it is, I will spare you the soup and come straight to the fish course (mentioning only that soups in most places in Greece tend to be wholesome and tasty, without great pretensions: meat, or fish or vegetable soups generally cooked with tomato and fortified with some kind of small pasta; the pulse soups of butter beans (*fassólia*), dried peas (*bizélia*), or lentils (*fakés*), which are solid soups cooked in oil and often the mainstay of weekday peasant diet; and the well-known *avgolémono* chicken soup with egg and lemon beaten into it).

Fish (*Psári*)

Greece is undoubtedly a fish-lover's country; more so, in a way, for fish-loving visitors than fish-loving natives, for there is an overall shortage of first-quality fish and very little of it reaches the ordinary market. You will find it plentiful in hotels and restaurants, which take the pick of the catch.

You will need to make up your mind fairly quickly about your views of the octopus (a Greek word, '*octapódi*', for a very popular Greek delicacy). Having forced myself on several occasions to try it, in spite of an initial revulsion from its appearance, I am entitled to say that I find it at best an inferior kind of lobster and at worst a superior kind of rubber. This, however, is not everyone's view. There must be something about it that escapes me, judging by the enormous trouble which the fishermen take to 'tenderize' the sucker-studded tentacles: they spend hours on end alternately slapping the monster hard against a rock and swirling it round in a gentle kneading action until it is fit for the pot. Served plain-boiled with oil and lemon, stewed in wine and tomato, or air-dried and grilled on a naked flame. The last method is, to my mind, most palatable.

In the same family, in a culinary if not zoological sense, is the squid or ink-fish (*calamaráki*). Crisply fried when they are very small, I find them extremely light and appetizing. Not worth eating when they are somewhat larger. There are also cuttle-fish (*soupiés*). No comment.

Most familiar kinds of shellfish are served – and a few not so familiar. Oysters (*strídia*) of the Portuguese type are now widely cultivated and no longer a rare delicacy which had to be flown in specially from Salonika. They are often plump and seem to last most of the year round. The commonest type of mollusc (if that's what they are) is a kind of clam (*kidónia*) which is also worth trying; it is a little tough, but has an attractive nutty flavour. That is as far as my acquaintance with the family goes. I have not yet essayed the larger pink-shelled thing which contains a vivid orange-coloured blob, nor the sea-urchin which is also regarded as edible.

Then there is all the range of many-legged sea animals known by various inexact descriptions such as shrimps, prawns, crayfish, lobster, etc. In Greece there seem to be three main types: *garídes*, *caravídes*, *astakós*, in ascending order of size. I have no idea exactly where these fit in to the precise scale of crustacean terminology, nor does it matter much, since they taste about the same – and very good, too. Served boiled, fried or grilled as a rule.

When it comes to fishes proper, I am even more out of my depth in attempting to correlate Greek fish-names with the precise fishes you know. The answer may be that there is no exact correspondence, with each locality possessing its own variety of certain main types. It is certain, however, that there is a wide range of very fine fish swimming in Greek waters, and that they are generally much fresher by the time they reach your plate than in many countries where they undergo a more elaborate transportation and marketing process.

Some Greek fishes are at once fairly familiar: the sardine (*sardélla*), best of all when crisply fried in little flour-stuck clusters; the sole (*glóssa*), a little less distinguished, I find, than its more northerly cousins, but still very good; cod (*bakaliáros*), which is a poor man's fish, often eaten with a pungent garlic paste; red mullet (*barboúni*), a favourite in Greece, with a strange muddy flavour. Some of the best fish is not easily identifiable: *marída*, which resembles whitebait, excellent when very small, worthless when it begins to grow into adulthood and becomes a *gópa*; a variety of big sea fish which are full of delicate flavour – *synagrída* is probably the best and is strangely translated in the dictionaries as 'red snapper', although there is no suggestion of redness anywhere on or in it. *Fagrí*, a pinkish blunt-nosed fish, is excellent grilled; and *sfirída* is probably best plain boiled.

Meat (*Kréas*)

Fish nomenclature may be confusing, but the fish itself is usually familiar enough. It is not quite the same with meat, which presents some distinct differences of substance. In general, the differences seem to be three: animals apparently do not grow to the same size; they are slaughtered sooner; and they are dissected into totally different joints. The resulting cooked dishes are often difficult to identify in terms of well-known culinary landmarks, although they are not necessarily the worse for that. Lamb (*arní*) is by far the most popular meat. But the only lamb worth eating is much younger and smaller than the meat you may be accustomed to. It is called *arní gálaktos* (milk lamb) and is as tender and 'unmeaty' as its name suggests. Served roasted on a spit (*tis soúvlas*), in the oven (*psitó*), fricasseed (same word) and in several other ways. The tiny cutlets (*païdákia*) grilled over charcoal are usually excellent. Ask for a kidney or two (*nefrá*) to be grilled with them. Many Greeks think highly of the more exotic odds and ends of the baby lamb: the whole head, complete with eyes, brain and tongue, is gratefully gobbled (these are *mezédes par excellence*), and even the testicles come in for gratified attention. They are politely known on the menus as *amelétita*, or, in other words, things not to be 'studied' or paused over! How far you investigate these more obscure aspects of gastronomy is for everyone to decide for himself. I would advise you to be only modestly cavalier. Practically any food (as I realize more and more as I write these lines) sounds fairly revolting in the process of elaborate description; but many of these special Greek titbits are truly good to taste. This is the case especially with the various charcoal-grilled specialities at the *psistariés*: *kokorétsi*, a yard-long 'sausage' fashioned from chopped livers and lights skilfully bound in about a hundred yards of the sheep's small intestine; *splinándero*, a spiced length of chopped spleens stuffed into the large intestine; *donnér*, a strange conch-shaped structure of compressed meats grilled on a special vertical revolving spit and thinly sliced from the browned exterior surface (good with raw onion); *exohikó*, another kind of grilled 'sausage' made of spiced chunks of pork fillet.

Pork, in general, is very good. But young sucking pig, *gourounópoulo*, crisply roasted on the spit, is one of Greece's great dishes. There is nothing to compare with it in the beef category. Beef, like lamb, is eaten very young. Except for the cheaper and coarser kind, known as *vodinó* and not much thought of, it is all what we should call veal. This meat, *moschári*, is generally eaten in various stewed forms, pot-roasted or as grilled chops. *Stifádo*, chunks of veal stewed in oil, mounds of small onions and various spices, is probably the most interesting of these dishes. Steaks, as they are known elsewhere, disappear in the process of unfamiliar dissection, leaving only the fillet steak, known as *bon filé*, which is excellent of its kind but, to my taste, duller than other kinds of steak. *Rosbíf*, as in other countries outside England and America, generally means sliced roasted fillet steak.

For the rest, liver (*sikótti*) is not often good; brains (*mialá*) are tender and cooked in a variety of ways (sauté, fried in breadcrumbs, cold boiled); tongue (*glóssa*) is eaten cold or hot with a piquant caper sauce. All these things are regarded as inferior kinds of meat and are among the cheaper items on restaurant menus. Chicken, too, is generally somewhat cheaper than ordinary meat; but, except at one or two exceptional *tavernas* where spit-roasted chicken is a speciality (see later), the Greek *kottópoulo* tends to be on the scrawny side. Not so with the turkey, *gallópoulo*, which is not only good but has the rare advantage of not being entirely restricted to certain arbitrary days on the calendar. Game of all kinds, *kinígi*, served in a variety of *tavernas* in season, is the inevitable result of the Greek passion for setting out in hordes with shotguns. (The *stifádo* (onion stew) made of hare (*lagós*) instead of veal is a noted Greek delicacy; you are welcome to try it.)

Vegetables (*Hortariká*)

Most of the common or garden ones: potatoes, tomatoes, cabbage lettuce, peas, beans, cauliflower, spinach, leeks, beetroots, carrots, etc.; and a few not so common: okra or ladies' fingers (*bámies*), globe artichokes (*angináres*), egg-plant (*melidzánes*) and a great variety of wild greenstuff gathered from the mountains and eaten as boiled salads smothered in oil and lemon (*radíkia*, *vroúves*, *antídia* and several others about which I am totally unqualified to express a view). Sadly, almost no mushrooms. Greece is too dry generally for their growth;

where they do grow wild, they are so unfamiliar that people do not know how to distinguish the edible from the poisonous ones. This has created a prejudice against the mushroom and nobody cultivates them. All the mushrooms you may eat in Greece will be out of a tin – i.e. almost tasteless. Less sadly, almost no brussels sprouts. The few which are grown are luxury commodities, very small and full of flavour. *Volví*, an earthy-tasting little onion-like bulb, are worth a try; and cucumbers in season (*angoúria*) are excellent. You cannot go far wrong on vegetables. But keep in mind that the line of demarcation between 'vegetables' and 'salads' is not the same as other peoples'. Greenstuff which we would normally regard as suitable only for a hot boiled vegetable to accompany other food is often served, with oil, as a cold salad; and various foliage normally used for cold salads tends to turn up as hot side-dishes. It is too complex to describe in detail, but make sure you know what you are ordering.

Cheese (*Tirí*)

It is almost impossible to be reliably informative about Greek cheeses. Like wines in Greece, cheeses tend to be produced, without standardized industrial processes, in very small quantities in each locality. The scientific organization of cheese-making is a recent development which has not yet progressed very far. I recently struck, for instance, a cheese produced by a new factory in Lamía: it was a brilliantly successful cross between a fine cheddar and a mild gruyère. But, before I could spread the news of the discovery to my friends, the trial quantity turned out by the new cheesery had been snapped up and there was no more on the market.

This largely domestic or, at most, small unit production of cheese makes it difficult to be positive in one's judgment of any particular type. The two main standard types, found throughout the country, are *casséri* and *fétta*. The former, in my experience, varies from just tolerable to totally inedible: it is a soft, soapy cheese which, when it has any flavour at all, tastes of mildew. Avoid it. *Fétta*, on the other hand, varies from horrid to superb. It is a white cheese made of goat or sheep milk. At its worst, it is pasty and acrid; in mid-range there are some nice dry varieties with a pleasant tangy flavour; and, if you are lucky, you may come across a really mature and creamy *fétta*, such as the cheese which is turned out – but only in very small quantities – in the region of Mount Parnassus. Extremely good also is the version of *fétta* turned out in a few of the islands, one of them Zanthe, where small rounds of the cheese (which elsewhere is made in barrels) are formed and soaked for maturing in vats of olive oil.

For grating over pasta, the hard and salty *kefalotíri* is suitable enough, though not so good as parmesan. Then there is the wide range of cheeses, slightly higher up the price scale, which are known as *graviéra* (a corruption of 'gruyère'). With big holes, small holes or no holes at all, this type of cheese is made in many areas of the country and, like the rest, is unpredictably variable in quality. Crete is the biggest and best-organized centre of *graviéra* production, and some of this island's cheese is excellent – fairly creamy and always rather more pungent than the Swiss type. But the new factory in Lamía has now got into its stride and there is no Cretan cheese I prefer to that brilliant mainland *graviéra*.

Another fairly new experiment is a Greek version of the Italian *provolone*. It is an undistinguished imitation of an undistinguished cheese. Many visitors enjoy *manoúri*, an unusual kind of cream cheese which comes wrapped in large silver-paper 'sausages'. It is extremely bland and gentle, not to say insipid. Much improved, in my view, by a generous shaking of pepper. *Mizíthra* is a crumbly and even more unsalted version of the same thing – to the point where it hardly resembles cheese at all. Many people, in fact, eat it with sugar as a dessert.

Occupying the same gap between cheese and dessert is one of Greece's greatest delicacies, yoghourt (*yaoúrti*). Once again, quality varies. But in general it has very little to do with the bodyless sourish stuff produced industrially in most other countries. Greek *yaoúrti* is rich, smooth and substantial. The average type is served in expendable plastic cups and is always good, but not so rich as the kind (often known as *yaoúrti silivrías*) which comes in earthenware dishes from which portions are scooped. Another distinct type is that which is made by allowing the milk to drip through white muslin bags which can often be seen hanging outside cottages as you drive through the villages. This type (*yaoúrti sacoúlas*) is the richest of all, but is sometimes over-stiff and over-sour, needing loads of sugar. The Greeks, quite rightly, regard *yaoúrti* as a basic and particularly digestible food. It is certainly a food which visitors should bear in mind: if you find your digestive system needs a rest from coping with an overdose of strange food, *yaoúrti* is the answer: it is light, delicious and makes a really satisfying meal in itself. Eat it, as the Greeks do, with a slice or two of brown bread or maybe a piece of fruit. You can eat it without sugar, but the added sweetness, to my mind, is always an improvement. And do not just sprinkle the sugar over the top; *yaoúrti* improves enormously by having the sugar well stirred in with your spoon.

Dessert (*Gliká*)

The Greeks have a sweet tooth and go to enormous lengths to gratify it. I doubt if there is any town in the world which has so many splendid *patisserie* shops as Athens, and Greek pastrycooks regularly win prizes in international contests for the most elaborate and original samples of their not inconsiderable art. There is no time of day a Greek would think it out of place to stop off for a cream-smothered pastry chased down with a glass of iced water.

The variety of such things is endless. Those most typically Greek (although Turkish, I believe, in origin) are the many variations on the theme of honey, almonds, custard and pastry: *baclavás*, *hanúm bourék*, *copenhági*, *kataïfi* (which looks just like certain well-known cakes of shredded breakfast food), *galaktoboúriko*, *logéres*, *trígona* and many others. I find them all too sweet and sticky, but they are all worth a try, especially *galaktoboúriko* when it is still warm from the oven. The same goes for *bougátsa*, a flattened version of the same sweet which is always served hot, with cinnamon and icing sugar, and can be found in special shops and stands devoted to this trade in the popular quarters of the big towns. It is very good indeed. Another hot sweet served in several *tavernas* in the winter is *sphíngos*, a freshly cooked egg-doughnut of considerable culinary distinction.

Specially good in Greece also are chocolate of all kinds and ice-cream. The latter comes in great variety (including very good pistachio) and seems to be less 'neutralized' than the factory-produced ice-cream of other countries. In summer, the water-ices made with real fruit (lemon, strawberry, peach, apricot, etc.) are notable. And there is one splendid oriental type of ice-cream served the year round, often in ice-cream parlours which serve little else: this kind of ice-cream (*pagotó*) is called *kaïmáki*, a thick creamy concoction tasing of real milk and served with cherry syrup. It certainly qualifies for your notebook.

Fruit (*Froúta*)

The high standard of Greek sweets should tempt you to go on beyond the main course or cheese stage. But not if it means going without fruit. For visitors from countries where most fruits are expensive luxuries imported, unripe and out of season, and individually wrapped in cotton wool from which they seem to derive their flavour, the abundance, freshness and natural ripeness of fruit in Greece comes as a revelation of what fruit can be. That nearly all fruit in Greece can be eaten only in season is the inevitable but, considering the variety available, hardly inconvenient result: in winter (with considerable overlaps into autumn and spring) the orange (*portokáli*) is by far the most notable (ranging from the opulent Jaffa type to the juice-flooded blood orange), followed by a large variety of apples (*míla*) and pears (*achládia*), but it is in summer that Greece bulges with its gush of ripeness, each kind of fruit reaching perfection before its predecessor has quite faded out. The medlar (*moúsmoulo*) is not in itself a distinguished member of the family, but its coming is welcome as a sign that its handsomer relations are on the way. The cherry (*kerássi*), when it comes, is as large as a plum. The strawberry (*fráoula* and not forgetting the wild wood-strawberry flown in from Corfu in gay baskets) is *not* flavourful in inverse proportion to its size. The apricot (*veríkkoko*), nectarine (*rodákino*) and yellow peach (*yarmás*) are so good that the best are now unfortunately snapped up by sun-starved Europeans further north. The Greek melon (*pepóni*) lasts well into the autumn and is an intriguingly orange-green cross between the cantaloupe and the honeydew – the best of both worlds. Water melon (*karpoúzi*) amazes by the amount of fragrant liquid it contains. (When, I wonder, will some public benefactor produce the perfect fruit – the pipless water melon?) Grapes (*stafíllia*) are lush and dew-clouded, with none so totally captivating as the amber seedless grape of Corinth (the *stafída* which, when it dries in the sun, becomes the raisin in your Christmas pudding, but, when you eat it fresh, is like a draught of pure gold). And, to crown the procession, the August arrival of the fig (*síkko*), its purple juices sweet and pungent with the accumulated sunshine of a whole Greek summer.

There is no need, in sensitive recompense for such of the above gifts of Greece for which you may feel grateful, to avoid ordering Turkish coffee. *Kaffés toúrkikos* is the national coffee of Greece and, before the invasion of the instant, French, Italian and American varieties, it was the only coffee of Greece. In some of the older surviving mansions you may still see the little pantries which used to be devoted exclusively to the mysteries of coffee-making, with rows of tiny brass and copper long-handled individual coffee-pots in which, if you can believe the nostalgic coffee addicts, the brew used to be prepared in no less than thirty-seven different combinations of sweetness, strength and specific gravity. The extent of boiling, the manner of stirring and of pouring into the tiny cup were of decisive importance in determining the final product. That this ceremonial was not entirely superfluous is suggested by the fact that, very occasionally, a cup of Turkish coffee can taste better than any other kind. Currently, the procedure is normally very much simplified: whether you order your coffee sweet or unsweet, weak or strong, the hastily boiled brew of powdered coffee, water and sugar does not seem to vary a great deal. Whether you prefer it to the kinds of coffee you are used to is a matter of individual mood and taste. If the coffee used is very good and fresh, and the powder grains have been properly precipitated by careful boiling, the biggest drawback remains the inadequate size of the cup. To produce the result most likely to gratify an uninitiated palate, order your coffee *métrio vrastó* (i.e. medium-sweet and clear-boiled) – and, if one or two small gulps are not enough, order a double (*dipló*).

The Greek for Alka Seltzer is Alka Seltzer. It can be purchased, in handy individual foil wrapping, at any kiosk.

Part II
Key Decisions

Introductory

If I have succeeded, even modestly well, in the objective I set myself at the outset, the reader who has come thus far will be better equipped than he was to fit his first-hand impressions of Greece into an intelligible and comprehensive pattern. I am not sure that much is to be gained by an attempt to suggest what those first-hand impressions should be. So much depends on considerations of time, budget, personal interests and – above all – physical endurance. For the visitor who likes his planning done for him, there is no dearth of agencies and organizations. The individualist, by definition, desires no guidance from me or anybody else. But somewhere between the two there may, I suppose, be a substantial number of newcomers to Greece whose preference for being left to their own devices stops short at a refusal to heed some well-intentioned advice. For them, in the pages which remain, I offer a few suggestions about the practical planning of their visit: where to go, what to see, where to eat and sleep, how to apportion time between the vast number of competing attractions.

It is hardly necessary to add that, since this is not a guide book, my advice is both personal and selective. Personal, because, like anyone else who lives fairly consistently in one place, I have dug my own rut of habit and preference. I am prepared to admit that there may be many remarkable things and places in Greece of which I do not even suspect the existence; and I myself am constantly discovering new delights and reluctantly revising my habitual enthusiasm for old favourites. Selective, because I want most of all to avoid any encouragement of the restless tendency to attempt a total exploration of the country in two or three weeks. Greece is dangerous in this respect. Tourists happily set off, year after year, for their favourite resort in France or Spain or Italy, with scarcely a thought for the vast and attractive regions of those countries which they never attempt to penetrate. There must be thousands who have spent blissful weeks there without approaching within hundreds of miles of Paris, Madrid or Rome. The same people in Greece tend to fret in nervy frustration when, even after exhausting expenditure of physical resources, they have to relinquish large numbers of towns, islands and archaeological sites on their 'must' list. I cannot urge too strongly the proposition that it is no more possible to 'do' Greece in one short visit than it is to 'do' any other country. And it is even more difficult in Greece than in most places to reconcile the urge to fulfil the demands of academic or educational curiosity with the pleasures of a relaxed holiday. The suggestions I have to make are an attempt to pursue a middle course from which each visitor will deviate as individual taste directs. The important thing for mental repose is a realization that compromise is inevitable; you will be happier and more fulfilled if the compromise is deliberately and cheerfully made. There is, after all, no longer any need for visitors to bring with them a 'see Athens and die' kind of attitude. Greece is now sufficiently accessible to warrant the supposition that your first visit is unlikely to be your last. So why not leave a few of your 'musts' for next time?

9 Inevitable Athens

It is difficult to imagine a visit to Greece which does not include at least a short stay in Athens. Its own features of direct tourist interest are paramount, even if quite few: the guide-books tell us that they can be exhausted (including the Acropolis, the main museums and all the lesser attractions) in one week or, at a pinch, in three days. I have known people between planes, with the aid of a taxi and a good guide, improve considerably on that. But this is the wrong way to approach the problem. An intensive pursuit of ancient marble among the dust and bustle of a sprawling modern city, especially in the heat of summer, is not my idea of a good time – and it will not be yours when you've tried it. And Athens gives you every encouragement to follow a more leisured and rewarding pattern: geographically, it is perfectly situated to serve as a base for short one- or two-day excursions to nearby mainland and island spots you will want to visit; and, as a dominant communications hub for the whole country, you will find yourself passing through the capital very often, even if your ultimate destination is a long way off. So there is no need to rush things. The Acropolis and the National Archaeological Museum will have much more meaning if you make their acquaintance at easy intervals in the course of a relaxed stay in the capital rather than in a frenzy of intense sight-seeing. Treat Athens not as a city to suck dry of interest, ticking off the guide-book entries as you go along, but (like the Athenians themselves) as a back-cloth to the totality of Greece and, from time to time, as a haven of cosmopolitan comforts after the comparative rigours of a prolonged stay in the Greek outdoors.

It is no great hardship to stretch your stay in Athens beyond the minimum time required merely for coming to terms with its comparatively few antiquities. It is true that, viewed simply as a collection of streets and buildings, it possesses few of the attractions of the world's great capital cities. It lacks London's sense of history, the grandiloquence of Paris, the towering magnitude of New York. It has neither the allure of age nor – in spite of its infancy as a modern metropolis – the clean-limbed expansiveness of youth. For all the recent demolition and reconstruction, the ceaseless din of drills and concrete mixers, the carving of new roads and the expanding ocean of neon lights, Athens remains essentially a gigantic village: a tiny heart of spacious tree-relieved squares and avenues (covering an area smaller than the central parks of other cities) merging quickly into a maze of twisting lanes in the commercial sections where the flood of two-footed traffic over-flows the narrow pot-holed pavements to join battle with the impatient file of wheels. Then, through the no-man's-land of the older residential districts with their faded pink stucco houses and nameless one-man enterprises, breaking out into the endless white field of one-storey suburban cottages stretching up to the northward mountains and down to the southward sea. A city of undisciplined vitality and colour where the naked anatomy of an urban society in its daily functions is clothed in the merest fig-leaf of cosmetic concrete; where public buildings are either obsolete reminders of a rapidly out-distanced past or brash witnesses to the functional fashions of the present; where the only truly noble structures – the scattered relics of Greek antiquity – seem at first sight to have dropped at random from the sky, to have no organic integration with the city they have made famous.

It needs a little subtlety and a few days spent idly in the city to become aware that this first impression, quite often a source of shock and disappointment, is superficial. In their most significant context, the Parthenon and the lesser ancient buildings we associate indissolubly with the city of Athens are the inspired architectural expression of man's affinity with and adoration of his natural environment. And, for all the imperfections of Athens today as a town-planner's nightmare and an ugly duckling among the sophisticated capitals of Europe, I fancy that the gods who were worshipped on the Acropolis as the embodiment of a sublime alliance between man and his physical world would still choose to be honoured in Athens rather than in any of the most imposing capital cities on the globe. For nowhere else in the world is it possible to the same extent to live immured in the comforting shell of urban isolation and at the same time preserve an exhilarating and continuous closeness to the bland elements of nature which tenderly envelop the city on all sides and in all seasons.

Take a look at Athens, all of it, as soon as you can. There are several first-rate vantage-points easy to reach. The *Acropolis* itself, or the strange extrusion known as *Mount Lycabettus*, afford reasonably good bird's-eye views (the latter, pending the installation of the projected cog-railway, also providing modest climbing exercise for the worried middle-aged). The view from the hill of *Philoppápos* (opposite the Acropolis hill) and from the rooftop of the new *Hilton Hotel* is even better. But none is so graphically complete, in my opinion, as the sight of Athens from the little corniche road at *Castélla* on the way to the yacht harbour at Turkolímano. Stand at the open railing at the highest point of this road and look inland over the Bay of Pháleron. There you will see the whole breathtaking expanse of the straggling city, nursed between the gently lapping waves at its sandy shore and the encompassing arms of the three low mountains spread in an arc to the north: *Mount Hyméttus*, buzzing with its honey bees and waiting to receive its unbelievable flush of deep violet at sunset; *Mount Pendéli* a little further round to the left, with its gaping reminders of the Parthenon marble's origins; and, closing the circle to the west, the evergreen conifer slopes of *Mount Párnes*, highest of the three. Is there

another city in the world, I wonder, so perfectly protected from the extremes of warmth and wind by the tempering circle of water and high ground? Is there another city where, from a seat in its most central café, you need less than half an hour to be plunging into a warm blue sea or taking your fill of the light mountain air? Is there another city where you can sit in spring, summer and autumn on an apartment house terrace and breathe a heady blend of pine from the hills, ozone from the sea and jasmine from a thousand balconies and courtyards?

These attractions, it is true, will be more apparent if you find yourself staying at the less congested end of town in the area of *Constitution Square*. Here you will be close to the great open expanse of the square itself, with its tufts of bitter orange trees; close to the broad embassy-filled Queen Sofia Avenue (the nearest thing Athens has to an imposing tree-lined Parisian boulevard); close to the Royal Palace and its garden and to the pleasant Záppeion Park, the only considerable patch of green in the centre of the city. The hotels in this area are inevitably more expensive than those which cluster around the denser section of the town towards Omónia Square. But, point for point, they are considerably less expensive than their equivalents in most other countries. Nor are they any longer so desperately few as they used to be: the best-known of all, the *Grande Bretagne*, has recently acquired a new face and an extensively renewed interior; the *King George* next door, another of the older luxury establishments, has had two completely new floors added to the top; the *Athenée Palace* is the first of the post-war hotels which have set a fashion for simple luxury, suggesting classical grace and lightness by the liberal use of marble and light metals – a style which has been successfully followed in most of the new first-class hotels: the *Amalia*, the *Olympic Palace*, the *Alexiou*, *Minerva*, *King's Palace*, *Attica* and several others, culminating in the simple magnificence of the giant *Athens Hilton*, architecturally acknowledged as one of the finest hotels in the world (have a look at it, even if you stay elsewhere, and be sure to compensate yourself for the strangely truncated view of the Parthenon from the roof by looking backwards to where Athens spreads beautifully northward into the foothills of her three satellite mountains).

If, of all these excellent hotels, I prefer the *King George*, it is only because my personal tastes run to plush and chandeliers rather than to austerity, however nobly classical in inspiration. This is a comparatively small hotel, furnished and decorated with amplitude and good taste by its proprietor Mr Basil Kalkanis (whose own art-collection in his sixth-floor apartment is sometimes shown to favoured guests) and run with stern efficiency by his vivacious wife. At every point, and especially if you occupy one of the more spacious new rooms at the top, it is a hotel which suggests a gracious place to live in rather than a superior kind of transit camp. And its terrace restaurant (to broach a pulsating topic slightly out of turn) serves about the best international food in Greece in conditions of dignified comfort worthy of the accompanying view of the Acropolis.

To stay in this area of Athens does not necessarily commit the visitor to one of the more expensive hotels. There are (in addition to some old relics which are not highly recommended) a few new second-class hotels in the vicinity: the *Pan*, the *Plaka* and the *Royal* are in this category. But most of the good new modestly priced hotels are clustered in the vicinity of *Omónia Square*, a quarter of Athens which is much closer than the more spacious areas further south to the genuine hum and hustle of the city. But the distance between the two areas is so small (about ten to fifteen minutes on foot) that it need not be taken heavily into account. One of the very first of the new-look second-class hotels in this area was the *Alice* – and it continues, I believe, to give excellent value for money. It has been followed by several others of which I understand the following are the most reliable: *Arcady*, *Alfa*, *Atlantic*, *El Greco*, *Ambassadors* (why, I wonder, this passion for the initial A?).

For those with their own means of transport, or who can afford regular taxis over fairly long distances, there is a good deal to be said for staying just outside Athens so that café-squatting and sight-seeing can be co-ordinated with more relaxed pleasures of an unmixed vacational kind. There are some excellent hotels up towards the hills: the luxurious *Mount Parnes* perched on the summit of that mountain, complete with swimming pool and night club; and several old-style spacious hotels (such as the *Cecil*) in the region of *Kifíssia*, a delightful hill suburb full of flowers, imposing villas and the old-fashioned passenger horse-cab which has all but disappeared from Athens itself. While in the area, we may as well dispose of its most notable eating places (well worth a special visit even if you happen to be staying in town).

In *Kifíssia* itself: *Hàdzákos*: one of the best *tavernas* in all Greece, specializing in really plump chickens expertly roasted on a charcoal fire. Try also the various hot *hors d'œuvre* (especially the cheese pies). Good *retsína*.

Salmatánis: almost next door – a large variety of specialities roasted on the spit (young sucking-pig, pork fillet, lamb, chicken, etc.), combined with a large selection of ready-cooked dishes to be inspected in the kitchen opposite the garden where you eat. Try the *sphíngi* for dessert.

Bókaris: a less pretentious *taverna* specializing in various dishes cooked in sealed individual earthenware jars (*stifádo*, veal with pasta, etc.).

At *Tatóï* (a little way beyond Kifíssia in nicely wooded country close to the Royal estate, with a splendid view down to the coast): *Leonídas:* close to the village of Varibóbbi (where a good deal of the arms smuggling to Cyprus was secretly organized). This is probably the best showcase in Greece for really genuine and lavish Greek cooking. A large bustling establishment, equally hospitable midday or evening and (more important) summer and winter, for, in addition to its large open-air terrace, it has two huge indoor rooms complete with log fires. The spacious kitchen is a joy to wander in (but watch out for flying waiters and trays!). Take your pick of what you see; it's all good. But nothing quite equals the Leonídas sucking-pig, *moussakás* and home-made pork brawn. Excellent *kokinélli* wine, in addition to the full range of non-resinated bottled stuff.

The Auberge: a sophisticated dinner and dance restaurant set in charming country surroundings. Very fashionable and appropriately expensive.

At *Halándri* (a pleasant suburb closer to Athens slightly off the Kifíssia road: one or two very unpretentious *tavernas* in the main square (I have no idea of their names, but you will find them just by looking) with charcoal grills and simple country food. Only for summer. In the square also are a couple of confectioners (one called *Vársos*) specializing in that delicious *kaïmáki* ice-cream.

At *Ekáli* (a wooded health resort further up the road from Athens beyond Kifíssia): here are the only *tavernas* specializing in the curious *peinirlí* concoction I described earlier. Worth a visit.

At *Filothéï* (just about where you turn off the main road for Halándri): *Zafíris:* the summer quarters of one of the most noted *tavernas* in the Pláka district of Athens. Set in a pleasant circular garden, with tables widely spaced under the trees, Zafíris serves a large variety of birds: I don't personally like game, but his chicken, stuffed with rice, minced meat and pine-nuts and cooked slowly till it falls off the bone, is something I always go back for. If you are lucky enough to hit the right season, ask for one of his home-grown nectarines to finish with.

Most people who have the taste and the means to stay just outside Athens will prefer the coast for its choice of sandy beaches. Many people find that to spend the morning swimming and sunning, and the afternoon and evening in town is the ideal way of organizing the best of both worlds during your stay in the capital. There is an increasing number of hotels available on the coast for this purpose. I do not recommend those which are closest to Athens, at Pháleron or even a little further west at Kalamáki. The beaches they front on are not ideal for bathing, and the saving in distance is negligible. The beach becomes really attractive beyond the airport, at *Glyfáda.* Here there are several small new hotels and one large one (the *Congo Palace*) which make a good base for seaside activities. But none is as attractive as the *Astir* group of luxury service bungalows with its own private beach, beach sports and catering. These bungalows are fashionable, expensive by Greek standards, and extremely difficult to get unless you book very far in advance. The same goes for some new service flats in the same area.

Further along the coast (but still within less than half an hour of the centre of Athens) there are several other splendid beach resorts at *Voũla*, *Cavoúri* and *Vouliagméni.* All these places have excellent hotels:

the *Cavoúri Hotel* is a new building with comfortable balconied rooms and exceptionally good plain cooking (the purple marble floor of the dining room, cut from the bed of the sea and full of the sliced and polished skeletons of sea-creatures is worth a visit in itself). At Vouliagméni there is another group of luxury bungalows very similar, and possibly even more attractive, than the one at Glyfáda. Also fashionable, full and financially fierce (always, of course, in Greek terms – I doubt if similar accommodation could be had in many other countries for as little as £9 a day for two people including breakfast and one meal). The even newer complex of restaurants and private beach chalets at *Lagoníssi* is similarly attractive; but it comes into another category in being about twenty-five miles out of Athens along the road to Cape Soúnion.

Once again, the best *tavernas* and restaurants in this seaside area are worth an excursion even for those who stay in town. The accent, naturally, is on fish. Here is a quick list, travelling from west to east along the coast.

In the *Piraeus* itself: *Vassílenas* (to be found through a maze of back-streets only by persistent questioning). This is unique both in atmosphere and in the food served, the epitome of the *mezés* approach to eating in Greece. Imagine a small dingy room, bare of decor and furniture except for a few wooden tables. Sawdust on the floor planks. You are greeted by Vassílenas himself, a tall lugubrious-looking man in workaday clothes. 'Greet' is not really the right word, for he generally says not a word, indicating a free table merely by a slight inflection of the head. There is no menu, for Vassílenas does not mean to admit that his customers know better than he does what is good to eat. There is no kind of exchange or conversation between proprietor and guest. The process is automatic: as soon as you are seated, the first course of the meal will be set silently before you, together with a jug of wine (it is said that Vassílenas has been known to defer to a customer's preferences to the extent of exchanging his good *retsína* for a non-resinated wine, but I would not like to guarantee that this is true). With an implacable rhythm, and in continuing total silence, the first course is followed by a succession of others at fixed intervals, whether you have finished the preceding one or not: a vast variety of cunningly-prepared fishy *hors d'œuvre*, developing gradually in scope and volume until you are reeling under the steady rain of food. Some people, warned in advance and having fasted for the past twenty-four hours, have been known to last through until the sixteenth course – which is generally a plump chicken braised in a casserole. Personally, however hard I try to discipline myself into skipping some of the earlier courses, I have never yet got beyond course thirteen or fourteen. A waste of very good chicken. One or two rules to bear in mind for your excursion to Vassílenas: it is open only at night (the rest of the day is devoted to cooking); never go if you have had lunch that day; and, most important of all, never be tempted by the delicious strangeness of some particular dish into asking Vassílenas how he prepares it – you will receive only a stony stare, or at most a twisted little grin, in reply. For Vassílenas is a man who likes to keep his secrets. For this marathonian meal, there is a fixed charge – somewhere about 15*s*.

In the harbour of *Passalimáni*, just east of the Piraeus proper, there is *Diásimos*: a good all-purpose seaside *taverna*, with an equal emphasis on fish and meat specialities. The bouillabaisse, a thick brown fish soup with great chunks of fish in it, is a meal in itself.

The next bay further east is the yachting harbour of *Turkolímano*, one of the most picturesque spots in the vicinity of Athens, with the Royal Yacht Club overlooking the forest of bobbing masts and caiques. The slim black hulk of *Eros*, the second-string yacht of Mr Niarchos, is a regular resident. The harbour is lined with a continuous string of fish-restaurants, among the best in Greece, and certainly in the prettiest setting. I generally eat at *Zéfiros*, or the neighbouring *Prássina Trehandíria* ('Green Fishing Smacks'). But there is very little to choose between any of these fish *tavernas*. They all specialize in first-quality fish, caught that day and cooked without frills. Each restaurant, too, has its own concessionaire selling first-rate oysters and clams. Walk, first of all, into the *taverna* itself – right back to the kitchen area where you will choose your fish from the refrigerated drawers. Give your order and then cross the road skirting the harbour to find a table at the edge of the shore, either under a sun-canopy or under the sun. Order your shellfish as you pass the oyster stand. Most of the fish is served grilled or fried. The live langoustes are split and baked in the oven with fresh butter. And a speciality worth trying is shrimp cooked in individual casseroles with fresh tomato and white cheese. Good country-style bread (ask for it toasted if you prefer), *retsína* or other white wine, and village salad, with cheese and capers.

Nothing of note until we pass the Pháleron Delta (the point at which the broad double-track road from Athens reaches the coast). A little further to the east, at *Kalamáki*, there is the *taverna* called *Soupiés* ('The Cuttle-Fishes'). Open very late at night; very large variety of *mezédes* (fried sliced courgette and *zadzíki* – yoghourt with cucumber and garlic – among the favourites).

Continuing east, we reach *Glyfáda* and one of my favourite restaurants – *George's Bar-B-Q* – as he now proudly calls himself in neon lights. One of the few seaside places which does *not* specialize in fish. This is really a super *hassapotavérna* (butcher's tavern), with first-quality meat really well grilled. Lamb or veal chops, fillet steak, liver, etc. In season, a remarkable speciality is the *bóli*, a mixture of finely-chopped liver and sweetbreads stuffed into a flat membrane casing and grilled on charcoal. An equally memorable speciality is the *stámna*, chunks of veal or spleen delicately spiced and slowly cooked in their own juices in a tightly sealed earthenware vase. The vase has to be broken for the food to be served. Nothing at George's, however, is as welcome as the discovery that the art of serving really hot crisp fried potatoes is not entirely unknown in Greece. After the meal, home-made *halvá* (a sweet, pudding-like mixture of nuts and almonds) is usually provided on the house.

At Glyfáda also there are several excellent fish restaurants, quieter and more aristocratic than those at Turkolímano – but not so picturesque. *Psarópoulos* is specially noted, and is an expert in the very best cooking of *calamarákia*, tiny, tender ink-fish crisply fried.

The *Astéria* restaurant, also at Glyfáda, is a smart cosmopolitan restaurant attached to the same complex as the Astir beach bungalows. Very pretty neo-Greek decor; good, but not outstanding international cuisine; very pleasant for dinner-dancing at night, and a pleasant change from tavern food. Rather expensive.

Further on, reached by a winding road through the trees of the Cavoúri peninsula jutting into a very blue sea, the *Ipatía taverna*: very good home-cooking by the proprietress, who turns out some unusual specialities learned in her native Constantinople.

At *Vouliagméni*, close to the second group of beach bungalows, the

Oceanís restaurant, operated by Flóca, one of the best catering firms in the country. Very prettily-situated, refined decor, fussy service. Specializes in fish dishes of the somewhat more complicated international kind. Worth a visit one evening if you are feeling expansive; but somehow not quite as good as its pretensions.

One or two places along the coast are worth noting for occasions other than normal meal times.

At Pháleron *Katina* keeps a well-appointed seaside *patisserie* with deep armchairs and canopied swings overlooking the sea. Good Expresso coffee, a large variety of pastries and ice-cream, and cold snacks if you want. Speciality (only for those with an extremely sweet tooth): *kaïmáki* ice-cream served with a slice of the flat sweet almond cake known, from its Turkish origin, as *ekmék cataïfi.*

The whole coast is punctuated at regular intervals by establishments known as 'clubs' where, at night and until well into the early hours, the youth of Athens dance to juke-boxes or small orchestras. All these 'clubs' are entirely open to the public, and most of them provide a very pleasant and inexpensive end to the day for those who enjoy dancing in gay but dignified surroundings for no more than the price of a whisky or a fancy ice-cream. The *Silver House* at Glyfáda (popularized by frequent visits from Mr Onassis when he anchors his yacht Christina off the coast there), and the *Queen Anne*, a little further on at Voúla, are two good examples of the kind.

It is perfectly feasible, as you see, to have a fine holiday 'in Athens' without ever setting foot inside the city itself. But few will carry the leisured approach to Athens as far as that. The Acropolis and the rest await and cannot be denied.

It is by no means a bad idea, as a first reconnaissance of the city, to put away your maps and guide-books and board one of the special Athens sightseeing buses which, complete with guide, cover the main features of the city in a few hours. This is not, of course, the way to see the sights of Athens; but it is an extremely useful means of absorbing the general topography and making a preliminary selection of the sights you will later want to visit at greater leisure.

About the *Acropolis* itself I propose to say very little. I am entirely persuaded that no amount of literary commentary designed as a lesson in appreciation can alter the fact that each individual who climbs its slopes for the first or for the hundredth time, if he is honest with himself, sees its store of classical Greek art and architecture with the eyes of his own personal experience and sensitivity. At the most uninstructed and insensitive level, it can appear to be little more than a pile of unimpressive ruins (as I believe Bernard Shaw declared, in half-serious provocativeness). At the level of a mind which is romantically conditioned and substantively prepared by a thorough knowledge of ancient Greek civilization in all its aspects, the Acropolis provides a comprehensive and tangible memorial to a whole world of ideas and emotions. If I were obliged to formulate some snappy rules for peering at the Parthenon, they would be these:

1. Read as much as you like about it but, when you arrive in sight of it, forget everything you have read. Bring to it the same openness of mind, the same capacity for subconscious appreciation as you may possess for abstract painting. Forget the details, and let your mind absorb the whole, with the aid of whatever you may happen to know about the civilization which gave it birth.

2. *The Parthenon* is not on the arbitrary list of the world's seven wonders. Banish from your mind any notion that you will be confronting something memorable for its sheer size and impressive technique. The Parthenon is not like the Great Pyramids in this or any other respect. On the contrary, it is – like the other classical remains in Greece – the architectural expression of clarity and simplicity in thought, the manifestation in marble of everything which is the opposite of pomp and grandiloquence. Even the impressively ingenious engineering aspects of these buildings are modestly concealed: it is only in fairly recent years that careful measurement has revealed the extraordinary fact that the Parthenon, that apparently ultimate embodiment of rectilinear grace, contains hardly a single straight line; its seemingly flat horizontal base is in fact slightly convex; the columns taper gently towards the top and, instead of being quite vertical, lean ever so slightly towards the centre; the corner columns are about three inches thicker in diameter and set closer together to their neighbouring columns than the rest. These hidden applications of the laws of perspective, known to the Greeks either by experiment or instinct, combine to give the Parthenon, when seen from a distance, its unique

qualities of graceful symmetry as though, for all its massive stone, it floats rather than sits on the flat summit of the Acropolis.

3. It is, indeed, as a complement to the light and the landscape that the Parthenon should be viewed, rather than as a building in isolation. The Theseum temple, built a short distance away on precisely the same principles, seems dull and heavy in comparison. This is why I think several visits to the Acropolis are desirable: not so much for the purpose of a better acquaintance as to see its monuments in all conditions of light and weather. The pearly pink reflections of the early morning, the brazen yellow glare of a shimmering noon, the gentle peach and purple glow of sunset, and the mysterious shadows of bright moonlight all reveal the marbles of the Acropolis in a light which is different but equally right. It is more than I can say of the battery of artificial multi-coloured lights hurled at the Parthenon every night in summer by the well-meaning organizers of the Sound and Light performance.

4. Never be tempted by fatigue to leave the *Acropolis Museum* unvisited. It is a small, beautifully arranged museum in which the display of ornamental features is an indispensable complement to an appreciation of the architectural forms they once graced. Bear in mind always that the exquisite sculptured reliefs of Phidias which are now eye-level exhibits in a museum were once deliberately carved so as to look their best high up on soaring pediments.

It is not so much a rule as a strong suggestion that you should reverse the usual order of things by resisting the urge to rush off to the Acropolis before you have had at least one leisurely session at the *National Archaeological Museum*. There are museums in Greece which contain finer examples of specific periods of ancient Greek art (the extraordinary collection, for instance, of Minoan art objects in the museum at Heraklion in Crete, and the neolithic collection at Vólos). But, in addition to its own very notable star exhibits (the Mycenean Room perhaps most immediately impressive of all) the National Museum in Athens contains a logically-ordered array of art objects representative of every area and every period of ancient Greece, from the neolithic to the Cycladian, the Minoan and Mycenean, the archaic, the classic, the Hellenistic and Roman. There is no more comprehensive collection of its kind in the world, and no better preparation to an appreciation of the steps leading to and from the summit of the Golden Age. Try, as you make your way round the museum, to keep the thread of continuity in mind at the same time as you leave your mind open to the beauty of individual exhibits. And, unless you are specially interested in ceramics, concentrate your attention on the ground floor. The huge collection of vases on the upper storey is impressive in bulk, but repetitive and diversionary for the non-specialist.

Athens has, of course, several other museums. The *Benaki Collection*, based on the fruits of thirty-five years of the founder's art purchases in Egypt and Europe (mainly of Arab, Persian and other oriental objects) has been greatly expanded in the years since it was donated to the Greek State and is now the best exhibition in Greece of objects representing the decorative art, costume, events and personalities of the modern period of Greek history. This museum is an essential corrective for the visitor who becomes too involved in pursuing the mementoes of ancient Greece. The same might be said of the *Byzantine Museum*, although the accent there is specifically on Christian art, especially ikon painting. You can get back to ancient Greece by a visit to the museum of the *Agora*, the heart of the ancient city of Athens next to the Acropolis, where lavish American funds have been responsible for a massive restoration of the pillared stoa. For myself, the very perfection of the restoration and the shining white new pillars (directly opposed to the current rules of the Greek archaeological officials who restore ancient monuments only when sufficient of the original material is present) drains the Agora of much of its interest. There is more emotional pleasure to be had in the sight of other virtually unrestored monuments, such as the *Theatre of Dionysus*, and in some of the best examples of Byzantine ecclesiastical architecture such as the eleventh-century church of *Kapnicaréa* and the twelfth-century miniature gem of a church neighbouring on the modern cathedral of Athens and making it look gaudy and uninspired.

Between visits to these and the other specific sites of interest I have left unmentioned (not entirely for reasons of space!) there is considerable enjoyment to be had in just wandering round the town with one or two landmarks in mind. The *Zάppeion Gardens*, for instance, while not remarkable as city parks go, provide an airy and fragrant place to put your feet up and watch the nursemaids trying to impart their own shaky basic French and English to their infant Greek charges. Close by, the *Stadium* is a structure which always arouses in me a kind of nostalgic admiration. Built for the first modern Olympic Games in 1896, entirely of white marble, it is a quaintly elongated arena which holds a mere 40,000 spectators. Not only is that far too small a number for the purposes of the mass attendances drawn by the Olympic Games of today, but the sharply elliptical shape of the track and arena is quite unsuited to the geography of modern athletic performance: spectators on the marble tiers are in constant danger of being winged by javelins and discuses flung in ancient style but with modern skill and strength. Just the same, there is something about this stadium which arouses admiration, not for its intrinsic beauty alone, but also for its evocation of the less scientific athletes of a bygone day, complete with flowing moustaches and long short pants.

In Herod Atticus Street, leading up from the Stadium towards town, you will certainly stop for a moment to admire the giant Evzone or Cretan guards on sentry duty outside the *Royal Palace*. They are very tall men to guard a palace so small that, when state receptions are held there, only about two hundred guests can be squeezed into the ballroom. Do not neglect, however, to look at the same time at some of the new residential apartment blocks in this street: they are among the most luxurious and pleasantly situated in Europe.

And before leaving the area of the Stadium, there is one more call you might make – unless you have a constitutional objection to cemeteries. The *First Athens Cemetery* is more than just a burial place, containing the graves of most illustrious modern Greeks from the War of Independence onwards; it is an exhibition of lavish sculpture in marble which speaks eloquently and movingly of a continuous tradition. Most of the distinguished sculptors of modern Greece (curious that so many are natives of Tínos) have put some of their best work into the marble tombs of this cemetery. The 'Sleeping Girl' by Halépas, a reclining figure of the beautiful daughter of a well-known Athenian family who died tragically young, is one of the masterpieces of romantic realism in sculpture.

Walking further into the centre of town, it is stimulating sometimes to leave the strictly tourist beat and approach closer to the routine life of the city. The area of the Stock Exchange in Sophocles Street, the serried file of drapers and textile shops in Hermes Street, leading to the area close to the cathedral where you can buy all kinds of church accoutrements from a tallow candle to a carved golden chalice; the Athenian 'flea-market' at Monastiráki, with one or two fine antique shops improbably squeezed among old iron, ruined furniture, copies of American-style clothing and the interminable clangour of the brass-smiths; walking up Athinás Street, with its accent on ironmongery and paint-shops, you can have a brief look into the crude immediacy of the central meat and fish market opposite the Town Hall, and pass on to Omónia Square where the only escalators in Greece (leading down to the underground station for the Piraeus) and the patch of struggling grass surrounding mostly dormant fountains, recently installed at great cost, have done very little to add dignity to the square's habitual bustle.

It may be found refreshing, too, to join the Athenians from time to time in some of their own organized spectator entertainments, at intervals between attending Festival performances and watching folk-dances. There are several large football stadiums in and around Athens where the intensity of crowd partisanship compensates for any deficiencies in the quality of the game. Down by the coast at Pháleron, there is the pleasantly-appointed horse racing track where, every Wednesday and Sunday afternoon the year round, you can prove the proposition that success in picking the winners does not necessarily depend on a close acquaintance with the contestants. And, when the long day is done in summer, be sure not to waste the cool fragrance of midnight by hurrying off to bed. Nothing is more soothing, more strengthening for the battles of the next day, than to join in the mass Athenian sortie to the open-air cinemas. This, in effect, is a developed form of café-squatting. There is a film to be seen, it is true (either a good old one or a third-rate new one); but the act of watching the film is secondary to the pleasure of sitting in a walled garden, protected from whatever chill breeze the evening may have engineered, sipping and sucking at various cooling potions placed by the waiters on the little iron tables set among the armchairs. Counting the audiences who watch the show free of charge from the balconies of the surrounding houses, I would say that about half Athens is thus soothingly occupied most nights in summer between 11 p.m. and 1 a.m.

The café life of Athens, however, continues round the clock. It is well that you know where it is to be found in its most convenient and elevated form.

The large cafés clustered round Constitution Square and its vicinity need little introduction. They are all, by definition, eye-catching and conveniently placed for the leisured observation of life as it passes through the central hub of the city. An exception is the *City Bar*, hidden among the airline offices and opening into an unexpected patio far from the traffic noises; *Papaspírou*, of the more conventional pavement-type, is new and stays open latest; the café of the *King George Hotel* serves superior refreshments, albeit rather too slowly; around the corner on Jan Smuts Street is *Zónars*, commanding the most vital intersection of University Street – a good all-purpose café, complete with bar and restaurant inside; only the transition to deep cane armchairs on the pavement marks the entry into the domain of *Flóca*, probably the most expensive and aristocratic of all the cafés; and, on the opposite corner from Zónars, try *Orfanídes*, not so much a café as a pavement bar with a specially good line in ham, cheese and salami served with draught beer and *oúzo*; finally, in the same street, the best coffee in Athens at the stand-up café so popular with the Athenian intellectual fringe that the '*Brazilian* crowd' has acquired a distinct social connotation.

Further afield, there are several equally popular café centres. At Kolonáki Square, the heart of Athens' 'Mayfair' district, pavement-sitting is diligently pursued amid the apartment blocks containing the headquarters of the major socialites and minor consulates. The *Hellenikón* is a good spot for the purpose; but not so chic, for all its chrome and glass, as the dowdy-looking *Byzantium*, a carefully-preserved replica of a Greek village *cafeneíon* in the fashionable heart of the city, complete with rush-seated chairs, a hubble-bubble smoking machine which can be hired for four drachmas, and an endless variety of jams to which the clowning chief waiter attaches arbitrary pet names with overtones of political and social satire. ('Two Fidel Castros, four nuclear fissions and an extra-sweet married bliss' is the kind of order you hear shouted to the kitchen.) It is a gay place, open all night; excellent for car enthusiasts who may see all the fastest models in Athens gathered on the road outside. Do not be alarmed when your bill appears to total hundreds or thousands: it is one of the quaint customs of this establishment to calculate in tenths of a drachma instead of whole drachmas. Nobody quite knows why.

Another all-night establishment with a similar name is the *Byzantine Café* attached to the Hilton Hotel. A circular pavilion-type structure with a huge central chandelier and other features suggestive of ecclesiastical decor. Useful for night-time refuelling if you have missed dinner, but lacking the direct contact with the passing pavement parade which is the essence of a genuine café.

This element is provided in good measure by a very fine café which dominates Victoría Square (sometimes known as Kiriakoú Square), the *Perféct*. This stays open well into the early hours and is conveniently sited for visitors who are staying at the Omónia end of town. Different from the other cafés in drawing its clientele mainly from the surrounding local residents who use it almost as a kind of club. Distinguished also by the specially high quality of its ice-cream and *patisserie*.

A similar centre of residential café life is worth a visit one evening in the district slightly further afield (going north up Patissíon Street) at *Fokíonos Négri*. This is a pleasant street, divided by a green strip with playing fountains, where the evening air in summer is particularly cool and aromatic. Several excellent cafés, including a branch of *Flóca*, the *Select*, the *Quinda* (favourite of theatrical circles), *C'est Ça*. Cars totally banned after dark.

Fokíonos Négri also contains one or two *tavernas*, worth noting for their pleasant surroundings more than for the distinction of their food. (although *Angelópoulos* is reasonably good – stuffed spleens). But before we get drawn into the vital topic of where to eat in Athens, a brief catalogue of the pleasanter bars and night-clubs: for expansive drinking, the bars of the big hotels (the Grande Bretagne, the Athenée Palace and the King's Palace have very well-stocked bars, while the Hilton has bars of considerable beauty and American-style precision); for matey drinking, the jostling bar of Zónars is all you need; for picturesque drinking, try *Apótsos* in Stadium Street – look for it carefully, for it has a tiny frontage leading into two dark saloons of which the walls are improbably decorated with enamelled plaques advertising various British comestibles of Victorian associations; for subdued, restful drinking, nothing is better than the little basement bar called the *Seventeen*, at 17 Jan Smuts Street – a dimly lighted room with good soft music, well-filled bookshelves and a blazing log-fire in winter, not to mention the biggest drinks in town; for profligate drinking, the collection of sailors' bars mainly congregated in the back-streets leading from Constitution Square towards the Acropolis.

The rooftop night-club of the *Hilton Hotel* is one of the few organized for both winter and summer operation. Most of the others close or shift quarters seawards during the summer months. The best are the *Athenaía* (low-roofed, lively, good jazz), the *Coronet* (accent on décor), the *Embassy* (reputedly good but unknown to me) and, for strip-tease shows, the *Arizona* and the *Flamingo*. None of these establishments provides the atmosphere or the facilities suggested in the phrase 'Athens by Night'; they are devoted to the satisfaction of eminently respectable bourgeois notions of an evening out, with prices which are correspondingly modest and predictable. The sleazier aspects of Athenian night-life, conservative enough by some standards, can be glimpsed by way of some of the smaller basement enterprises, with quaintly spelt enticements in English neon, in the general direction of Omónia Square.

There are few restaurants in Athens itself as good as those already listed in the outlying sea and hill districts – which is another way of repeating that memorable eating in Greece depends more on the surroundings than on the food itself. There will be occasions, however, when it is inconvenient to eat anywhere except in town. The following are my own favourite places.

RESTAURANTS PROPER

You will not need guiding to the big central tourist restaurants: *Flóca*, *Zónars* and the dining rooms of the big hotels. They are all safe if unexciting purveyors of international food with a slight Greek accent. Of them all, only the *Tudor Room* of the King George Hotel seems to me to have special distinction for its combination of careful cooking and a fine view.

Of the smaller individual restaurants, *Costí* is probably the best from a strictly culinary point of view. This is the nearest approach in

Greece to the dining-room of one of the better English clubs: dark panelling, aged waiters with the manners of butlers, impeccably white cloths and polished silverware, hushed tones and really good plain cooking. Not exactly a gay place, but especially indicated if you have serious business to discuss over your meal.

The *Pantheon*, lately somewhat out of fashion but still serving about the largest selection of Greek and international dishes in Athens. A large, barely decorated room where the recent discontinuation of the three-piece palm-court orchestra has done little to remove the general gloom. Go with a big party to neutralize the surroundings, for the food is worth while – lobsters and any of the dessert dishes specially good.

The *Papákia* ('Ducklings'), an attempt to achieve what Athens lacks so notably – a small speciality restaurant with a carefully tended ambience, created here by candlelight and folk-art décor. A refreshing change from the frankly utilitarian décor of most Greek restaurants. But one wishes that the food (including the house speciality of duck with green olives) was really good instead of nearly good.

Relaxed dining with a splendidly close view of the Acropolis at the *Diónysos* restaurant, a new and successful addition to the modern pavilion-style establishments intended primarily for tourists, but none the worse for that. Adequate international-style food enhanced by romantic surroundings. The ground floor operates as a café and snack-bar throughout the day.

A little off the beaten track, not too far from the Hilton Hotel, is the *Mayeménos Avlós* ('Magic Flute'), a Swiss-style café-restaurant serving food unusual in Athens, including *fondue* and excellent ravioli. Stays open late. Gay and crowded.

For cheap, utilitarian eating there are several adequate restaurants in the central Athens area. Many of them make a special point of looking after bewildered tourists: *Vassílis*, *Kíssos* and the *Corfu* are among the best. But none, to my mind, is as good as the unattractive-looking *Ideal*, half-way between Constitution and Omónia Squares. Certainly not a place to linger in. But if you can put up with sharing a table and dispense with some of the other niceties, this is where you will find, throughout twenty of the twenty-four hours, the hottest, cheapest, freshest and most varied food in town. Good fried potatoes; French and German aids to menu decoding.

TAVERNAS

Your acquaintance with the quaint quarter of old Athens known as the *Pláka* will almost certainly be made in search of one of the scores of well-known *tavernas* which abound in the area. They vary from basic chair and table places, through garish local colour places to the big dinner and dance *tavernas* with cabaret numbers at night. None of them is notable for its food. *Saḯtis*, in the first category; *Vákhos* ('Bacchus') in the second; and *Vráchos* ('The Rock') in the third, are possibly among the best from a food viewpoint, although there is little to choose between any of them. In a slightly different category, *Da Piero*, run by an expatriate Italian left over from the occupation, is somewhat cosier than the rest and has a fairly good line in pasta dishes together with Italian and Greek songs.

Of the many *tavernas* in the other areas of town the *Tzáki* ('Fireplace') has a good but subdued cabaret programme; *Yerofínikas* ('The Old Palm Tree') has a pleasant and unsuspected garden; the *Sphíngos* (name both of the proprietor and of the excellent doughnuts he serves) and the *Stéki Tou Yánni* ('Johnny's Place') have food which is a distinct cut above average for town *tavernas*. *Norók* (the Rumanian word for 'joy'), open only at night, is run by a Greek-Rumanian and has some unusual dishes reminiscent of both national origins; the only place in Athens which knows the secret of good pickled cucumbers and red cabbage.

I have left one of the very best till last. Almost, but not quite, in the Pláka district, *Adám* is appropriately a combination of the best elements of a *taverna* and a well-run restaurant. The surroundings are pleasant: a cosy room with a soft-playing piano in winter, and a series of tiny flat roofs in summer. The menu is ambitious and varied. The proprietor gives every diner his personal attention and advice. Be guided by him, but save some space for the best and most inexpensive *crêpes suzettes* you have ever eaten. The excellent home-made cherry brandy placed before you at the end of the meal is on the house.

Before you finally leave Athens, or preferably on odd days to add variety between town and suburb schedules, there are several worthwhile sites in the immediate vicinity of the city which can be visited comfortably without rising at daybreak or missing dinner at one of the above restaurants. Many of these day trips are a convenient pretext for trying out new beaches, especially those on the broad sandy coast of eastern Attica (Porto Ráfti, Loútsa, St Andrew and Marathon) and, if you are willing to push on about thirty kilometres beyond Eleusis, the remarkable beach at Kinétta for those who prefer fine pebbles to sand, and water which takes you quickly out of your depth.

Soúnion, site of the temple to Poseidon on the extreme tip of Attica, is a steady favourite. I confess that I personally find the view of the temple much more exciting from the sea, as the Cape is passed on the way to one of the Cyclades Islands, than it is from the land side – even if it denies the opportunity of searching for the initials of Lord Byron scratched in the marble. But the trip is worth making for its use of the new corniche road which was one of the first, and is still one of the prettiest, of the ambitious post-war tourist developments in Greece. On the return to Athens, use the old road which dissects the so-called *Messóyion* (or interior) of Attica, with its own characteristic landscapes and rich vine-growing areas. Along this road is the luxuriant village of Marcópoulo where Athenians often stop to buy country-baked bread. From here, a short diversion leads to the new excavations at Brauron and to the beach at Porto Ráfti. Further along the road towards Athens is Liópesi where, at merry harvest parties, it has become the habit of the Athenian diplomatic corps 'gone native' to help in pressing the wine grapes with their bare feet at the now fashionable establishment of Mr Canakis.

Further north, the road which skirts the eastern flank of *Mount Pendéli* (worth a look for its marble quarries and the romantic ruined villa of the Duchess of Plaisance) leads to the sea at *Marathon*, site of the famous victory against the Persians in 490 BC. Apart from the vast sandy beach, the only feature of note in the immediate area is the simple tumulus built as a memorial to the 10,000 heroes of Miltiades. From the summit, however, there is a strikingly plain impression to be had of the topography of the battle. A word of warning if you are travelling by car: keep closely to the well-worn tracks through the pine-studded sand or you will find yourself bogged down with the rear wheels turning impotently. Not usually a tragic predicament, since there are men who make a living in summer by wandering round the area armed with large shovels and planks for digging out the unwary. But it is better to forestall trouble. Another word of caution: do not confuse Marathon by the sea with the Marathon Lake. The latter is several miles inland, and is reached by an entirely different road further west. Your visit to the Marathon Lake, which supplies Athens with its drinking water, is best combined with a trip into the Kifíssia and Ekáli area. It is a visit worth making, not only for the pretty winding road but for the impressive landscape gardening of the site where the huge dam, made entirely of rough-hewn marble, holds back the artificial blue lake. You will probably have time on the same day-trip to go on to the pretty archaeological site at *Amphiárion*, dedicated to the hero who was among the seven chieftains who besieged Thebes and who was later invoked as an oracle. Except for the theatre, the site is in considerable ruin. But it is well worth visiting, if only for the magnificent view of the sea across to Euboia as you descend to it from the village of Kálamos.

The convent on the lower slopes of Hymettus at *Kaisarianí* is another close objective which removes you with remarkable speed from the atmosphere of the city. The little tenth-century church of the convent contains some fine murals executed at a considerably later date and restored with infinite patience by the nuns themselves. The whole area, which Ovid describes in lyrical verse, is a charming terrain of green woods and running water which, in ancient times, was brought down into Athens in conduits. From the convent, the road continues to the summit of Hymettus – a dizzy flirtation with sheer precipices which culminates in a surprising bird's eye view down to Athens Airport.

In the direction of the Peloponnese from Athens there are varying estimates of how much can be seen in a comfortable day-trip. Even with the new road, which cuts the fifty-mile journey to Corinth to one hour, it is wiser not to be tempted, as many tourists are, into continuing beyond Corinth as far as Mycenae or even Epidaurus. It looks comfortable enough in terms of miles, but it is hopelessly overloaded in terms of the number and interest of the features to be absorbed. Daphni, Eleusis and Corinth are more than enough for one day. Save the rest for when you decide to abandon your Athens headquarters and begin your travels further afield.

The church of *Daphní*, built in the eleventh century on the site of a much more ancient fifth- or sixth-century convent of which traces are still visible, is one of the world's outstanding monuments to Byzantine art, both as architecture and for the mosaic compositions it contains. The looming, fearsome head of the Pantocrator in the dome (faintly damaged by Turkish vandalism) is at once comprehensible and impressive. The other mosaics, apart from the obvious technical mastery of their construction, improve on acquaintance: they are especially remarkable for the subtle expressions of the religious figures, achieved through a medium so essentially inflexible as glazed morsels of coloured stone, and for the strange blend of stylization and freedom of line which contains the seed of the Renaissance in Europe. The wooded grounds surrounding the Daphní church, containing a tourist pavilion which is convenient if not specially notable for its food, are the site of the annual Wine Festival in the autumn. It is a mistake, however, to combine an afternoon visit to the church with the evening's wine-spree. The apertures through which light can enter the church are few and narrow; and only the full flood of the midday sun gives full value to the light and shade effects of the mosaics.

The compact archaeological site at *Eleusis* is hardly among the prettiest in Greece, overlooking as it now does a thriving industrial township busy turning out cement and iron – and the smoke that goes with them. It is also one of the more confusing ancient places, with traces of building spanning a period of some two thousand years – from Mycenean down to Roman times – all contained within its few hundred square yards. Of most immediate interest are the relics of features directly connected with the Eleusinian Mysteries: the Telestirion, or initiation chamber and the two grottoes in the cliff through which Persephone was snatched into Hades by Pluto, are two features which make an immediate and powerful impact on the non-specialist. The small well-arranged museum on the site contains some interesting fragments of statuary connected with the secret rites of Demeter.

Do not be discouraged at your first sight of *Corinth* after passing over the fascinating slit of water separating the Peloponnese from the Greek mainland at the Isthmus. The present town of Corinth was totally rebuilt after the great earthquake of 1928. It is uniformly dreary from end to end and, for a town of its size, is remarkably devoid of even the most elementary travellers' comforts. Pass quickly through this town and up towards the site of ancient Corinth which lies below the towering bulk of the acropolis with its Venetian fortifications. Only the very ambitious or very athletic will attempt the long climb to the top; and there is plenty to occupy a whole morning or afternoon at the site of the excavations. This is one of the most varied and appealing archaeological sites in Greece, dominated by the earthquake-jostled Temple of Apollo of pre-classical origin and by the still eloquent expanse of the Roman market place. Another absorbing feature of the site is the Fountain of Pyrene, an ancient bathing place which will interest hydraulic engineers as much as it does amateurs of art.

The ancient site at Corinth has a small tourist pavilion which is handy for refreshment. But do not linger at the cost of missing some of the other features of the Corinth area: the region of Perachóra, with its smooth expanse of inland water (good for fishing and water-skiing) is worth a special excursion – to reach it takes you through the large spa resort of Loutráki, about five miles from Corinth, where there are dozens of good hotels if you should decide, after all, not to return to Athens that day. Just before Corinth, also, on the road from Athens at a place called Áyi Theodóri ('The Saints Theodore') is the unprepossessing *taverna* of *Nicholas* which many of its partisans claim, not unjustly, serves the best food in Greece.

This, then, seems to be the point to make up our minds that, for all its flexibility as a base of operations, the time will come when being anchored to Athens is a hindrance to an uninhibited acquaintance with the attractions of Greece which lie further afield. When the capital had a near-monopoly of even passably good hotels, there was every reason for attempting to hang on as long as possible, even if it meant paying for rooms left empty during hurried absences overnight. This is no longer necessary. When the call comes, pack your bags and strike out boldly for new pastures.

10 Inventory of the Islands

There is a romantic appeal for all landlubbers in the very concept of an island; and for a landlubber on holiday there is nothing more intoxicating than the image of seclusion and idyllic seaside diversions which an island provokes. Greece has no greater assurance of an intense and continuing tide of tourism than the geographical accident of possessing 1,425 islands accounting for about one-fifth of all Greek territory – even if only 166 of them are classified officially as 'inhabited'.

The Greek islands do, indeed, afford in practice most of the attractions presupposed by idealized conceptions. In spite of their inexhaustible variety and their highly individual charms they are alike in their unfailing gift of sunny skies to be enjoyed in conditions of picturesque tranquillity, sea-tempered coolness and easy informality which are not always available on the mainland. The comparative segregation of the islands from each other and from the mainland enhances their attractions in ways more fundamental than the mere assurance of peaceful isolation and individuality of character: divorced from the regular and often corrupting contact of the outside world and living in a compact and self-reliant community, the islanders themselves tend to be gentler, more direct and more hospitable even than the mainlanders of Greece. For visitors, this is a factor of considerable psychological weight. It is remarkable how, even in the most popular islands flooded with thousands of foreigners, the native inhabitants seem to absorb the flood without any evident change in their daily habits and without stepping over the line which separates the polite duties of hospitality from the self-interested concerns of exploitation. On the mainland, a relatively thin concentration of tourists can subtly alter the whole flavour and significance of the places where they gather; the tourists themselves become an objective element of a landscape in which they cannot escape either from each other or from their own integral role in the scheme of things. On the islands, where the concentration of this foreign element is often far denser, the degree of contamination is always much slighter; the tourist slips gently into surroundings which he may observe and enjoy without disturbing fundamental patterns in that self-vitiating process which has more and more tourists chasing fewer and fewer tourist-free resorts.

It ought, then, to be a matter for relief and gratitude that the Greek islands are not the idle and exotic 'tourists' paradises' of popular imagination, not the 'azure-girt Mediterranean jewels' of the advertising copy-writers, bereft of an organic life of their own and totally geared to the parasitical satisfaction of an army of invaders each summer. For it is the identity of the Greek islands as integral and hard-working units of the country's life and economy, their history and traditions, and their paternity of self-reliant populations who live by tilling the land and fishing the surrounding seas, which make it possible for the visitor to luxuriate in their natural beauties in unmolested dignity and on equal terms with the natives. Yet it is precisely this advantage which often surprises and at first disappoints the unsuspecting visitor whose previous experience of Mediterranean islands, if any, is drawn from those like Capri and Majorca.

It is not long before the sensitive visitor realizes the great psychological benefits of this difference. But he must accept that certain practical problems are raised by the happy fact that the tourist is not the sun around which the world of the Greek islands revolves. Of these problems, the most immediate is that of transport. It is generally assumed that a tourist has only to go down to the Piraeus and board a waiting ship which will carry him on the island cruise of his dreams, dropping him off at a chosen island and waiting patiently until he is ready to be wafted over to the next. It is not, I am afraid, as simple as that. The concentrated service of passenger boats serving the islands takes account in many ways of the needs of tourists, both foreign and Greek. But it is geared, first and foremost, to the needs of the islands and the islanders themselves, for whom the ship from the Piraeus is the vital lifeline bringing their mail, the tools of their trade and much of their food and other basic raw materials as well as carrying back their produce to market on the mainland. The routes and timetables of the island services are integrated primarily with requirements of that kind, and the tourist, if he wishes to travel from one island to another, will find that he either has to return to the Piraeus first or, quite often, board or disembark at hours which reflect no deep concern for relaxed passenger travel.

There are two possible solutions to this difficulty for the tourist who must, at all costs, go through the motions of 'cruising' the islands. One is to have a private yacht and crew which, when you find yourself at Mytilene, will unhesitatingly point the prow of the boat towards Naxos when you say the word – a first-rate solution for those who can afford it. The other, with which most have to be content, is to buy a ticket for one of the several organized cruises which, in anything from two to fifteen or more days, will whisk you round an impressive list of islands, including most of those you have dreamed of visiting. I believe there are some people who, even in retrospect, claim to like this system. Respectfully, as they say in the law courts, I must disagree. I can imagine nothing so contrary to the very essence of a balanced and relaxed appreciation of the Greek islands as this kind of frenzied inspection tour. The phrase 'cruising the Greek islands' gives rise to an alluring image of carefree dalliance on idyllic playgrounds set in the blue-green waters of the Aegean. The reality, on a comprehensive tour of this kind, is less attractive: an exercise in perpetual motion which aims at exhausting in a few hours pleasures and experiences which should be enjoyed over days and weeks. It is hard to believe that the mere satisfaction of having set foot on an imposing list of different islands can compensate for the frustrations of an experience of which the most lasting impressions are of a ship's bunk in which jangling nerves and painful muscles recuperate in preparation for next dawn's attack on a new objective.

I cannot urge too strongly the wisdom of planning your acquaintance with the Greek islands over a cycle of years rather than days. The problem of choice involved is certainly perplexing, especially since every Greek you may ask seems to have a different favourite. 'Islandmanship', or the championing of islands which nobody else has ever heard of, is in great vogue these days. But the problem is not as insoluble as all that. For practical purposes, on the assumption that you have a week or two available, plan in terms of a few days spent in one of the near islands of the Saronic group and the remaining time in no more than one of the more distant islands. There is no need, for the reasons I hinted at above, to worry too much about avoiding the crowds. For those, however, who are especially sensitive to the company of fellow tourists, there is a kind of self-compensating sliding scale to be borne in mind: one of its extremes is occupied by the comparatively few islands of outstanding physical beauties and growing international reputation where large numbers of visitors (both Greek and foreign) arrive to enjoy themselves in conditions of considerable cosmopolitan comfort extending to smart boutiques and juke-box night haunts (designated as class 'A' for convenient identification in the brief descriptions of the islands which follow); at the other extreme of the scale is a much larger number of islands which are often of equal physical attraction but which have not yet fallen within the scope of recent efforts to develop the islands for tourism. These class 'Z' islands are candidates for consideration only by those whose enjoyment of great natural beauty can withstand the consistent absence of a varied diet, moderately soft beds and running water.

Between these two extremes are the increasing number of islands (I shall call them class 'M') which, often by virtue of the recent acquisition of a good Xenía-type hotel, have been promoted out of the Z category and will inevitably end up in the A category. For the time

ΚΑΦΕΝΕΙΟΝ

being, they offer their natural charms in conditions of modest comfort but without the added elements of cosmopolitan luxury and night-time entertainment which attract the really big crowds. These are no doubt the islands which will most interest the large group of determined but modestly sybaritic isolationists.

Size, finally, is another factor which comes into the reckoning. Crete and Euboia are both islands in the sense that they are entirely surrounded by water. But they are much too big to be regarded as islands in the sense of compact sea-enclosed territories which the visitor can identify and make his own in the space of a short stay. In *Crete*, the Minoan palaces near Heraklion and that town's breath-taking museum will certainly be among the objectives of every visitor to Greece sooner or later – even if he makes no attempt to penetrate the island's beautiful but rugged mountain interior. In *Euboia*, the archaeological site at Erétria, the secluded beach reached through the famous fig-growing area at Kími, the pleasant Lucy Hotel at Chálkis and the thriving seaside spa at Aidipsós with its hot bubbling springs in use from Roman times, are all features which will provide pleasant punctuations to a tour of one of the most beautiful regions of Greece (where I have my own private – not to say secret – Shangri La). But visits to both of these technical islands are better regarded in terms of mainland excursions rather than as typical island holidays.

With the ground thus cleared for the momentous choice, there is need for only a few final words of caution: the climate of the Greek islands, and with few exceptions the accommodation and general facilities of life for tourists, places them firmly in the category of mid-summer resorts. Greeks go to the islands at the height of summer to escape the heat of the mainland. You should, if possible, do the same. The combined effect of the surrounding sea and the prevailing winds is distinctly cooling. In seasons outside the two-month range of high summer (July and August) the cooling process can often be more emphatic than is compatible with the full enjoyment of the outdoor life. The possibility of some rain is also increased, especially in the Ionian group to the west. A cool wet afternoon on the mainland is a nuisance which can be modified by a suitable change of plans. The same kind of weather on an island, where enjoyment depends totally on your freedom to join with the sun and sea in a state as near as possible to nakedness, is much more than a nuisance; it is a disaster. This is not intended to frighten you, or to suggest that it is impossible to enjoy the Greek islands in spring or autumn. Nor are the dangers equally great in all the islands – the Dodecanese, for instance, tend to have warm stable weather even in winter. But the wise tourist will not rush off to the islands as soon as he arrives in May or June. Nor will he leave the islands till last if he arrives in September or October. So far as possible, he will arrange his programme so that his stay on the islands coincides as closely as possible with the middle summer weeks. And even then he will not forget to take a pullover and a warmish suit for the evenings.

Much of your time among the islands (and not a little, for that matter, anywhere else in Greece) will be spent in the sea so a few hints will not be out of place.

Bathing accidents in Greece are very rare. Tides and currents, as in most Mediterranean waters, are negligible. And, in addition, the very limpidity of the water in most places reveals at once any lurking dangers. Rocks and the depth of water can be spotted by the least experienced of bathers. The commonest nuisance, the sea-urchin with its painful hedgehog spines, can almost always be avoided if you watch where you are treading in shallow waters. They are not all that common. Nor are jelly-fish, of which the commonest type is a large sponge-like creature which – apart from its somewhat repulsive appearance – is quite harmless and sting-free. On the beaches, wasps, horseflies and other forms of insect life are much rarer than they are on more temperate stretches of sand. They are hardly ever seen.

Occasionally, there will be a shark-scare. Sharks do exist in Greek waters, and, in the course of the last several years, there have been a very few authentic accidents from that cause. A careful watch is kept by fishermen, and any sighting of a shark is at once reported to the authorities who send out hunting parties to shoot the invader. But most of these scares are false alarms, frequently occasioned by the sighting of dolphins – than which there could be no more harmless and delightful creature. Sharks, when they do appear, almost never venture out of deep water. Danger from them can be ignored when bathing from a beach at normal distances from the shore. But there is, I suppose, a fractional danger in bathing from a boat some distance out to sea. On the whole, however, the threat is not taken very seriously. Certainly not by the small fisherboys who, whenever there is shark-scare, will offer themselves to tourists, in return for a five-drachma coin, as 'shark-bait', and swim around in the water to the seaward side of the prudent bather!

All in all, there is only one common danger you need worry about: the danger of failing to reckon with the power of the Greek summer sun, especially when there is (as often on the islands) a strong cooling breeze. No amount of preventive greasing or curative lotion will avoid or repair the damage (which can ruin an otherwise splendid holiday) if strict precautions against over-exposure are not taken.

Two islands of the *Saronic Group* fall within my A category: Hydra and Spétsas. Both are close enough to Athens – as are all the Saronic islands – to make it possible to see them on short excursions, especially if the hydrofoil boats are used to get there.

Hydra (pronounced Ídra) is, I suppose, the Greek island with the biggest international reputation, partly due to its use as the backcloth to several films shot in Greece. I can understand an initial enthusiasm for this island. Its landscape is picturesque to the point of drama, especially when first seen from the sea: a tightly enclosed blue harbour full of brightly painted fishing caiques and fronted by buildings of island simplicity with an extra touch of aristocratic dignity, rapidly giving way to the sharply rising bulk of flat-roofed white houses perched on the hillside to form the vision of cubist clarity which the painter Ghíkas has exploited to such good effect. Within the island, an added attraction for visitors is the possibility of visiting some of the traditional old mansion houses belonging to the wealthy families which supported the island's maritime and commercial fame during the last century. These houses still contain the style and the furnishings which are typical of a strongly native tradition and prosperity but at the same time bear witness to the influences of a constant interchange with the cultured European world.

It is the sharp rocky line of Hydra, its tortuous ascending lanes, its steep precipices plunging into the sea, its mainly treeless austerity which compel a fascinated admiration of the landscape. But it is precisely those features which deny the basic requisites of an equable island vacation. The sense of being oppressively enclosed within the steep flanks of the hillside, the constant necessity to move either up or down – never just along, the lack of any expanse of sand, or even pebble, worthy of being called a beach, are features which are diametrically opposed to the ideal island attributes of restful gentleness. My experiences in Hydra foodwise have not been very happy either. It is an island which grows almost nothing of its own and strangely, considering the number of guests it receives, seems to import very little of what it lacks across the short stretch of water from the Piraeus. I may have been unlucky, but my lasting impression of the island's diet is one of frugal monotony. For me, the ultimate disqualification of Hydra as a fit place for a relaxed vacation is the obtrusive presence on the island of a motley foreign colony, bizarre in dress and behaviour, which performs the empty motions of a bohemian tradition created long ago by a few real artists and writers who found inspiration in Hydra but who have long since been driven out by the inanity of their imitators. Like the landscape of Hydra itself, their arrestingly picturesque qualities will be found to have an unnerving kind of fascination. A day or two on Hydra, if you have time, will not be wasted. But take your real island holiday elsewhere.

On *Spétsas*, for instance. This is a real Greek island, long popular with Athenians on holiday. It has as long and as impressive a seafaring tradition, as a visit to its charming museum will disclose. And it has the calm gaiety, the wide choice of sandy coves and beaches, the open spaces, horse-and-buggy rides and simple fishing population which are the true essence of the islands. Its growing popularity with foreign visitors has added A class elements of sophistication to these simple virtues which have been enhanced rather than spoiled by the fact that they are set off by good and plentiful food, comfortable beds and one or two merry night spots. It is an island I recommend without hesitation, indeed with considerable enthusiasm.

A travel note for those with their own means of transport: Spétsas can be reached by an interesting and not too arduous overland route which terminates just opposite the island at Pórto Héli in the Peloponnese. From there you can reach the island by boat in a few minutes, leaving your car (for which you will have no use on the island) securely parked under cover at the *taverna* on the land side. The thing to remember about this route to Spétsas is that the road leading down to Pórto Héli branches off the main road just a mile or two from Epidaurus; so it is possible to have Spétsas in mind as a restful terminal point for your tour of the five-star archaeological sites of the eastern Peloponnese (Mycenae, Argos, Epidaurus, etc.). There is a similar possibility for those who are not travelling under their own steam: a boat service which, in summer, regularly connects Spétsas with the key Peloponnesian town of Náfplion.

Two M class islands of the Saronic group are *Póros* and *Aígina*. The former, approached through a beautiful fjord-like passage framed by green hills, is very unspoiled and offers an excellent combination of sea and country pleasures (the latter extending over the narrow channel which separates the island from the mainland, to include for the adventurous the site of Troizene fifteen miles away, where the legend of Phedra was born). The latter, Aígina, is even closer to Athens and combines good but simple facilities for a seaside vacation with considerable archaeological interest, of which the Temple of Aphaia is the most celebrated feature.

Closest of all to Athens in the Saronic group is the island of *Salamis* – a Z class island in spite of its accessibility and its resounding historical fame. It is a strangely neglected island in many ways. Even its archaeological treasures (and they must be many) lie almost undisturbed under the ground. It is not, I suppose, an island of immediately striking natural beauty. Its most picturesque spots and attractive beaches are somewhat remote. Yet, as I write these lines in the early morning, the sun is rising over an oily-flat sea haze, the wakening commotion of little birds in my palm-tree has just died away, and the only sounds are the chug-chug of the returning *gri-gri* fishing boats following their mother-boat in stately procession like circus elephants joined trunk to tail and the occasional clatter of motor-bikes carrying the islanders to work in the rich market gardens or the main naval base of Greece. In many ways, Salamis is as near to a typical Greek *working* island as it is possible to get, for all that the bustle of the Piraeus is only half an hour away. Those who have come to love its unspoiled charms pray that it may long continue to be the neglected ugly duckling of the Saronic. Certainly, the island is still without a hotel or a restaurant worthy of the name. It is not a 'staying' island. But it is certainly a 'visiting' island for those who have a car. From Athens, drive to Pérama west of the Piraeus (an ugly concourse of small shipbuilding yards and refugee-squatters' houses, lying just below the hill where Xerxes watched his fleet being smashed in 480 BC) and cross on the ferry which leaves every half-hour. In fifteen minutes you land at Paloúkia and can drive inland towards the island's capital Koúlouri, or towards the beaches at Selínia and Moúlki. Pause in the capital long enough to inspect the colourful courtyards of the houses, filled with pots of basil and geraniums. Observe also the touch of blue added to the whitewash of the walls to reduce the glare of the summer sun. Between Paloúkia and the smaller landing-stage at Kamateró is the Romanza Bar, a tiny tavern on a promontory where the simple food is served with rare attention to detail. For the return, take the road which leads out beyond Koúlouri along the pine-skirted coast road towards the fine old monastery of Phaneroméni. After a visit to the church and cloisters, the near-by ferry will take you across to the mainland at a point on the old Corinth road close to Mégara, about half way between Athens and Corinth.

To sum up the Saronic, Spétsas is my firm recommendation for a longish stay; and as many of the other four islands as time allows for brief visits.

Your choice of the second island to visit for a longish stay (assuming you propose to heed my advice to limit yourself to two only) will very likely be made between the three remaining A category islands – one in each of the main groups: *Corfu* in the Ionian group, *Mýconos* in the Cyclades and *Rhodes* in the Dodecanese. There are no others which properly qualify for an A rating.

Corfu and Rhodes, at extreme ends of the Greek archipelago, have several features in common. Both are big islands, with an extensive road system and several separate centres of interest. But both have a single distinct focal point (the main town in each case) and are just small and compact enough to convey a true island character. Both islands, by virtue of their geographical positions and their comparatively recent incorporation into the modern Greek state, have a characteristic patina of alien influences superimposed on the basically Hellenic features which are found supreme and unmixed in the Cyclades.

Corfu has any number of points which explain its leading place in the island stakes. It is, in the first place, among the most accessible of all the islands from Europe, linked both by the ferry and a regular air service from Brindisi and by several boat services from Venice. The town itself, with its Italianate architecture retaining hints of both Byzantine and British influence, is one of the most attractive in all Greece. The beaches are broad and delectable. The countryside, open, green and gentle, lush with olive trees, hibiscus and bougainvillea. It has pleasant surprises, like the cultivation of the Chinese (cumquat) orange from which good liqueurs and preserved fruits are made and the relics of the British occupation which ended in 1864: the stately Victorian-style palace of the High Commissioner, beautifully restored and containing a nice collection of chinoiserie, and the continued habits of cricket-playing and ginger-beer drinking. The Achilleion Palace built for Elisabeth of Austria in 1890 and recently converted into one of the smartest and certainly the most beautifully situated gambling casinos in the world. Excellent Theotóki wine, with a faint sparkle on the tongue. Lots of local colour in the shape of fêtes and dances, and the peasant women balancing pitchers on erect heads or sitting in the fields tending their sheep, their white pleated blouses, black bodices, long dark skirts and kerchiefs setting off quizzical wrinkled faces reminiscent of Vermeer's Dutch ladies in a pastoral scene by Renoir. Excellent hotels, ranging from the luxury beach bungalows of the Miramare through the chic Corfu Palace, the aristocratically furnished Mibcle (a converted private château), the B-category Xenía with its startlingly good restaurant and magnificent view over the picturesque 'mouse-island' from the heights of Canóni near the royal summer estate at Mon Repos, the sound and utilitarian Astir near the harbour, down to any number of smaller but still comfortable establishments.

If Corfu is not my own favourite island, I think it is because my preference is for smaller places in which the visitor enjoys the best outdoor diversions the island has to offer without becoming divorced from the main stream of the island's life. In Corfu, the best vacation spots are 'resorts', more or less remote from sights and sounds of the island's hub. Indeed, the most attractive spot of all, at Paliocastrítsa where the bathing in deep rock-studded water and the fresh lobsters hauled out of their sea-pens and sent straight to the kitchen are features worth travelling a long way to enjoy, is about the remotest of all. This is a drawback which is partially neutralized by having your own transport on hand; but even that facility does not entirely dispel the sense of isolation which robs a stay in a Corfu resort of the exciting immediacy felt in some other islands where the harbour jetty is the centre of activity for the islander and visitor alike.

Rhodes, big as it is and containing as it does a considerable scattering of widely separated tourist sites, does not suffer from the same disadvantage. Here the order is reversed: the main beaches and hotels are clustered round the colourful town which remains the hub from which the visitor can make his day excursions to the archaeological site of Kámiros, the valley of the butterflies and the memorable citadel at Líndos, repository of the relics of practically every civilization which Greece has known.

This main island of the Dodecanese, just a stone's throw from the coast of Turkey, has a number of other special attractions. The climate, first of all, is about the best in Greece – several degrees warmer in winter and cooler in summer than that of Attica. By a strange accident of history (the island was turned over to Greece only in 1945 after more than thirty years of Italian occupation) there is not a complete Customs union with the rest of Greece, and many commodities, especially European imports which attract luxury tariffs elsewhere, are unusually cheap. Greeks who visit Rhodes have to pass a Customs check before boarding their ship or plane for home! The countryside is sub-tropical in its profusion of bright flowers and vegetation. The town of Rhodes itself is unique in its contiguous reminiscences of Turkish bazaars and the medieval ramparts and palaces of the crusader knights, impeccably restored by the Italians. A wonderful island for idle wandering in colourful streets and alleys, for exhilarating country excursions, for varied archaeological browsing, bargain shopping and perfect bathing (the year round, some people claim) either from open beaches or from the exclusive private preserves of the cosmopolitan Hôtel des Roses or the Miramare bungalows. And all only an hour and a half by slow plane from Athens.

In Greek terms, the attractions of Rhodes (and they are considerable, especially in seasons which are climatically doubtful in other islands) are distinctly exotic. The undiluted flavour of the Greek islands resides in the groups closer to the centre of the archipelago and more continuously connected with the flow of Greek history. Of these groups, none is more Hellenic in every sense of the word than the *Cyclades*. And, of the Cyclades, no island is more captivating than *Mýconos*. Of all the A islands of Greece, and making every allowance for the fact that it is the favourite of almost everybody else, it is the one which gives me the most intense and ever-renewed pleasure. It would be easy to join those who say that Mýconos, a small island with but one tiny centre, has been ruined by the tide of tourists and to advise my readers to steer clear. Certainly, I could wish it were less popular, that there were fewer juke-boxes and boutiques selling various improbable transformations of sponges and sea-shells. But it would be a dereliction of duty to counsel abstinence from a first glimpse of an island which, for all its recently acquired excrescences, continues to cast its spell over me after the twentieth glimpse.

It is purposeless to attempt here to describe why this is so. The objective features of this miniature island are either well-known or at once ascertainable on arrival: its three hundred and more chapels, its sentinel windmills on the hilltops, its icing-sugar houses with their incomparably plastic line, its famous ceramic museum, its proximity to the absorbing islet of Delos – the deserted relic of the first United Nations headquarters, its outstandingly fine beaches and penetratingly blue sea. What cannot be known until it is experienced is the sense of freedom and excitement conveyed by the combined testimonies to a purity of tradition carried to the point where the blindingly picturesque ceases to be a mere optical experience and becomes a unique spiritual revelation. Big words, I know. But this is a big little island. One of these years, you must go. If some meteorological friend can tell you in advance when the summer winds are likely to die down for a spell, so much the better.

Almost every group of Greek islands has one or more examples which fall within my M category. In the Ionians, *Cephalonia* and *Zanthe*, now recovered from the disastrous earthquake of 1953, both offer comfortable facilities for a longish stay in surroundings of considerable maritime and pastoral charm. Zanthe in particular, more generally called Zákinthos, known as the Flower of the East when it was part of the Venetian Empire, has a gentle flower-perfumed flavour of its own and picturesque reminders of the Venetian style of architecture with its cloister-like arched arcades. The island may have lost most of its formerly active renown, but a sensitive visitor quickly detects the traces of the island's prolonged contact with Europe, its total freedom from Turkish domination, and the brilliant literary and artistic traditions which were carried on there up to the last century. Zákinthos is still an island with a lyrical soul; the home of Greece's national poet Solomós, born there in 1798; the natural habitat, to this day, of the romantic serenades of the Ionian. There is also, as I think we said before, that unforgettable Verdéa wine. I have never tasted better than that which is served with such pride by the hospitable owner of the Mimosa *taverna*. Try it after a morning's bathing from the five miles of sand on Lagána beach.

The other main islands of the Ionian are distinctly in the Z class. Lefkáda, in particular, is one of the most beautiful of the group, with its stretches of fine-grain pebble beaches and its surrounding clusters of tiny islands creating a fjord-like pattern which has led a famous German archaeologist to claim that this island, and not the one now called Ithaca (also in the Z group) was the real Ithaca of the *Odyssey*. It appears that the shipowner Onassis has been developing an interest in the tourist possibilities of this splendid island. He is quite right. But until something is done to make a stay even modestly comfortable there is not much point in recommending it.

Of the M islands in the Cyclades, I would prefer *Paros* and *Santoríni* for prolonged stays providing genuine island atmosphere, good bathing and the necessary minimum of specific features of cultural, natural or archaeological interest. The volcanic origins of Santoríni, in particular, provide some unique landscape features and a memorably colourful sunset. Further east, against the coast of Asia Minor, the M islands of *Mytilene* (Lesbos), *Samos* and *Chios* offer similar attractions in a somewhat more lavish setting, and with a more colourful emphasis on local tradition.

But, in this general area of the Aegean, the M island I would urge you most to stay in is *Skyros*, the largest of the Sporades group. Well on its way towards the A class, Skyros is still a comparatively uncrowded island which combines many of the characteristic Aegean features with several of its own. Based on the exceptionally well-run Xenía hotel, the visitor soon discovers that Skyros has a rare quality of open contact with nature in which the sea and the countryside behind it are curiously intertwined. The waves break on the beaches with more determination than is common elsewhere, and the fields seem to be larger and greener. The island is full of grottoes, and the rocks are the home (until they are rudely removed) of Greece's finest lobsters. Inland, the miniature horses of Skyros still tread out the wheat on the circular threshing floors, and the island's craftsmen produce their captivating pottery, decorated with thick splashes of white paint, and the carved furniture for which Skyros is famous throughout Greece. It is also as most visitors are surprised to find, the place where Rupert Brooke was buried. An island to be explored and enjoyed at leisure. The handiest way of reaching it, unless it happens to be the day for the weekly boat from the Piraeus, is by the regular service which leaves from Kími on the island of Euboia.

Skíathos, with about the finest beach in Greece at Koukounariés, and *Skópelos*, a reef-enclosed island of great picturesque attraction, are two other members of the Sporades which will one day work their way into the A grade. For the moment, however, they rate no more than a Z.

Appropriately belonging to no group at all, but sitting in splendid isolation off the coast of Thrace to the extreme north of Greece, is the circular paradise of *Thássos*. It is, without question, my favourite M island of all. It has been a favourite with many people in their time: Phoenicians, Thracians, Romans, Saracens, Venetians, Genoans, Turks and Egyptians, for almost a whole century up to 1902. Even the Russians, for a brief period (1770–1774), were attracted to the island and there are still traces of their occupation – the only example, I believe, of a Russian invasion of Greek territory – in the church of the main town, which is of Russian rather than Greek Orthodox character.

What drew this motley succession of foreign rulers to the island was mainly its identity as a rich trading centre sustained by considerable deposits of gold and silver, to begin with, and of iron ore later. The iron workings, operated by the German Krupp organization under a concession which has just ended, once occupied 10,000 workers. The headquarters of the mining company is a huge German-style villa at the port of Limenária, towards the south of the island. This may, it is said, now be turned into a hotel for tourists.

Limenária has an excellent beach. But the incomparably finer attractions of Thássos lie further north, around the ancient port of Liména, where the bottom of the harbour is paved with stone flags! The beauty of this part of the island is hard to describe in words and has no equal in Greece. It can be imagined only in terms of an alpine landscape of thick woods and running streams which has become inexplicably detached from its habitat and has turned up to form the background to warm sandy coves hollowed out of a crystal sea. In some places, such as at Makri Ámmo ('Long Sand') where a group of beach chalets has just been completed, the forests do not merely form a background to the seascape, but descend in richly wooded tongues of land down to the white sand of the sea-shore.

The interior of the island is dotted with villages which hide in the mountains. Many of them are of great antiquity, like Panayía and Theodórou, and provide handy objectives for exhilarating forest walks. (In Thássos, the way to detect the age of a village is to observe whether it is visible from the sea; none of the villages which can be seen from the coast are among the very oldest, which were always built out of sight of potential enemies.)

But Thássos is not only the Greek island with the most impressively exotic physical attractions; it is, for me, unique in Greece for the evocative power of its archaeological remains. A little aside at this point about what might be called 'ruin reactions' would not be out of place:

It is not always consciously realized, although it is really very obvious, that the vestiges of ancient Greece are not confined to those places where, for reasons of their own, the archaeologists have concentrated their excavations, turning those places into 'archaeological sites'. The entire subsoil of Greece is a repository of the past, and many of the finest individual relics have been discovered, not by the archaeologists, but by some uninstructed navvy digging a sewer or the foundations for a block of flats. It was a party of sponge-divers who, in 1900, found fragments of statues on the sea bed off the coast of Anticýthera, which an underwater expedition later discovered to have come from a sunken galley containing the famous fourth century BC

'Youth of Anticýthera'. A fisherman in the Bay of Marathon five years later pulled out the exciting 'Youth of Marathon', created in the workshop of Praxiteles; and it was some other fishermen, a few years after that, who struck in their nets off the coast of Artemission part of the statue of Zeus hurling his thunderbolt, one of the fifth-century masterpieces now in the National Museum, as is the marvellous 'Kouros' found only a few years ago by sewer-diggers in the Piraeus.

Trained archaeologists of a large number of nations have been working continuously in Greece, together with their Greek colleagues, for more than a hundred years. The underlying impulse for most of them is the excitement of discovery. But their professional discipline insists on the primary importance of minute classification and interpretation. There is often a large gap between what is 'significant' for the specialist and what is exciting and meaningful for the layman, who is moved by evidence of living links between the past and present (as when a chance spade strikes an ancient masterpiece) more than by the systematic exploration of a site from which all life seems to have fled. This is not, of course, an absolute proposition. Often, as in the case of Mycenae, Epidaurus, Delphi and the Athens Acropolis, the majestic qualities of the landscape itself give an automatic aura of grandeur and emotive power to the ruins. Elsewhere, as at Corinth and Mistrás, the very completeness of the ruins which have been excavated gives a thrill of immediacy and comprehension. Or, as at Knossos in Crete, comprehension may be assisted by an artificial reconstruction of the ruins to a degree which earns the gratitude of the non-specialists but, more often than not, the wrath of the experts. At many other archaeological sites – and one of the most famous of them is Olympia – the complex researches of the archaeologists have failed to redress the vast disorder of the scattered ruins. Sites like these, which the guide books describe in detail and which have tourists chasing off on earnest expeditions of self-improvement, resist our best efforts to synthesize them into a living and meaningful whole. They remain dead, cold and speechless.

For me, to return to our island subject, no archaeological remains are more eloquent in their simplicity and directness than those of Thássos. They are all confined within a radius of less than half a mile inside an ancient rampart which surrounds the old harbour and is pierced at intervals by sculptured gateways into the old town. In other circumstances, the whole of this area might have been an exhaustively documented archaeological site. But the excavators arrived too late. By the time archaeologists became really interested in Thássos, the area had been fairly thickly covered by the pretty but unpretentious new houses of the current inhabitants. What remains of ancient Thássos, dominated by the breathtaking theatre above the town (which still has tall trees sprouting among its tiers) is now to be seen in the stones and statues and plinths which pop up inconsequentially among the houses and on street corners. Archaeologists working in Thássos cannot hide their chagrin at having to terminate their excavation of an ancient wall abruptly because it has reached the courtyard where Mrs Papadopoulos is hanging her washing on the line to dry. But, for the rest of us, it is this very informal contiguity of the impressively old with the current life of this tree-shaded town which achieves a unique synthesis in which both the significance of the old and the charm of the new are movingly enhanced.

On the map, Thássos (where there is a Xenia hotel) may seem discouragingly remote from Athens. In practice it is not so. A daily plane flies to Kaválla in an hour and a half; from there passenger and ferry boats cross to the island every day in about the same time. Your visit to Thássos can be easily combined with an exploration of the much-neglected attractions of northern Greece. Which brings us back to a brief consideration of the Greek mainland outside of Athens and its immediate surrounds.

11 Mainland and Minorland

Considerations of time and endurance often make it necessary to leave Greece without personal verification of the fact that, outside of Athens, the islands and a few well-charted sites of interest on the mainland fairly close to the capital, there is a whole country waiting to be explored. It will come as a pleasant surprise if, on one of your visits to Greece (probably not the first), the process of uprooting yourself from a cosy base in Athens is undertaken not only for the purpose of moving headquarters to an island but as the prelude to a more extensive acquaintance with the neglected attractions of the mainland. The important thing here, as with the islands, is not to attempt an impossibly ambitious programme on a nomadic grand tour. It is much more rewarding to choose a convenient base and see as many of the surrounding features of interest as you have time for. You can always choose a different centre of operations on a subsequent visit. The principle of selective compromise.

The first mainland objective for most visitors, the *Peloponnese*, is curiously not a real part of the mainland at all. The Greeks, in fact, distinguish the Peloponnese from what they call 'mainland Greece'.

This is not just a geographical quibble in acknowledgment of the Corinth Canal. From ancient times down to the present, the Peloponnese has cultivated an independent kind of identity. It was the centre, often in rivalry with Athens, of some of the most powerful centres of ancient civilization; its inhabitants claim for themselves a more dominant streak of racial purity; and, at the time of the modern War of Independence, it was in the Peloponnese that the flag of revolt was first raised and most gloriously sustained in battle. A sensitive visitor can instinctively appreciate the subtle flavour of personal pride and political potency which is entailed in the fact of being a Peloponnesian.

There is no need for me to trace the justly well-trodden mainline of the so-called 'Argolid' antiquities from Corinth through Mycenae, Argos, Tiryns, Náfplion and terminating at Epidaurus. There is probably no similarly compact area of Greece which contains so many centres of compelling interest. The danger is that this geographical concentration of such major and separate points of interest may produce a wholly disproportionate concentration of the time consumed in visiting them. This is almost certain to happen if the mistake is made of using Athens as a base for the tour. It would be forgivable if there were no pleasant alternative. But *Náfplion* is more than a pleasant and conveniently central base for the purpose: it is, in its own right, one of the most fascinating towns of Greece, repaying a stay of several days even if it were surrounded by desert instead of the richest archaeological treasures of the country. The smiling harbour, the towering Palamídi fortress (1,000 steps to the top), the quaint Venetian streets and the castle on the rock of Boúrzi in the harbour (a good, but somewhat expensive, hotel and restaurant), the odd relics of Turkish occupation (there is now a cinema housed in what remains of a mosque) and a museum of unusual interest are only a few of the features which make this town, the first capital of modern Greece, an instant favourite with every visitor and a relaxing contrast to the austerity of the ancient remains to be visited in its vicinity.

For a satisfying appreciation of those remains, do not hesitate to use the services of a guide – if possible one specially engaged in Athens rather than the guide-caretaker on the spot. It goes against the grain with many people to resort to the second-hand rote-recited wisdom of a guide. They need have no such worries in Greece. The young ladies who usually perform these functions are not only personable and well-trained, but totally immersed in the operation of passing on to a stranger a small part of their own constantly renewed enthusiasm for their country's treasures. They really believe in their job with a missionary zeal, and it is often surprising to find that they have enough energy left over to act in addition as nursemaid, counsellor and general organizer on a tour.

A few minor suggestions on your visits to the sites in this area: at *Mycenae*, do not necessarily take your food or refreshment at the tourist pavilion – the Belle Helene, an inn where archaeology has become almost a part of the furniture, is often a pleasant alternative; before leaving *Argos*, a short trip along the road towards Trípolis brings you to the branch for Kefallári – a shady spot for a meal by the side of a running stream fed by a clear cool cataract; if there is the possibility of timing this tour to coincide with the *Epidaurus* Festival, prefer that time to any other (mid-June to mid-July) but make sure of your hotel in Náfplion in good time – there is a world of difference between Epidaurus at rest and Epidaurus in action; do not leave the area of Náfplion without swimming from the beach at Tolón – far pleasanter than the other near-by beach at Mili.

The best base for a study of the western side of the Peloponnese (including Olympia) is *Patras*, the third town in Greece which has lost its former eminence as an important shipping centre but still retains the charm of its Ionian style architecture and the easy logic of its street-plan. Strangely, Patras is still without a modern hotel. Rather than submit to the dubious comforts of the so-called A class establishments I always stay myself in an officially rated third-class hotel, the Mitropolis, which I find offers effectively the same facilities with considerably greater willingness and at much lower cost. Evangelátos is the best general-purpose restaurant in the town. Down the coast towards Pýrgos and Olympia, the Trocadero and the Parisienne are fairly lively dinner-dance places for the evening. But the best food of all is at a little *taverna* in the old part of the town, called the Old Patras (Paliá Pátra). The main square of Patras is among the few unspoiled ones of its kind – a wide square terrain with fountains in the centre and entirely surrounded by arched arcades. It is here that you may ask to visit the old Municipal Theatre, one of the very few copies of an old-style European opera house still standing in Greece.

An excursion of unusual interest from Patras is to the winery of the Achaia company, famous for the sweet Mavrodaphni wine. The cellars here contain the barrels specially reserved for the Greek Royal Family, and there is a quaint little bar where you may taste wine *ad lib.*, or buy a few bottles cheaply. It is not a bad idea to combine a visit to Achaia with a meal on the road at the pleasant Koúkos *taverna* which has a good line in chicken and really good home-baked bread.

Further afield from Patras, a day excursion to the forest of Metóchi (a paradise for game hunters) or the enormous smooth sands of Killéne is worth thinking about.

The normal approach to Patras, along the narrow road from Corinth, is often taken at a gulp. It should not be, for there are not a few places worth lingering over. *Xilócastro*, a pleasantly wooded beach area about twenty miles out of Corinth travelling westwards, tends to be overrun in summer by holiday campers. But that is no reason to pass by the delightful Valkánia (Balkans) Hotel. Even if you have no time to stay overnight and breakfast on the balcony outside your room over the fragrant garden, a stop for a meal will bring home the truth that, in the right surroundings, there is nothing so good as carefully cooked simple food.

Just outside Xilócastro, a left turn off the main road winds twenty miles up the mountain to reach Tríkala, an attractive summer hill resort and a growingly popular centre for the still infant sport of skiing in winter.

Towards the fruit-growing centre of *Aígion*, probably the sweetest-smelling town of Greece, is the starting point of the rack and pinion railway which climbs from Diakopto up to Kalávryta by way of tunnels through a gorge full of rushing cataracts. Special panoramic cars are used on this train, and it is one of the most scenically impressive excursions in Greece. At Kalávryta still stands the giant plane tree outside the monastery where the flag of revolution was raised in 1821. And, from the intermediate point on the cog railway at Zagloroú, it is easy to reach the Great Cavern monastery (Mega Spélion) with its giant cave and miracle-working ikon.

Beyond Aígion, just short of Patras, it is difficult to pass without stopping at one of the gentle bays in the region of *Labíri*, perfect for swimming to the accompaniment of the lemon-blossom perfume from the orchards stretching right down to the beach. In this area, at Lóngos, is a specially good seaside tavern, famous for its grilled lamb chops.

Assuming that you have been from Patras to Olympia, if only to see for yourself whether my own coolness towards the latter famous site is justified, the best move towards a new Peloponnesian base is along the road to Trípolis – a fine mountain route which no longer suffers from its former poor surface and which passes through some splendid scenery. A walk around the village of Langadiá and a stop in the hill resort of Vitína on the way are both pleasant diversions. The new base I would choose is Sparta or Kalamáta, depending on whether you attach most importance to the very eloquent remains of the Byzantine town at *Mistrás*, or to the Mycenean ruins of the Palace of Nestor at *Pylos*. In either event, do not hurry through *Trípolis*. It is a thriving town in the middle of a rich dairy-farming area, sufficiently high to be cool and leafy in summer. The park and pavilion of the near-by ancient settlement of *Tegéa*, supported by an improbable association of Athenian lawyers who come from that area, provide an unexpectedly fine site for a picnic and a chance to view an impressive restoration of a basilica-style Byzantine church. The Tegéa lawyers also support a large school which teaches domestic arts to young girls – the exhibition of embroideries and other samples of popular art, which can be seen if permission is asked at the school, is worth half an hour of your time.

There would be a further point in favour of making for Sparta rather than Kalamáta if it were possible to travel over land down to that fascinating relic of a medieval town at Monemvásia. For the moment, however, the land route is all but impassable and Monemvásia is accessible for practical purposes only from the sea. For those who possess a jeep, the choice between Sparta and Kalamáta is academic, for there is the semblance of a road over the magnificent Taëgetus mountain connecting the two towns. The construction of a good road over this route, one of the most spectacular in Greece, can only be a matter of time.

Back on the 'mainland proper', the first target after hoisting anchor in Athens is almost inevitably the 'navel of the earth' at *Delphi*. This is a visit which can be made independently of Athens, as an adjunct to a tour of the Peloponnese, by using the convenient ferry linking Aígion with Itéa, just below Delphi. But do not make the error of attempting to combine Delphi with a journey to or from western Greece by using the road which links the ancient site with the delightful seaside resort of Náfpaktos – unless you do so in the knowledge that you will be sacrificing tyres in the interests of scenic wonders. Whatever route is used, the important thing is to allow a minimum of two days. The common practice of squeezing Delphi into a single day-trip from Athens is barbarous and inexcusable (even on the plea of better quickly than not at all). In theory, one day gives you all the time needed to visit the not enormously extensive ruins and the small, if high quality, museum. In practice, you will be missing more than half the point. The overwhelming impact of Delphi lies not in the ruined relics of ancient cults and political alliances, but in the wild and mysterious majesty of its situation among the eagle crags of Parnassus. Like Mycenae and Epidaurus, but to an even more forceful degree, Delphi is meaningful because of its testimony to the uncanny wisdom of ancient peoples who instinctively appreciated the inevitability of a site where the very aspect of nature merges with the divinity which is worshipped there. Unless you give yourself time to absorb some of Delphi's natural magic, even if it is only to the extent of a leisured breakfast early in the morning on a balcony overlooking the great chasm, or a brief walk in the nearest hills beyond the spring of Castalia, your impressions of Delphi are bound to be disappointingly limited to the roar of tourist coaches down the solitary narrow street of the town. Ideally, considering the constricted situation of the town and the growing flood of visitors, it is best to avoid Delphi at the peak of the tourist season. But, if that cannot be arranged, it is vastly better to possess the flexibility even of a short residence than to be one of the jostling crowd of day-trippers.

A tip or two for those who travel to Delphi from Athens by their own transport.

It is quicker to use the longer route via the new Lamía road, to the point where it turns off for Thebes. When Livadiá is reached, pause for one of the excellent *souvlákia* sold in the main square; or, better still, ask your way to the waterfall which lies just off the main route (all you need say is '*ta nerá*' – the water) and stop there for a meal, in sight of the peasant women washing their gay blankets in the stream, by the side of a torrent of water which, in summer, seems to reduce the temperature by at least fifteen or twenty degrees. The relief will be doubly welcome if you are among those inquisitive travellers who, before reaching Livadiá, are tempted to penetrate into the dusty bowl of the drained Lake Copais area where, in the region of Gla, there are some fascinating Mycenean remains, including a smaller version of the beehive tombs at Mycenae itself. On the road from Livadiá to Delphi, a short diversion to Distomo takes you within striking distance of the monastery of Ossios Loukás, one of the earliest Christian buildings in Greece, containing mosaics regarded often as superior to those of Daphní. Do not be dissuaded, finally, when you have regained the main road to Delphi, from making a brief stop at the village of Aráchova. In spite of its rash of tourist shops, this is a genuine Parnassan village, famed for its wine and honey and remarkably faithful still to its pastoral colour and traditions. I have had a special fondness for this place ever since I stopped on one occasion to buy a jar of honey: as I walked towards a house where I had been told the honey on sale was specially good, I heard the handbell of the town-crier who came to a halt near by and began to intone, in a scarcely penetrable country accent, the following delightful announcement to the villagers clustered around: 'John Carvellis is missing. Should anyone see him, would they please tell him to go straight to the *cafenéion* in the square where they are waiting for him to start a game of *koúpes* [a favourite card game], for this is a day on which card-playing is allowed.'

Moving north, the prosperous but otherwise unremarkable town of *Lamía* is a place you can hardly avoid – not to stay, but as a junction of roads leading to three different regions any one of which makes a splendid new base of operations.

Southwards, the road leads through the narrows of *Thermopylae* (no longer so narrow as in ancient times, on account of coastal silting) where the sight of steam rising from the ground and the acrid fumes of sulphur suggest the volcanic nature of the area. Indeed, a little further on the road reaches the fashionable and spaciously laid-out spa of *Camména Voúrla*, by no means a bad spot to set up shop for a few days. The hinterland of rich wheat country, the area the Greeks call Roúmeli, is one of the most fertile in Greece and the one which is noted for its preservation of all that is bravest and heartiest in the Greek rural tradition. A short journey from Kamména Voúrla brings you to Atalánti where a frequent ferry service crosses to the northern end of the island of Euboia – the easiest way to see this charming part of the island and its spa at Aidipsós without travelling the length of Euboia on the partly poor road from Chálkis.

The road eastwards from Lamía reaches the large town of *Vólos* (good beaches and the remarkable neolithic museum) and continues into one of the most attractive and as yet unspoiled holiday areas of Greece: the region of *Mount Pelion* with its diadem of charming villages amid the streams and apple orchards. A stay at one of the villages in this area (Portariá, Makrinítsa, Zagorá, Tsangaráda, Milliés and St John are among the most attractive) is the closest approach to an ideal combination of island and mainland pleasures. For, on this peninsula which virtually connects with the Sporades islands, an unspoiled beach is never far away (white pebbles below Zagorá and fine sand below Tsangaráda). The architecture of the village houses in this area, especially at Makrinítsa, is of the kind which becomes inextricably involved with the memories of this outstandingly beautiful area of the country.

Beauty of a different kind, much more reminiscent of alpine sights and smells, is to be found going west from Lamía as far as *Karpeníssion*, a mountain village on the slopes of Timfrístos. This must be one of the best centres in Greece for those who enjoy any kind of mountain activity, from easy forest walking to serious climbing, without (so far as I know) a single archaeological distraction. It is possible to recommend this little-frequented mountain resort without qualms ever since it acquired the blessed gift of a Xenía hotel. The tiny village of Mikró Chorió close by is even more spectacularly situated. But it has not yet been similarly blessed, and I cannot lightly recommend anyone to repeat my experience of sharing a bedroom with a family of six.

From Karpeníssion, the road on the map travels temptingly on towards Agrínion in western Greece, a good start towards a trip either to Míssolonghi, just south of Agrínion, or northwards up to Yánnina, the colourful town on a lake in Epirus. But this is another of those beautiful routes which can only be travelled in grim determination or in simple error. The approach to Míssolonghi and Yánnina for most people has to be by the more conventional route of the recently promoted 'national' road which runs down the west of Greece and is primarily intended to serve those who disembark from the Corfu ferry at Igoumenítsa.

Árta, with its famous medieval hump-backed bridge and sprinkling of Byzantine churches, is a reasonably good base-point for this area. Once again, a Xenía has come to the rescue; it is impressively situated, in this case, within the enclosure of the town's crenellated castle. The town of *Míssolonghi* to the south is not in itself immediately endearing. But its reminiscences of Byron and the War of Independence are worth the visit: especially the old wall within which the townsmen endured the famous siege, and the modern Park of Heroes, a truly inspired and tasteful monument to the rebellious spirits of so many nations who came to help Greece's liberation struggle. There is a strange fascination also in the town's geographical situation on a giant lagoon where fishermen go about their business with nets cast from curious flat-bottomed boats.

Yánnina is a good alternative base: absorbing in itself as a colourful repository of Balkan and Turkish features, and as a centre for an acquaintance with the wild mountains of Epirus and the hardy inhabitants who have a particularly impressive record in all the liberation struggles of Greece. In the town, a converted seventeenth-century mosque enclosed within the castle overlooking the lake (reached through the old quarter where silversmiths ply their trade) contains a fine collection of relics linked with the powerful Ali Pasha – an Albanian who was appointed ruler of the area by the Turks at the end of the eighteenth century and who broke away to set up an independent dominion extending as far as Thessaly. Just a mile or two north of the town are the famous stalactite caves at Pérama, discovered quite recently, and among the most impressive of their kind in Europe. In the other direction, there is the site of the most ancient oracle in Greece at Dodóni and its extremely well-preserved theatre, considerably larger than the one at Epidaurus.

The road down to the next possible base-point at *Kalabáka* (useful only for its proximity to the strange cluster of monasteries at Metéora) passes through Métsovo, an exciting mirror of the landscapes and folklore of the whole Epirus region. The customs of the area, preserved within these mountain enclaves, may be observed just by spending an hour or two in the village. But a more concentrated and organized presentation is available in the unique museum which a wealthy native family of Métsovo has created out of its old mansion house.

The *Metéora* (i.e. 'hanging') monasteries, perched on strange vertical spikes of land and at one time accessible only in contraptions like balloon-baskets hauled up on ropes, certainly have their rarity value. It is for the other-worldly landscape more than for the monasteries themselves that the area has become one of tourist interest – to the extent that Kalabáka, until recently a dismal town with nothing cosier than an E-class hotel, has now been granted the accolade of the Xenía. To that extent, I am not prepared to dissuade anyone from a trip which I could previously have counter-indicated on the grounds of accommodation alone. Just the same, I am compelled to pass on the fact that, for me, the whole of this peculiar region, with its nightmarish extrusions of black and yellow fingers of rock, is oppressive and unattractive. Others may well find it thrilling.

The final base-point on the mainland and, after Athens, the most intrinsically worth while, is the Macedonian city of *Salonika.* The Greeks call it the 'co-capital' and treat it as such. But it has a long way to go before it is similarly ranked by foreign visitors, of whom only a small fraction even consider Salonika as a possible centre on which to base a part of their stay in Greece.

This is unjust – and unwise. Salonika is not only a town of many attractions in its own right. It is a gateway into an understanding of the whole medieval period of Greek history when, next to Constantinople, Salonika was the most flourishing centre of the Byzantine Empire. No town in Greece conveys such an immediate impression of the country's position at the crossroads between East and West.

The impression has been accidentally enhanced by the fact that, after the great fire in 1917, the major part of the city was rebuilt to modern Western standards of architecture and town-planning. Yet the considerable remnants of the old quarters of the town are there to point the contrast, with their maze of twisting alleys where oriental pastry shops, coppersmiths and carpet merchants crowd together.

A leisured round of Salonika's impressive Roman and Christian monuments can be achieved in material conditions of no little comfort. In many ways, it is a city which has absorbed the tempo and standards of western European life more thoroughly than Athens. The University of Salonika, for instance, is – by common admission – considerably more advanced in its methods; the new theatre built by the Society for Macedonian Studies has no equal in Greece; shop windows have a distinct European flair not easily found in Greece's first capital; Salonika contains, so far as I know, the only self-service restaurant in Greece – and, while we are on the subject of food, I doubt if Greece has another restaurant as good as the Olympus Naoussa.

Of the Roman remains in Salonika, the two most striking date to around the end of the third century AD: the Arch of Galerius and the near-by Rotunda which contains the oldest mosaics in the city. Of the more numerous Byzantine monuments, the beautifully restored fifth-century church of St Dimitrios is possibly the most imposing; but there is no finer example in Greece of the plastic genius of Byzantine brick-work than the fourteenth-century church of the SS. Apostles. Salonika also has an archaeological museum and a representative museum of popular art.

There are many near-by sea and country excursions possible to add variety to a stay of several days in the city: the hill resort of Panorama and a string of beaches and fishing villages along the shores of the Thermaic Gulf. But, when you have seen all you want of the city itself, the best use for Salonika is as a base for some extensive visits to the much-neglected attractions of northern Greece – an area so different from the rest of the country in its climate, the fertile richness of its landscapes and the specially solid intelligence of its people, that some acquaintance with it is an essential complement to a balanced picture of the country as a whole.

Travelling eastwards from Salonika (intending either to return to base there, or to continue on good roads straight through into Constantinople) the route passes alongside a lush rocky coast not too different from the famous coastline of the Pacific between Los Angeles and San Francisco. Above, the impressive peaks of the Pangeon mountain; below, rich fields of grapes and tobacco, giving way later on, around the broad delta of the Nestor River, to broad expanses of flat

rice fields and pheasant-filled forests. *Kaválla* is the main town of this area, its huge tobacco warehouses in solid evidence of the origins of a considerable prosperity. The town has much interest of its own: the overwhelmingly rich fish market, the imposing Turkish aqueduct and domestic architecture to match, some odd features of the former Egyptian occupation (including the house of Mohammed Ali, ancestor of Farouk, which contains the most fascinating devices for protecting the harem from all possibility of male invasion). The Bátis beach, just outside the town, is an up-to-date spot for very good bathing.

A very short distance outside Kaválla, on the elm-arcaded road which leads to Drama, is the ancient site of Philippi (after which is named the pleasantest hotel in Kaválla). The site is one of the most intriguing in Greece: notably for its huge theatre, converted for gladiator contests; the truncated but somehow very noble remains of a sixth-century Byzantine basilica; and the Roman forum with a system of running water and latrines which surpasses any other example I know of Roman genius in this vital field of engineering.

If he has a minimum of two or three days in hand, an unaccompanied man can compensate himself for the lack of female company by a visit to the one 'country' in the world where no woman (or even an animal of the female sex) is allowed to set foot: the independently administered monastic state of *Mount Athos.* This is the easternmost of the three finger-like peninsulas, about twenty-eight miles long and up to four miles wide, which poke into the northern Aegean east of Salonika.

The monastic community of Athos, with its twenty monasteries of various national branches of the Orthodox Church dotted throughout a green mountainous terrain, is now a thousand years old. It is the world's greatest repository of Byzantine records and treasures. For specialist scholars it is a primary source of material. But, even for the casual tourist, a visit to the Holy Mountain (*Áyion Óros,* as it is called in Greek) is a plunge into a vast medieval hermitage which time has ignored. The calendar is still thirteen days late; and the Byzantine hour of twelve is rung out at sunset.

The experience is unique. But, in the physical as well as the spiritual sense, you have to be prepared for a taste of medieval frugality – not to say noxiousness. Enjoyment of a visit to Mount Athos demands a mental adjustment to the crudity of its living conditions. Transport from one monastery to another, if not undertaken in compliance with the biblical exhortation 'go on foot in imitation of Christ', is at best accomplished on the back of a mule (not exactly male, but definitely not female). Flies abound everywhere. The food provided in the monasteries – and there is nowhere else to eat – is all but inedible. And sanitary facilities are, not to mince our words, repulsive to the point of inducing total inhibition of the natural functions.

With the right mental approach, however, these discomforts are worth enduring as the price of a glimpse into a society of unexampled historical interest and a landscape of rare unspoiled attractions. From Salonika, there is an infrequent direct sea route to the Holy Mountain. But a more useful approach is by road to Tripití where a boat runs out to the main harbour at Daphní. But certain formalities have to be completed first. Mount Athos guards its independence jealously. Nobody can enter without special permission. In the case of foreigners, permits are issued almost automatically (on payment of 100 drachmas) either by the Foreign Office in Athens or by the office of the central government in Salonika. On landing at Daphní, passports have to be handed in to the local police (they wear a special uniform bearing the emblem of the Byzantine two-headed eagle). Passports are returned to visitors when they leave. The permit then has to be presented to the authorities inland at Karyés (a four-monk council called the *epistasía*) and, in return, the visitor is given a document which guarantees free board and lodging at any of the monasteries. A donation dropped in the monastery collection box (say, 20 drachmas) is morally compulsory. Take care to arrive at the monastery you are aiming for before sunset. If, as you approach in the growing dusk, you hear the sound of a great iron bar being struck on a chunk of wood, hurry the last part of the way – otherwise you will find the monastery gates firmly barred for the night.

Theoretically, there is no limit to the duration of free hospitality provided by the monks of Mount Athos. But the growing tide of tourists has lately compelled some practical departures from the ideal. Some of the more 'popular' monasteries, such as the biggest, Áyia Lávra, have posted notices informing guests that they may not stay longer than forty-eight hours unless they have come for serious study and research in the monastery archives.

From Salonika westwards, the countryside is full of interest. The geography of the main features is also particularly handy in suggesting a tour (totalling about 240 miles) which can be comfortably completed in two days and makes a whole circle including Édessa, Flórina, Castoriá, Kozáni, Vérria before arriving back in Salonika.

The trip starts off with a rapid injection of interest as, just before Édessa is reached, you turn slightly off the main road to find the very recently discovered capital of the Macedonian Kings at Pella with its splendid mosaics of the Hellenistic period, one of them showing Alexander at the hunt.

Édessa, once the capital of Macedonia, is now chiefly a centre for summer excursions attracted by its 300 foot waterfall and its cool leafy shade. *Flórina*, further on, is a similarly attractive fruit-growing centre without, so far as I know, any special features of scholastic interest. Shortly beyond it, the road gives a spectacular view of the two lakes Prespa, which Greece shares with Yugoslavia and Albania; it then dips sharply south to arrive at *Castoriá*, standing on its own entirely Greek lake. The material existence of Castoriá is largely dependent on its traditional practice of a specially skilful branch of the furrier's art: the matching and piecing together of tiny remnants of fur into whole skins. The craftsmen of this tiny lakeside town can be found engaging in this skill in practically every fur centre of the world. But it is on its seventy Byzantine and more recent churches that Castoriá depends most for its tourist interest: they are by far the best source for an appreciation of the development of religious architecture in northern Greece, and their carefully restored murals give a vivid account of west Macedonian sacred art throughout the period from the tenth to the eighteenth centuries.

The route back to Salonika, via Kozáni and Vérria, passes over the lower slopes of Mount Vermion (an increasingly popular ski resort in winter) and, tantalizingly, reveals some spectacular glimpses of *Mount Olympus* to the east. One of these days, when the urge to penetrate every nook and cranny of this provocative country has been allayed, that is where you may well retire, joining the gods on their perch among the green peaks, surveying the Greece you have discovered in replete and Olympian omniscience.

12 Footnote on Booty

I am not among those who regard the shop windows of a foreign country as one of the more compulsory attractions, ranking in interest – in Greece, let's say – somewhere between the Acropolis and the tomb of Agamemnon. Nor have I ever been entirely persuaded of the reasons why, as soon as I set foot outside my own country, it becomes a matter of life or death to engage in the systematic and expensive accumulation of all kinds of hardware, software, chinaware, rubberware, beachwear, slumberwear, neckwear and every other kind of ware or wear which, in the normal way, I would not dream of favouring with a second glance. I am, in this matter, a stout defender of the airline companies, which not only do their best (albeit so often in vain) to discourage this kind of excess by imposing stiff prohibitive fines per kilo, but also thoughtfully provide excellent alternatives in the safe international currency of Scotch whisky, French perfume and American cigarettes.

In this attitude, my wife tells me, I am unreasonable and perverse – not to say intolerably selfish. No visit to a foreign country, she says, is complete unless we remove with us a good suitcaseful of objects which are *typical of the country*, and which *cannot be found elsewhere* or, if they can, *not nearly so cheaply*. It is apparently by the aid of these elusive treasures that we will remember the country of their origin; and, more important still, it is by their unstinted distribution that our friends will remember us.

My own obstinate impression remains that, somehow or other, and especially in view of the Shrinking World, the Common Market and similar modern inventions, items which are typical of one country tend to be pretty typical of most others. And, if they are not, then they are by and large not terribly useful – as, for example, a ten-gallon Texas hat inscribed with the words 'Giddalong Cowboy' and (in smaller print) 'Made in Japan'.

However, since roughly half my readers are likely to share my wife's view of the question, I am obliged by a sense of duty to offer my advice on the question of booty. It is, let us suppose, the day before you are due to leave Greece, and that extra suitcase is gaping accusingly empty on the luggage rack of your hotel room. What do you do?

The honest answer would be that it is already too late to win a first prize for booty-manship: some of the best items for a collection of this kind are to be obtained most cheaply and most conveniently in the different regions of Greece where they are the products of local tradition. You should have thought about that on your travels round the country. I do not mean to advise, of course, that you should encumber your journeys through Greece with things like four-gallon cans of first-quality olive oil from Kalamáta or ten-pound heads of gruyère-type cheese from Crete. But there are a number of compact and conveniently carried articles you might bear in mind:

The characteristic pottery of Rhodes, with its oriental and Persian-inspired designs.

The delicately ornamented pots and vases of Skyros.

Skilfully worked silver items from Yánnina.

Pieces or garments of raw silk from Kalamáta.

Embroidery and lace from Crete.

Fox-furs from Salonika, excellent for making small rugs.

A box of Turkish delight from Sýra (where the water is supposed to be ideal for this abstruse manufacture).

A goat-hair holdall, maybe, from Samos, or even a bottle of that island's sweet wine.

Certainly a bottle of genuine Verdéa wine from Zákynthos.

A jar of honey from Thássos or Aráchova.

From Delphi, a half-dozen individual miniature iron spits, decorated with brass motifs, for making nostalgic *souvlákia* when you get home.

A chunk of wax-covered caviar from Missolonghi.

A hand-made beach shirt from Spétsas.

A cedar-wood pitcher from Vitína.

A salami sausage from Lefkáda.

A natural sponge from Kálymnos.

If this wisdom, in your case, comes after the event, there is no need to despair. Almost all of the above trophies can be obtained in Athens, if possibly at some slight extra cost. The main drawback about this procedure is that you will have to seek out your prizes in one of a hundred arty-crafty shops operated specially for tourists where the genuinely attractive articles are almost lost in an ocean of tasteless mementoes, including fake classical-style vases with pictures of the Parthenon, leering 'ancient' masks, plaster statuettes of the Praxiteles Hermes, and a weird collection of peasant-style Greek clothing which looks quite attractive in a Greek shop window but which makes any woman look like a tourist poster when she wears them at home.

With care and persistence, however, you can find some pleasant gifts in these all-purpose bric-à-brac establishments. Just the same, it is generally safer and quicker to prefer one of the more selective speciality places. In one of the art galleries, as I have suggested earlier, you may easily pick up an attractive modern painting for much less money than its equivalent would cost at home. Or, at even less cost, you can find really attractive samples of modern Greek ceramic art (for instance, a piece by Valsamákis) or of primitive-style modern costume jewellery. There is also an interesting new shop called 'The Clock' almost opposite Hadrian's Arch, a co-operative venture launched by an impressive group of leading Greek artists. The samples of their work on sale are not cheap. But they are mostly first class, and highly varied – from sizeable pieces of furniture down to hand-painted screens and carved miniatures.

Gramophone records of popular Greek music are now available in much greater numbers than ever before. Beware of the unvarnished *bouzoúki*, which will sound even worse when you get it home. Theodorákis and Hadzidákis are rightly the most popular composers for this purpose.

Of the high-quality selective shops specializing in popular art, none is more reliable and full of tasteful things than the shop which sells objects made throughout Greece under the supervision of the Queen's Fund (an organization for the encouragement of the popular arts and crafts). This shop in Athens (adjoining the King's Palace Hotel) has anything from attractive basket-weave bread dishes, to a vast variety of embroidery, wood-carving and even massive hand-made carpets. If I had the space, the prize I would personally covet in this collection would be one of the brilliantly coloured long-tufted woollen rugs which fit superbly well into any kind of modern house décor. They are known as 'floccáta' rugs.

Another speciality shop worth visiting is the tiny establishment run by Mrs Richardson, an Englishwoman who has developed a unique manufacture of homespun textiles made of silk and wool. These materials are wonderful for draped dresses and curtains. She also has unusual ties.

A shop devoted to the handcrafts of Crete is called Diploús Pélekis (near the office of the newspaper *Vima*). Here you can buy some fine samples of Cretan embroidery and lace, among other things.

If you wish to abandon the principle of buying 'typical' items, and decide merely to look for pleasant gifts of any origin, some of the smart, but not expensive, boutiques in the area of Jan Smuts Street will be worth visiting. The Quartier Bleu is, I fancy, one of the better ones.

Higher up the scale of acquisitive ambition there is, of course, the whole range of objects which come under the heading 'archaeological' – the ancient vase, or coin or delicate ikon you have eyed enviously in the museums, or even the fragment of ancient stone you have thought of pocketing while the attention of a guard was turned elsewhere. It is not true, as many people believe, that all such objects are strictly 'not for sale'. But the laws on the subject are precise and strictly enforced. Anyone who finds any kind of ancient object in Greece (and it is happening all the time when people dig their gardens or the foundations of a house) is obliged to turn it over to the archaeological authorities. If the experts judge it to be important enough for a museum, they will pay the finder at a fixed rate of compensation (not very generous by free market standards) and keep it. If the object is not of museum standard, it will be returned to the finder with a clearance certificate. It can then be sold on the open market.

There is a simple lesson to be learned from this state of affairs: if you are offered an ancient object at a price which seems unreasonably cheap, it is either a fake or it is a black-market 'smuggled' piece being sold off by a needy owner (like the pair of lions which, to my astonishment, I was once offered by an amateur excavator in Salamis in a whispered aside – at the time I was not aware of his hobby and imagined that he had been left with the remnants of some circus on his hands!). If the price seems suitably high, then the piece *may* be genuine – but do not buy it unless the shop or the owner can produce proof that it has been cleared by the authorities for free sale. The best rule of all, if you are seriously anxious to buy an antique of some value, is never to do so alone, but always on the advice of some Greek acquaintance who can introduce you to a dealer guaranteed to be reputable.

The most durable purchase of all, and one which is attracting an increasing number of buyers, is a piece of Greece itself. There are few visitors who, at some time during their travels through this land of sun and sea and mountain, have not toyed with the idea of making some of it their own. They would be surprised to learn how few are the practical obstacles to this apparently unattainable ambition. Greek law places no restrictions on the ownership of land by foreigners. The formalities are exactly the same as for Greeks, except in the case of land adjacent to the frontiers, for which a special permit has to be given. Cost? Much higher, it is true, than it was even three or four years ago. The average price of land even in undeveloped beach areas which a foreigner might consider has doubled or trebled in that time, and is still rising quickly. This is the time to strike; it is still possible to buy a plot of beach in some idyllic and unspoiled corner of Greece, big enough for a simple house and breathing space around it, for as little as £100–£200. It is an intriguing thought that, including the cost of building a simple house with local materials or putting up a prefab (making sure, if it is of Scandinavian design, that it is suitable for warm climates), you can establish a foothold in Greece for little more than the cost of a single holiday. The most obstinate practical difficulty you are likely to strike is the Greek system of inheritance and land tenure, especially in the less prosperous parts of the countryside: by the time a parcel of land has been inherited by a few generations of sons its ownership has often become so scattered that even your tiny chosen morsel may have three or four different landlords. The negotiations involved in the process of achieving unanimity may turn out to be a lengthy and extremely delicate exploration of peasant psychology. The experience will be instructive. And the reward of your perseverance will be the most permanent and satisfying expression of all the riches of sight and mind which Greece has showered on you: a pledge to her of your loyal gratitude, and to yourself of a determination to return.

YUGOSLAVIA
BUL
ALBANIA
MACEDONIA
Kaval
Florina
Edessa
Salonika
Castoria
Verria
Kozani
Livadia
Mt. Olympus
EPIRUS
Yannina
Pindus Mts.
Meteora
Kalabaka
THESSALY
Volos
AE
CORFU
IONIAN ISLANDS
Arta
Eretria
SKIATHOS
SKOPELOS
SKYROS
Lamia
Aidipsos
EUBOIA
Thermopylae
LEFKADA
Agrinion
Mt. Kandili
ITHACA
Nafpaktos
Delphi
Chalkis
Aulis
Thebes
Missolonghi
Patras
Aigion
Marathon
Mt. Parnes
CEPHALONIA
Xilocastro
Kalavrita
Eleusis
Megara
Mt. Pendeli
Athens
Corinth
SALAMIS
Mt. Hymettus
Piraeus
Saronic Gulf
Mycenae
Epidaurus
AIGINA
Methana
ZANTHE
Olympia
Argos
Nafplion
POROS
Tripolis
Tegea
Cape Sounion
IONIAN
SEA
PELOPONNESE
HYDRA
SPETSAS
Mistras
Sparta
Kalamata
Pylos
Monemvasia

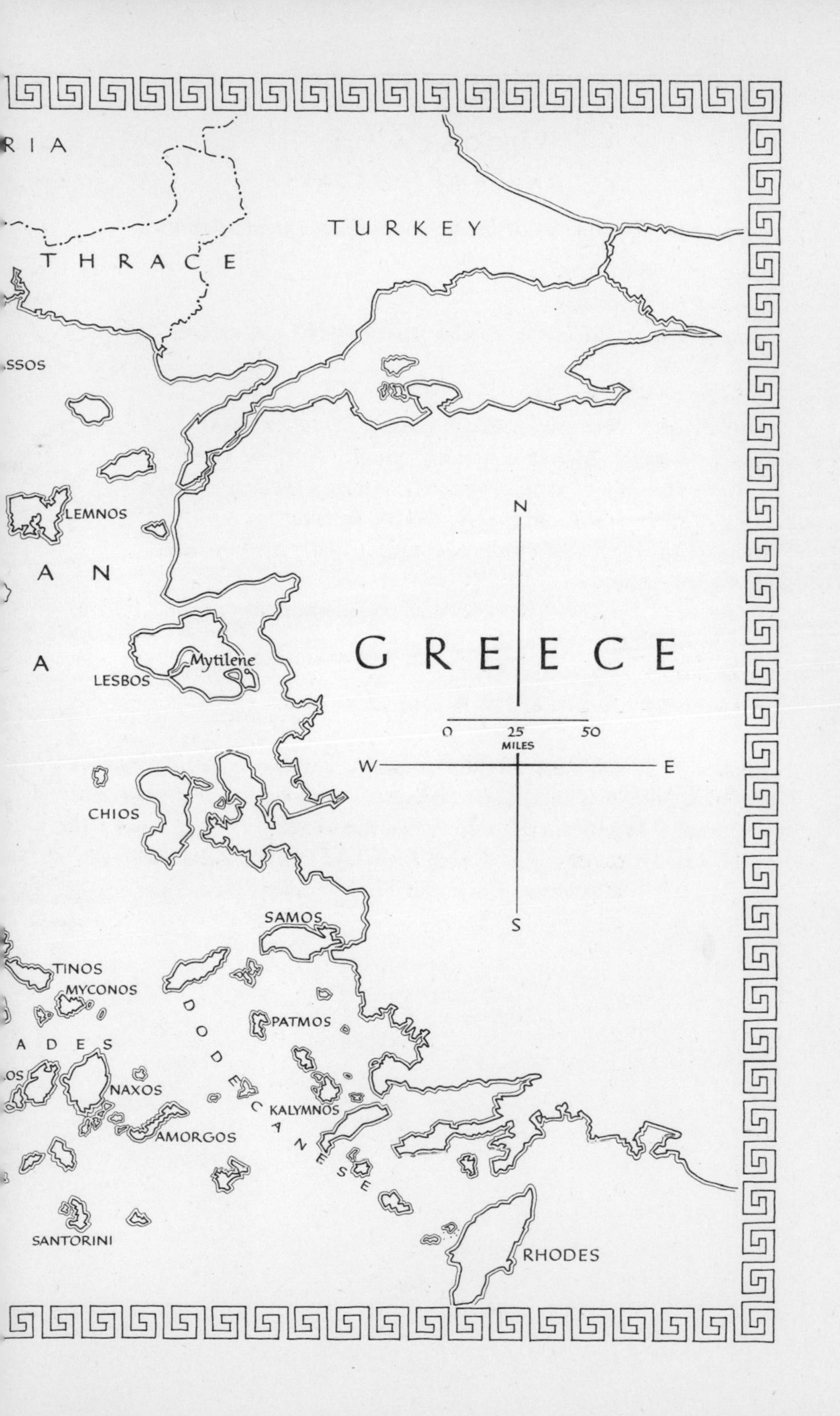

RIA
TURKEY
THRACE
SSOS
LEMNOS
A N
GREECE
A
Mytilene
LESBOS
N
0 25 50
MILES
W
E
S
CHIOS
SAMOS
TINOS
MYCONOS
PATMOS
ADES
OS
NAXOS
KALYMNOS
AMORGOS
DODECANESE
SANTORINI
RHODES

TABLE OF HOLIDAYS

Full holidays (shops, banks and public offices closed all day)

1 January New Year

6 January Epiphany

Clean Monday Movable holiday, first day of Lent, usually February or March

25 March National Day

Good Friday Movable holiday, usually March or April

Easter Monday Movable holiday, usually April or May

1 May Holiday of both labour and spring-time connotation

Feast of Holy Spirit Movable, usually in June

Feast of SS. Peter and Paul Movable, usually also in June

15 August Holiday of the Virgin

28 October National 'Óchi' day, in commemoration of 1940 defiance of Mussolini

25 December Christmas Day

26 December Equivalent of Boxing Day

There are, in addition, certain religious holidays generally accompanied by half-day closing or truncated office hours. The main ones are: 5 and 7 January (each side of Epiphany), the day before and after Good Friday, the day after Easter Monday, 3 October (St Dionysios), 24 December (Christmas Eve), and 31 December (New Year's Eve).

BIBLIOGRAPHICAL NOTE

For the general reader and tourist in search of practical and background information there is no shortage of books in English. Many of them are published in Athens and can be found at the central kiosks and bookstores. Few of these are better than hasty compilations of well-worn material. The brightest and best of them is probably the annual Tourist Almanack published by 'Hellenews'. For motorists, the road map published by ELPA, the Greek Automobile Club, is also helpful and up-to-date. There are also several handy phrase-books, best selected by thumbing over the pages and deciding which suits individual taste. Among the better central bookshops of Athens, with well-stocked shelves specializing in books about Greece, are Eleftheroudákis (in the arcade between Stadium Street and Karayiórgis Servías Street) and Kauffman (28 Stadium Street and 11 Voukourestíou Street). English-speaking assistants at these shops will give the visitor all the guidance he needs on the literature about Greece.

Of books on Greece published abroad, the following are the most rewarding of those I have read:

GENERAL GUIDES

There is not much to choose between the several very compendious guides. They all have the advantage of comprehensive coverage, and the disadvantage of insufficient selectivity for the general tourist. The *Guide Bleu* is certainly as useful and well-meaning as any.

Of the slightly less ambitious publications, the *Nagel Guide* seems to me the most easily manageable. It is certainly the most up-to-date. And its front section in small print on general topics of history, language, etc. is well conceived.

ANTHOLOGIES

There are several collections of essays and travel-impressions by Greek specialists. My favourites in this range are:

Introducing Greece, edited by Francis King (Methuen, 1956) which contains good material on Athens, Attica and Delphi (by Ian Scott-Kilvert), the Peloponnese and the Aegean (by Robert Liddell), Crete and Thessaly (by Peter Sheldon) and several other excellent treatments of various geographical areas of Greece.

Greece, edited by Dore Ogrizek (McGraw-Hill, 1955), published in the World in Colour series, with an introduction by Jean Cocteau. This anthology contains, in addition to some well-reproduced photographs and illustrations, a wide and generally entertaining selection of essays on various aspects of Greece, both geographically and thematically conceived. The authors are mostly French.

HISTORY

The least tiring and most up-to-date of recent general history seems to me to be *A Short History of Modern Greece, 1821–1956*, by Edward S. Forster (Methuen, 1957).

STUDIES IN DEPTH

Mani, by Patrick Leigh-Fermor (John Murray, 1958) remains one of the most illuminating of the 'sentimental' approaches to Greece, seen through a deep study of one particular geographical area.

Aegean Greece and *The Morea*, by Robert Liddell (Jonathan Cape, 1954 and 1958) are similarly enlightening, if rather more businesslike.

An Affair of the Heart, by Dilys Powell (Hodder and Stoughton, 1957) is a warm and effusive word-picture of Greece, seen through memories of and renewed acquaintance with a small archaeological area near Corinth. A little sugary for some tastes.

Greek Horizons, by Helen Hill Miller (Charles Scribner's Sons, New York, 1961) has the same sentimental – but nevertheless moving – approach to modern Greece, seen in the light of its ancient civilization.

In a lighter vein, but at least as perceptive as any of the above, is Osbert Lancaster's *Classical Landscape with Figures* (John Murray, 1947). It has the added attraction of the author's own fine drawings.

FOR YACHTSMEN

A Companion Guide to the Greek Islands, by Ernle Bradford (Collins, 1963) is a chart to help those bent on a boat's-eye view of Greece.

FOR THE CONSCIENTIOUS

One of the most illuminating accounts of the social life of the Greek countryside is contained in a study produced for Stanford University in California by Ernestine Friedl. It is called *Vasilika, A Village in Modern Greece* (Holt, Rinehart and Winston, New York, 1962). A small book. But one which contains more essence, more excitingly conveyed, than most of the more 'literary' accounts of Greek life.

FOR WOMEN

If they cannot leave thoughts of the kitchen behind on holiday, and wish to know all about the origins and idiosyncrasies of Greek cooking (in addition to a comprehensive list of practical recipes), no book is more useful than *The Home Book of Greek Cookery* by Joyce Stubbs (Faber, 1963).

FOR CHILDREN

And to keep the children usefully amused while you are doing your Greek swotting on the beach, there is a small but charmingly instructive book written specially for the young: *The Land and People of Greece*, by Francis Noel-Baker (A. & C. Black, 1956).

Index